EVERYDAY FUTURES

EVERYDAY FUTURES

*Language as Survival for
Indigenous Youth in Diaspora*

STEPHANIE L. CANIZALES

AND

BRENDAN H. O'CONNOR

STANFORD UNIVERSITY PRESS
Stanford, California

Stanford University Press
Stanford, California

© 2025 by Stephanie L. Canizales and Brendan H. O'Connor. All rights reserved.

No part of this book may be reproduced or transmitted in any form or by any means, electronic or mechanical, including photocopying and recording, or in any information storage or retrieval system, without the prior written permission of Stanford University Press.

Library of Congress Cataloging-in-Publication Data
Names: Canizales, Stephanie L., author. | O'Connor, Brendan H., author.
Title: Everyday futures : language as survival for Indigenous youth in diaspora / Stephanie L. Canizales and Brendan H. O'Connor.
Description: Stanford, California : Stanford University Press, 2025. | Includes bibliographical references and index.
Identifiers: LCCN 2024049894 (print) | LCCN 2024049895 (ebook) | ISBN 9781503636545 (cloth) | ISBN 9781503643352 (paperback) | ISBN 9781503643369 (ebook)
Subjects: LCSH: Maya youth—California—Los Angeles—Social conditions. | Maya youth—California—Los Angeles—Language. | Immigrant youth—California—Los Angeles—Social conditions. | Immigrant youth—California—Los Angeles—Language. | Guatemala—Emigration and immigration—Social aspects. | Los Angeles (Calif.)—Emigration and immigration—Social aspects.
Classification: LCC E99.M433 C36 2024 (print) | LCC E99.M433 (ebook) | DDC 305.23086/9120979494—dc23/eng/20241029
LC record available at https://lccn.loc.gov/2024049894
LC ebook record available at https://lccn.loc.gov/2024049895

Cover design: Gabriele Wilson
Digital illustration: Valeria Weerasinghe, *Avanti*, 2024, Italy

The authorized representative in the EU for product safety and compliance is: Mare Nostrum Group B.V. | Mauritskade 21D | 1091 GC Amsterdam | The Netherlands | Email address: gpsr@mare-nostrum.co.uk | KVK chamber of commerce number: 96249943

To Indigenous children and youth—from Pico-Union in
Los Angeles, to Guatemala, Palestine, and beyond—who, amidst
unthinkable violence, are relentless in their future-making.

To all those committed to making youth's imagined futures real.

CONTENTS

Acknowledgments   ix

Introduction   1

1   Becoming the Maya Youth Diaspora   27

2   Preparing for the Future   62

3   Measuring Adaptation   95

4   Surviving as Future-Making   118

Conclusion   155

Notes   179

References   191

Index   211

ACKNOWLEDGMENTS

Research for this book began in July 2012, when Stephanie met the Maya youth of Voces de Esperanza at a Starbucks in Pico-Union, Los Angeles. Without their kindness, generosity, curiosity, honesty, and open minds, this book would not exist. We are grateful to all the Maya young people who opened up about their lives and everyday futures.

Everyday Futures is a product of five years of collaboration between Stephanie and Brendan. Our first endeavor began in October 2019 when we set out to contribute the chapter "From *Preparación* to *Adaptación*: Language and the Imagined Futures of Maya-Speaking Guatemalan Youth in Los Angeles," to Doris Warriner's edited volume *Refugee Education Across the Lifespan: Mapping Experiences of Language Learning and Use* (2024). An advancement of this argument is presented in Chapter 2 of this book. We are grateful to Doris Warriner and our peer reviewer for feedback on our original theorization of *preparación* as part of the immigrant incorporation process.

We then began work on a second paper, "'Maybe not 100%': Co-Constructing Language Proficiency in the Maya Diaspora," published in 2023 in the *International Multilingual Research Journal*. Here, we stretched our understanding of Maya youth's use of percentage talk to measure adaptation. Thank you to editor Jeff MacSwan and the reviewers of this journal article for their incisive feedback, which refined our argument in the paper and informed our elaboration of this process in Chapter 3.

We are grateful to Doctoras Inmaculada García-Sánchez and Ariana Mangual Figueroa for inviting us to contribute our article, "Thresholds of Liminality: Discourse and Embodiment from Separation to Consummation Among Guatemalan Maya Youth Workers in Los Angeles," to their special issue, "New Horizons in the Study of Language and Liminality," in the *International Journal of the Sociology of Language* (2023). The central argument of this paper is presented with greater precision and detail in Chapter 4. Writing this paper together was a turning point for our collaboration as the editors' critical suggestions during our writing and revision process helped us understand the guiding frameworks and historical context needed to tell a fuller story of Maya youth's use of language for *sobrevivencia* in diaspora. It was after the completion of "Thresholds of Liminality" that we began to write this very book project.

At different stages, the manuscript benefited from the editing efforts of Kim Greenwell at Acad/Edit and Jean Lee Cole, Rachel Fudge, and Cathy Hannabach at Ideas on Fire. We're grateful for their careful attention and suggestions for improving the book.

Marcela Maxfield at Stanford University Press has been steadfast in her enthusiasm for this project. We're fortunate indeed to have found such a supportive editor.

Thanks also to Valeria Weerasinghe for her vision and artistry in creating the cover art for this book.

Everyday Futures represents a deep intellectual partnership cultivated over the last half decade. We hope this work inspires future generations of migration and language scholars to engage in interdisciplinary work to address critical issues in the immigrant incorporation and coming of age.

From Stephanie

The young people I met in 2012 introduced me to the issues of unaccompanied child migration and child labor exploitation in Los Angeles, giving me a window into the phenomena unfolding across the United

States and globally and how Maya youth were uniquely vulnerable and resilient in these processes. This set me on the path to uncover why and how. My early thinking on this topic is reflected in articles published with *Ethnic and Racial Studies* (2015) and the *Journal of Ethnic and Migration Studies* (2019). I am grateful to editors and reviewers at these journals for encouraging me in this line of research.

As the years progressed, I set out to broaden my scope, to tell stories of Central American and Mexican young people growing up under such conditions. My first book, *Sin Padres, Ni Papeles* (2024), encapsulates many of their shared experiences. I am grateful to the University of California Press for the opportunity to develop my research on unaccompanied migrant youth's material and emotional incorporation process.

While I am proud of these prior works and what they offer to sociology and other fields, I have long felt dissatisfied by how the complexities and multidimensionality of the Indigenous youth experience were lost when I tried to tell a broader Latin American–origin unaccompanied immigrant youth story. I first shared my frustrations with Brendan when we met on February 14, 2019, the day I visited Arizona State University for a research talk.

I was admittedly a bit intimidated. I'd never spoken to a linguistic anthropologist about my research before and wondered how long or short our thirty-minute meeting would feel. I vividly remember the morning rain that created puddles on the university courtyard as Brendan and I walked, and I told him about how Maya youth talked about language proficiency percentages. I shared my observations about how young people would attend just "enough" adult English-language school to get better jobs, earn better wages, make more friends, or just feel safer in Los Angeles.

Brendan and I stopped to sit on the steps in front of ASU's Old Main while I told him about the simple premise of Voces de Esperanza but how it provided a space for rich conversations about unaccompanied Maya youth's everyday lives, week after week, and a lifeline for the group. I remember confessing to Brendan that I had ethnographic and interview data about Maya youth's language proficiency and learning and did not know what to do with it. He told me I could send him some excerpts if I wanted him to have a look. I did a few days later.

I cannot put into words how thankful I am to Brendan for embarking on this project with me. There have been times throughout this writing process that the descriptions and analysis take me back to the field. The conversations and spaces come alive again as I read this book's pages. I can see youth's faces and hear their voices; I can visualize the spaces I participated in so clearly because of the rich descriptions and deep analysis our partnership produces. This, I believe, will bring readers closer to understanding Maya youth's experiences in Los Angeles and empathizing with their realities in Los Angeles. I could not wish for anything greater to come from this work.

Brendan, I would not be able to tell Maya youth's stories in this way without your curiosity, care, and craft. I am grateful for your attention to detail and patience. I am grateful for every conversation where I could share details about participants' personalities, mannerisms, and the dynamics of my interactions with them. I am grateful for your attentive eye (and ear) to interview transcripts and fieldnotes. You brought something truly special to this work, and I thank you.

I also owe immense gratitude to my mentors for encouraging this project, the second book to come out of the data I collected while a sociology PhD student at the University of Southern California. There, my advisors Pierrette Hondagneu-Sotelo and Jody Agius Vallejo oversaw my work. Pierrette's constant encouragement to "read widely and deeply" encouraged my exploration of literature outside sociology, which had only nascently examined the Indigenous immigrant experience in the US at the time of my data collection. Manuel Pastor Jr. and George Sanchez, graduate school committee members, encouraged my exploration of the heterogeneity within the Central American and Mexican populations and how converging and diverging histories of Los Angeles and migration could produce such different realities for communities living side by side in the city. I thank them for their support and enthusiasm for this work.

Several generous funders made this work possible. Stanford University's Center on Poverty and Inequality; University of California, Davis Center for Inequality and Poverty Research; the USC Center for the Study of Immigrant Integration (now Equity Research Institute); the USC Latin American and Latino Studies Program; the National Science Foundation Sociology Program; the USC Tomás Rivera Policy Institute; and the USC Department of Sociology, which funded data collection and early analysis. Awards from the John Randolph and Dora Haynes Foundation, the American Sociological Association's Minority Fellowship Program, the Ford Foundation Fellowship Program, and the University of Wisconsin-Madison Institute for Research on Poverty supported several years of analysis and writing. The UC Merced Chancellor's Postdoctoral Fellowship supported writing for this book.

I wish to also thank colleagues and friends from across the University of California. I began writing this book while an assistant professor of sociology at UC Merced. I am an assistant professor of sociology at UC Berkeley as this book goes into press. Thank you to my writing accountability groups, faculty mentors, and department chairs at each campus for their support throughout this process.

I am, of course, also grateful to my family—especially my mom, Kendrick, Brianna, and my grandparents, Mamá Chita and Papá Peter—for their encouragement in my professional endeavors. I am indebted to my partner Antonio Diaz for the safe space we create together and call home, where I can hide away and write for hours without a single worry about the outside world. I love you, AD. And to Dobby, my most loyal writing companion. Since May 2012, two months before the research for this book started, I have been able to count on my sleepy cat to be by my side every time I sit down to write, and I just think that's so special.

From Brendan

I'm deeply grateful to Stephanie for inviting me into the world of the *jóvenes* and trusting me to help tell their stories. I've strived to keep that trust in the forefront of my mind and to take this profound responsibility seriously. I hope that what we've written together goes some way toward doing justice to the courage, optimism, and ingenuity of the youth. Stephanie, you've been a dream collaborator—thank you *de corazón* for broadening my horizons and pushing me to move our thinking in new directions. This has truly been one of the most enriching intellectual experiences of my career, and I owe it all to you and that first, brief conversation on a rainy day in Tempe.

I've been greatly blessed with brilliant, critical friends and colleagues throughout my academic journey. Here, I want to single out a few, past and present, who have particularly shaped my thinking about Indigenous peoples, languages, and lifeways, with deep respect and appreciation: Philip Stevens and Vanessa Anthony-Stevens, Saskias Casanova, and my dissertation advisor Leisy Wyman, whose ethical example remains a lodestar.

Jenn and Ellie O'Connor are my sun, moon, and stars. Thank you for believing in me and sustaining me with your love. I love you. Everything I do is for you.

I'm also thankful to the individuals and groups who gave me the strength to keep going as we were writing this book: Zen Desert Sangha of Tucson and my teacher Dan Dorsey Roshi; the Refuge in the Desert sangha of Recovery Dharma; the Franciscan Renewal Center in Scottsdale; my medical providers; and my family—farther away than I'd like, but always close.

EVERYDAY FUTURES

Introduction

Andrés was twenty-four years old when he sat down for an interview with Stephanie in Los Angeles, California. A double-needle sewer in an LA garment factory, he recalled his struggles with mental health and isolation after migrating from Guatemala as an unaccompanied fifteen-year-old:

> I would just cry. The only thing I could do was close the door to my room when no one was around and cry. Because . . . [I was] more fearful, it made me feel more unsafe to talk with other people. And I didn't want to talk anymore. It made me scared, because my self-esteem was already very low—"What will they think of me?" or "They're going to think the same as such-and-such a person," and I don't want to suffer. I prefer to hide myself or do something else like that but not talk because that's what I thought: That all the people, if they don't want us [here], that all the people talk like that.

Immediately afterward, Andrés switched course, telling Stephanie, "But now it doesn't affect me . . . I've gotten over it." In stark contrast to the image of newly arrived Andrés in the story—crying alone in his room, afraid to speak his language, and suffering from exposure to racist attitudes—Andrés, in 2013 and after nine years in Los Angeles, offered a full-throated defense of the value of Mayan language and culture. More than that, he affirmed that, over time, he had come to rely on *"mi raíz Maya"*—[his] Maya roots—to mitigate the suffering he experienced in Guatemala and the US as he pursued what youth called *sobrevivencia*. *Sobrevivencia* directly translates to "survival," but youth in the study used it to mean something more: the long-term ability to survive and thrive. First, as an individual endeavor and, later, in ways that would strengthen the diasporic community:

> For me now, being Maya, I'm proud. And that's what I am, Maya—I have my K'iche' language, I have my own culture, we have Maya ceremony, which has nothing to do with witchcraft like many people say. . . . It's the connection with nature, with Mother Earth. And [the way] I'm coming to understand everything now, I understand that it is healthy because they're not doing anything bad.

Andrés went on to describe observing his father's traditional practices, such as getting up early to watch the sunrise and feel the wind, thanking God for the sun and the air, and seeing all of nature as connected. In the past, Andrés said, he might not have understood the significance of these practices, but now he was coming to understand it. When he asked his father about this morning ritual, his father would tell him, "It's that we have roots where we come from, and never forget that, because we're not doing witchcraft."[1] For Andrés, believing in the value of his language and culture went along with the "confidence" to "get over" negative beliefs about *Indios*—what once affected him severely, he now saw as a symptom of others' narrow-mindedness:

> A lot of people think about it like that [as witchcraft] but it's not like that. So now it gives me confidence if people say, "You're an *Indio*." That's your problem, not mine, because I know what I'm doing.

At the time of their interview in the spring of 2013, Stephanie and Andrés were sitting at a picnic table in a community garden in Pico-Union, a neighborhood of Los Angeles where much of the Guatemalan immigrant community lives. Many, like Andrés, were from Indigenous groups in Guatemala and arrived in the US as speakers of languages from the Mayan language family. Andrés liked wearing embroidered shirts from the preppy retailers Hollister and Abercrombie. He had many of the physical features he and his Maya friends talked about as stereotypically "Indigenous" traits: straight black hair, dark brown skin, thick lips, and rounded teeth. An active participant in an informally organized support group for Indigenous youth called Voces de Esperanza, he was the first member to call Stephanie "teacher" because the group knew of Stephanie's aspirations of becoming a professor, and she often translated words or phrases for the group. The nickname stuck.

Though entirely his own, Andrés's story also broadly represents the language socialization and cultural adaptation processes we trace in this book. Many of the unaccompanied Maya youth workers who participated in this research shared stories that echoed that of Andrés to some extent, though they certainly did not all share the same outcome. In Andrés's retelling of his traumatic early days in Los Angeles, he used the common tactic of beginning the "complicating action," or central sequence, of his narrative in the past—that is, initially using the Spanish imperfect tense: "I *didn't want* to talk," "It *made* me scared," and so on—and only transitioning into the historical-present tense by the end: "I *don't want* to suffer," "I *prefer* to hide myself," and so on.[2] He did so not because he still felt that way; instead, in recalling the visceral feelings of isolation and shame post-migration, he dramatized them by shifting to the present tense, as they came alive in his memory and also created a scene for Stephanie.[3] When Andrés remembered, "I didn't want to talk," it is important to be clear about what he meant: He did not want to be heard speaking K'iche', his Mayan language, because he had already "suffered" tremendously in Guatemala and the US from others' discriminatory attitudes about Indigenous languages and peoples.

Like many youth in this study, Andrés recognized that there was a long history of such suffering. Early in the Spanish colonial encounter, the "ordering" of Maya people as colonial subjects was linked to the *reducción* (reduction) of Mayan languages, or their "[systematic] re-forming" into codes that were commensurate with European languages.[4] As anthropologist William Hanks put it, "Just as the spatial and behavior *reducción* transformed Indian lifeways, so too the linguistic *reducción* was wrapped up in the concerted effort to transform the Indian languages" from the Spanish perspective.[5] As a participant named Aarón said, Spanish speakers wanted to "change our language" and, to justify doing so, created a social hierarchy in which Maya languages "[didn't] have value" and Maya people were systematically denigrated. His account recalls Andrés's reference to colonization and Spanish attempts to stamp out "witchcraft" through the transformation of Mayan lifeways and language.

Examining the role of language in Guatemalan Maya youth workers' experiences *between* the disorientation of their displacement from Guatemala, their arrival in Los Angeles, and their relatively more stable positions as longer-settled Los Angeles residents years later is a primary goal of this book. Immediately following migration, youth felt *desorientado* (disoriented) but started to undergo what they called *orientación* (orientation) to the social structure of the new *sistema* (system) that they encountered in Los Angeles. The youth learned about their new and deeply stratified social worlds and acquainted themselves with the structures that determined their life chances and the circumstances of immigrant life in the present in a process of *orientación*.[6] For Indigenous youth, *orientación* gave insight into the efforts they would have to make to adapt or adjust to their multiply marginalized ethnoracial position as Indigenous within anti-Indigenous Latina/o Los Angeles, and as undocumented Latin American-origin immigrants within the anti-immigrant host society.[7] Participants referred to these efforts as *preparación* (preparation), which entailed gaining social and human capital—including linguistic capital—and other resources that they expected would benefit them in the future by promoting greater economic mobility and social inclusion.

Self-motivated *preparación* was necessary because Maya youth in Los Angeles did not have access to the familial or school-based environments that provide structured opportunities for "preparation" during the transition to adulthood to which other immigrant youth might typically have access.[8] As such, *preparación* was the dimension of the incorporation process in which youth's agency was perhaps most apparent: They did not have parents or institutions telling them what to do to succeed in the US but determined for themselves—from their "orientation" experiences—what they would need to ensure a successful future, and then positioned themselves accordingly. Shielding oneself from language- and race-based discrimination, as in the first part of Andrés's story, was typical of *orientación* (though not limited to that phase); by contrast, investing in learning Spanish or English, to varying degrees of proficiency, was one element of *preparación*.

Adaptación (adaptation) followed *preparación* and referred to youth's adjustments to and incremental advances in their social, material, and emotional positions stemming from their *preparación*. Attaining a less arduous or better-paying job because of having learned a certain amount of English was an example of linguistic *preparación* leading to economic *adaptación*. Taking public transportation to explore new parts of Los Angeles was an example of linguistic *preparación* leading to spatial and social *adaptación*. As in Andrés's story, being able to question and disrupt ideologies of Maya inferiority was an example of *adaptación* that relied on the emotional and spiritual dimensions of *preparación* that youth experienced in community with other Maya. Ultimately, youth expected that instances of *adaptación* would compound over time to transform their situations gradually and lead to what they called *sobrevivencia*, a more secure state of affairs in which youth not only were able to sustain themselves in diaspora but felt empowered to *be* themselves and encourage other Maya immigrants to do the same. *Sobrevivencia* was not "merely surviving"; it entailed an imagined future where youth's financial situations and physical/mental well-being, including their relationship to Maya language and culture, were relatively solid and assured.

Thus, youth described the time between initial migration and becoming long-settled, relatively stable members of the Maya immigrant community as a matter of interlinked processes of *preparación*, followed by *adaptación*, leading, they hoped, to *sobrevivencia*. Based on their accounts, we conceptualize youth's trajectories as an integrated effort at *future-making* or using language and other symbolic and material resources to set themselves up for socially and economically secure futures as immigrants and as teens transitioning to adulthood. Over the long term, as

Andrés's story suggested, future-making also entailed a transformation of many youth's relationships to Mayan identity and cultural practice in diaspora. Youth aspired to motivate others' engagement in similar processes of future-making, shifting Maya immigrants' relationship to Indigenous identity, cultural practice, and language. This conception of future-making draws on existing understandings of immigrant "home-making," though in a highly distinctive way, which we discuss in detail in Chapter 4.[9]

While all immigrants undergo processes of linguistic and cultural adaptation to their new societies, Maya youth experienced and conceptualized *preparación, adaptación,* and *sobrevivencia* in Los Angeles somewhat differently. This was, in part, because of their distinctive identities as youth who, like Andrés, often felt themselves to be phenotypically and linguistically identifiable (and inferior) as Indigenous and/or Maya in Los Angeles, as they had been in Guatemala. By and large, since the youth in this study migrated as unaccompanied adolescents and without direct guidance from parents or older relatives, they developed these emic conceptualizations of Maya immigrant incorporation (i.e., *(des)orientación, preparación, adaptación,* and *sobrevivencia*) in dialogue with each other—in work, education, and family and community life.[10]

Everyday Futures will show that many Maya young people who participated in this research described their experiences as Indigenous youth in Guatemala and upon arrival in the US in terms of *timidez y miedo* (shyness and fear), most often due to the discrimination and marginalization associated with life as undocumented Indigenous immigrants. Because of this, many felt compelled to "hide themselves" in Los Angeles (to paraphrase Andrés), concealing their linguistic and cultural backgrounds along with their ethnoracial identity and national origin. To be sure, the practice of strategically revealing and/or concealing one's marginalized or stigmatized identities to protect and preserve oneself and one's social status is frequently observed in immigrant communities. Scholars have observed such practices related to how undocumented immigrants treat their precarious legal status within an anti-immigrant society; few have considered how ethnic subgroups, like Indigenous immigrants within the broader racialized Latin American–origin immigrant community, navigate their stigmatized identities across nested contexts and how their stigmatization contours their physical, economic, and social stability and mobility over time.[11] This book reveals that, over long-term resettlement, some youth were able to use language to overcome the persistent challenges they faced as unaccompanied Indigenous young people to achieve a measure of individual social and economic mobility, moving from their difficult post-arrival circumstances to less onerous labor and living conditions, while becoming better incorporated within the Los Angeles community and, thus, better able to advocate for other Maya. We set out to describe how.

Sobrevivencia in diaspora required the strategic and adaptive use of multiple languages—Maya languages, Spanish, and English—to navigate "colonial codes of power" that were subtly different from those that Maya youth had already encountered in Guatemala.[12] As Andrés's story implied, for many, *sobrevivencia* also involved questioning language ideologies that stigmatized Maya languages and speakers as inferior and unfit for modernity, and reframing languages like K'iche' as resources for personal and community thriving in the US. These processes contour unaccompanied Indigenous migrant youth's future-making in diaspora.

Unaccompanied Children Migrating to the United States

This study of *sobrevivencia* was developed during a time of rising migration among unaccompanied Central American youth. The term "unaccompanied children" is statutorily used to refer to someone who is under the age of eighteen and has neither lawful US immigration status nor a parent or legal guardian to provide care or custody at the time of apprehension.[13] The unaccompanied Maya youth in this research were not legally recognized as unaccompanied minors, as they entered the US having evaded apprehension at the southern border. Yet they grew up as such, without the material support, such as housing, or the emotional support, such as discipline or supervision by an adult figure, present in the lives of youth who migrated with family. As such, Maya youth were forced to be materially and emotionally independent, responsible for securing their own financial and social stability—and oftentimes that of the families they left behind as well—during the critical developmental years in the transition between adolescence and young adulthood.[14] While we cannot enumerate unaccompanied youth entering the US without inspection, estimates of unaccompanied youth apprehensions over the last decade give important insights into the population's characteristics.

The unaccompanied migrant youth population has grown in size and diversity. From fiscal year 2009 to 2014, rates of unaccompanied Central American and Mexican child apprehensions grew from 19,688 to 68,541.[15] This number reached 76,020 by 2019 and 121,712 by 2023.[16] About 75 percent of unaccompanied children were between the ages of fifteen and seventeen, and 63 percent were identified as male.[17] In the US today, 93 percent of unaccompanied minors originate from Latin America, primarily Central America (77 percent) and Mexico (17 percent).[18] This distribution has shifted dramatically since 2009, when Mexican children accounted for 82 percent of apprehensions.

This study began in 2012, when the rates of unaccompanied minors from Central America were rapidly increasing; 2014 marked the first year that more Central American unaccompanied minors were apprehended at the US–Mexico border than those from Mexico.[19] Guatemalans have represented the largest proportion of Central American unaccompanied minors since the onset of the humanitarian crisis of 2014, when increased arrivals of women and unaccompanied minors at the southern border temporarily overwhelmed emergency service providers and law enforcement. In fiscal year 2023, the 49,463 Guatemalan children apprehended represented 53 percent of all apprehended Central American children (93,393 total) and 41 percent of all Central American and Mexican children apprehended in the United States (121,712 total).[20] Represented only by national origin, these estimates reflect bureaucratic processes that homogenize immigrant youth, flattening unaccompanied children's ethnoracial diversity. Based on rates of deportation of unaccompanied children from the US and Mexico who were returned to Guatemala, it is suggested that 95 percent of unaccompanied Guatemalan youth migrants are Indigenous, hailing "from rural communities in the departments of Quetzaltenango, San Marcos, Quiché, Huehuetenango, and Totonicapán" where the primary languages spoken are K'iche', Mam, and Q'anjob'al.[21] Other estimates suggest that between 75 and 90 percent of irregular migrants from Guatemala are Indigenous.[22]

Noting these population trends, this study builds on a burgeoning body of work that examines the disproportionate violence faced by Indigenous youth in migration and apprehension, in large part because of language and phenotype.[23] All unaccompanied youth struggle to find their footing in the US when they are transferred to the custody sponsors living in the United States by the Office of Refugee Resettlement, but Indigenous youth face several distinct challenges.[24] For example, Indigenous youth encounter language barriers in access to housing, health, and social services, and in schools and courtrooms.[25] Indigenous language interpreters are sparse.[26] If children's caregivers do not speak English or Spanish, Indigenous language–dominant youth's access to services necessary for their integration, safety, and well-being is severely limited since the adults assigned to liaise with service institutions on the children's behalf are also limited in their ability to access support.

Unaccompanied Indigenous youth, like Andrés and others portrayed throughout this book, who entered the US clandestinely, also found themselves outside of normative family living situations and formal legal and education systems. Because of this, and as noted above, they had to take responsibility for their own *preparación*—in other words, for acquiring the knowledge and skills required to adapt successfully to labor markets and community life in the United States. They set themselves up for success over the long term. This meant that unaccompanied Indigenous youth navigated migration to and incorporation in the US in ways that are typically associated with undocumented adult migrants: as low-wage workers managing local and transnational family and community life simultaneously.[27] Because the unaccompanied Maya youth in this research grew up as undocumented low-wage labor migrants responsible for their day-to-day survival, and often the financial support of left-behind families, they were subjected to the exploitation and opportunism born out of community resource impoverishment, including within immigrant communities.[28]

The poverty and marginalization of all undocumented immigrants in the United States are compounded for Indigenous immigrants, who are further exploited at work and discriminated against in the community in ways that reinforce their subordinate position in social, political, and economic hierarchies.[29] Thus, newly arrived Indigenous youth are particularly likely to encounter harsh conditions of poverty, employment and housing instability, and limited access to resource-dense networks that provide opportunities for mobility out of these constraints.[30] While a long line of literature touts immigrant communities as centers of bounded solidarity (the idea that members of a community are, at least in part, responsible for one another) and enforceable trust (the idea that the community will hold its members accountable for reciprocity in resource exchange), Indigenous immigrants are often marginalized within, or even excluded from, some immigrant communities.[31] Indigenous immigrants must grapple not only with the violence of anti-immigrant sentiment in the American mainstream but also anti-Indigenous sentiment in LA's Latin American–origin community. And, as the next section describes and the next chapter elaborates, unaccompanied Maya youth arrive in the US having already had to navigate their tenuous place within Guatemalan society, something that has shaped both the history of Guatemala and Guatemalan migration to the United States (Chapter 1).

Theorizing Indigenous Immigrants' Incorporation as Future-Making

Social scientists assert that immigrant incorporation happens unequally and unevenly in contemporary US society. This conceptualization challenges canonical migration theories, based on the experiences of pre-1965 European migrants, that describe inevitable incorporation trajectories that were a product of time.[32] Classical theories—critiqued for their White supremacist ideologies—argue that all immigrants will eventually be incorporated into a singularly dominant English-speaking, Euro-American mainstream. The incorporation of today's immigrants—who are diverse in national origin, legal status, ethnorace, social class, and level of education—is not seen as an inevitability nor as a uniform process.[33] Instead, stratifying systems of power, such as ethnic nationalism that justifies nation-state borders alongside racism and xenophobia that contribute to the social and legal production of the "other" and "illegal immigrant," have caused marginalized groups to experience incorporation as "differential inclusion," resulting in those groups' enfolding into US social, political, and economic hierarchies as "distinct and subordinate subjects, rather than as identical peers."[34]

Race and legal status powerfully stratify immigrants' incorporation prospects.[35] Latin American-origin immigrants and their descendants in the US, Indigenous and otherwise, have historically been racialized as "illegal" regardless of their actual legal status, which has affected their access to jobs, education, housing, health care, and social ties that promote incorporation and mobility.[36] Racializing illegality through anti-immigrant legislation, enforcement practices, and public media has created a homogenized and stereotypical image of Mexican or Central American-origin immigrants, thereby erasing the presence of Indigenous Mexicans and Central Americans in diaspora.[37] These homogenizing tendencies have been reinforced through research that centers the experiences of non-Indigenous Latin Americans and disregards Indigenous immigrants' distinctive trajectories of migration and incorporation. They also reflect a historical pattern of "flattening" cultural and linguistic differences among US Latina/o communities.[38]

Ethnoracial identity—and (non)Indigenous identity, more precisely—is a determinant of immigrants' social, political, and economic incorporation prospects.[39] Indigenous migration scholars acknowledge that the experiences of Indigenous Latin American immigrants and their descendants' communities are distinct from those of their non-Indigenous counterparts in the US in part because of their subordinate position within their origin country society.[40] Emerging scholarship highlights Indigenous immigrants' distinctive challenges, strengths, and incorporation pathways. It provides evidence of "hybrid hegemonies" or overlapping forms of discrimination and stigmatization that Indigenous youth confront as they work toward transnational futures for themselves, their families, and their communities.[41] Transnational anthropologist Giovanni Batz (Maya K'iche') asserts that "[b]eing Maya in Guatemala has often meant marginalization, exploitation, and victimization through state-sponsored violence and death. Being Maya in Los Angeles has less severe consequences but is still marked by marginalization, repression, and discrimination."[42] Indigenous immigrant youth contend with ethnoracial discrimination in the US, alongside the many other language, work, and legal status–related challenges that immigrant Latin Americans face in general.

Predicated on findings that today's immigrants are experiencing incorporation as "differential inclusion"—inclusion as "other" in a hierarchy of difference—and that Indigenous immigrants are especially marginalized, social scientists have moved away from the notion of incorporation as a linear trajectory with a single endpoint.[43] Instead, incorporation can be understood as a dynamic process that takes shape differently for different groups.[44] As a process, incorporation's trajectory is shaped by an individual's or group's social roles and responsibilities; access to material, social, cultural, and emotional capital; and social position within the opportunity structure accessible to them.[45] Because these conditions change throughout the life course, immigrant incorporation is theorized as an ongoing and iterative process that begins with *disorientation* in the destination society, a cognitive and emotional sense of unfamiliarity with its material and social organization, which is differentially experienced based on immigrants' intersectional social locations.[46]

Immigrant disorientation is especially acute for unaccompanied and undocumented Latin American-origin youth who are marginalized in US society due to intersecting axes of national origin, immigration and legal status, and age.[47] Over time, immigrants can become better *oriented* to, or familiar with, the rhythm of everyday life in the United States.[48] Orientation is more easily achieved for unaccompanied youth who are welcomed by long-settled relatives who can act as material providers, emotional caregivers, and cultural and institutional brokers. As mentioned above, *orientación* is often followed by *preparación,* as youth, once sufficiently "oriented" to the systems, institutions, and norms that make up their social worlds and their roles and responsibilities within each, may actively seek to prepare themselves for long-term success (material, but also social and emotional) as immigrants. *Adaptación* may follow *preparación* as Indigenous immigrants become equipped (materially, socially, and emotionally) to adjust to the society in which they first felt disoriented, reaping the benefits of the knowledge and skills they gained from preparation. Importantly, as immigrants undergo orientation, preparation, and adaptation within one social sphere (e.g., family, school, work, and/or community), they may gain new knowledge, resources, and skills that expand their social worlds and facilitate entry into other spheres, within which they may relive the path from (dis)orientation to successful adaptation over time.[49]

Framing immigrant incorporation as an ongoing and iterative process within and across institutions and societies over time allows scholars and policymakers to consider immigrants' experiences of mobility and inclusion within their distinct social and spatial contexts, even if the dominant society marginalizes them.[50] This has been called a process of "homemaking,"[51] meaning both "a set of practices and a perspective on migrants' ways of local incorporation" according to context-specific, relatively idiosyncratic interactions between immigrant newcomers and majority populations, as well as within immigrant communities.[52] Because interactions are central to homemaking as a form of incorporation, a singular homemaking outcome does not exist.

Like homemaking, our concept of future-making "embraces all the practices whereby people try to make themselves at home in a certain social context, on a variety of scales, given the structure of opportunities accessible to them."[53] However, as we will show, future-making takes into account immigrant youth's distinctive incorporation experiences over the life course, braiding together considerations of human development—for example, the difference between an adolescent who migrates and the settled young adult ten years later—and Indigenous immigrant youth's ingenuity and agency in working toward *sobrevivencia* for themselves and their coethnics. Future-making, then, is not a blueprint for incorporation. Rather, it is a conceptualization of immigrant youth's resourcefulness as they use materials and opportunities on hand to craft a local form of incorporation, "mak[ing] do with whatever is at hand."[54] In this formulation, *sobrevivencia* is a stable state of affairs imagined as one dimension of youth's future-making. It might even be linked to widespread concepts of *cosmovisión* among Latin American Indigenous communities: organizing frameworks that "[provide] individual and collective meaning and coherence to living" despite the disruptions of colonialism and migration.[55]

Given the distinct social position of Latin American Indigenous immigrants within hybrid hegemonies, it is worth examining whether and to what extent these communities enact future-making in diaspora. Furthermore, it begs the question of what practices constitute future-making for members of particular Indigenous communities, especially at different life stages and as they contend with anti-Indigenous racism and marginalization within the cultural and linguistic ecologies of the destination society.

The case of unaccompanied Indigenous youth migrating to the United States and arriving in Los Angeles builds on a rich body of literature demonstrating that Maya migration since the 1970s has led to the formation of multigenerational Maya communities in the US, within which identification with and expression of Indigeneity are complex. Ethnic studies scholar Alicia Estrada writes that "Maya diasporic identity can be understood as constructed, reconstructed, performed, and articulated through various cultural, economic, and symbolic exchanges and movements that occur between the immigrants' place of origin (Guatemala) and their residence, one of which is Los Angeles."[56] Empirical research has turned up examples like the weekend *mercado* on 6th Street, where Maya residents form community connections and exchange goods that they might not otherwise have access to.[57] Maintaining a diasporic identity may also include the use of Maya regional clothing to "continue claiming and transforming traditions" passed from parents to children;[58] the (re)production of Maya music, religion, literature, and language to resist Western impositions and reaffirm Maya identity;[59] and participation in hometown associations or cultural organizations that support intergenerational and transnational cultural exchange.[60]

Taking these frames into account, we revise the incorporation framework to move away from its association with notions of aspiration to Americanization and approximation to an idealized dominant identity and propose instead that Indigenous immigrants' efforts, and in this case, Maya youth's efforts, at diasporic future-making be understood as relatively idiosyncratic acts of resistance to their marginalization across national borders. As such, *Everyday Futures* looks closely at the role of language maintenance and language socialization in Indigenous immigrant youth's experiences of *preparación* and *adaptación,* which, in turn, were critical to immigrant Maya youth's *sobrevivencia*—their goal of surviving and thriving across multiple dimensions of life—and future-making in the United States.

Language and *Sobrevivencia* in the Context of Worldwide Language Diversity

While this book is about young Indigenous Guatemalan immigrants, it is also about language. The following chapters are devoted primarily to youth's language socialization in Spanish and English as elements of *preparación* and *adaptación,* but our focus on language includes the persistence of Mayan languages as community languages in diaspora. We deliberately seek to push back against the erasure of Indigenous languages in immigrant communities by highlighting the practices and processes that allow language to endure across space and time, as well as the factors that disfavor Maya youth's learning and maintenance of their native languages.

In this, we face an apparent difficulty: Neither of us speaks a Mayan language, and all data were collected in Spanish (with occasional code-switching into English from some participants). As the Mayan-speaking participants were a subset of the unaccompanied youth from the larger study, Spanish dominated in group settings (such as Voces de Esperanza meetings) and accommodation to Spanish was the norm in one-on-one interactions.[61] Depending on the individual, their time in the US, and their specific incorporation trajectory, it might not have been seen as appropriate to speak K'iche' in researcher-participant interactions (even if that had been an option; also, not all Mayan-speaking participants spoke K'iche', and languages like K'iche', Q'anjob'al, and Mam, while related, are not mutually intelligible). Our data show that some participants were reluctant even to admit that they spoke Mayan languages, much less speak them aloud to a US citizen. Still, this means that we rely on participants' *accounts* of Mayan language use in diaspora and their metacommentaries (statements) about Mayan languages—as well as their dialogic engagement with others' commentaries—to map the contours of the Mayan language ecology among Indigenous Guatemalan youth in Los Angeles.[62]

The participants' efforts at Spanish and English learning and Mayan maintenance took place against the backdrop of worldwide language shift, in which the reverberating effects of colonialism, Western-style schooling, mass migration, and climate disruption (among other forces) have led to an overall decrease in language diversity and, some portend, will result in the eventual extinction of smaller languages like K'iche'.

Quantitative analyses of the future of language diversity worldwide emphasize the inevitability of language loss, with one recent study estimating that 1,500 languages (of approximately 6,500 worldwide) could cease to be spoken by the end of the twenty-first century.[63] Calls to action around impending language loss frequently highlight the co-occurrence of high language diversity and biodiversity in geographical hotspots, noting that many of the same variables—for instance, density of road networks in each area, land-use patterns, regional climate disruption—affect the prospects of survival for both languages and species.[64]

Attempts to grapple with the scope of the "language crisis,"[65] past and present, have relied on versions of Joshua Fishman's Graded Intergenerational Disruption Scale to assess the extent of endangerment for specific languages based on intergenerational transmission or the lack thereof and the consequent prospects for reversing language shift.[66] There is good reason to pay attention to macro-level patterns of language shift and loss, as these phenomena are not evenly distributed around the world.[67] Finer-grained understandings of language endangerment may help to "focus attention" and limited resources "on areas where language vitality might become threatened" to a greater degree.[68] According to such measures, the most widely spoken Mayan languages, Q'eqchi' and K'iche', are still considered "threatened" despite having robust populations of speakers in Guatemala (800,000 and 1 million, respectively).[69]

In the interdisciplinary literature on culture and language evolution, research carefully points out that "these predictions are not death knells, but possible outcomes in the absence of investment in language vitality."[70] In recent years, however, Indigenous linguists and language activists, along with non-Indigenous collaborators, have challenged the "expert rhetorics" that have framed and continue to frame advocacy for so-called endangered languages. As linguistic anthropologist Jane Hill pointed out, messages intended to raise awareness of language threat are not always experienced as welcoming or empowering by communities of speakers,[71] who may be "exasperated" by the ceaseless enumeration of "last speakers" as a countdown to extinction.[72] In particular, Indigenous language activists and allies have taken aim at the very term "extinction"—what linguist Wesley Leonard has called the "e-word"[73]—as reinforcing a logic of elimination that rhetorically removes Indigenous peoples from colonial space,[74] placing their languages in a remote, pre-modern "sublime" category.[75] Others have also questioned the discursive power of academic linguists, missionaries, and biodiversity researchers (*inter alia*) to delimit Indigenous futures, asking, "Where is the locus of agency in declaring a language or culture extinct? And where is the locus of agency in resistance to both the label and the process?"[76]

These scholars' and activists' critique of "extinction" is not limited to its rhetorical power to erase Indigenous language and cultural practices. As Kaska linguist Barbra Meek argued and others affirm, scholarly definitions of language vitality do not always account for communities' understanding of the status of their languages, including the myriad ways they may "live" in everyday cultural practice (but may be invisible to outsiders).[77] Discourses of extinction are not just unhelpful; in many cases, they are inaccurate in that they "have not caught up to the reality" of present-day uses of Indigenous languages.[78] Colonial ideologies endemic to academic linguistics have been criticized because "the prototype [of] . . . a first-language speaker who ideally is rural and deemed to have not had much influence from socially dominant languages" is upheld as the most "authentic" (or only authentic) repository of linguistic value and knowledge.[79] Below, we review some of the alternative ways Indigenous linguists and language advocates have theorized language vitality before considering how these issues manifest for speakers of Indigenous languages from Latin America in the United States.

Building on Gerald Vizenor's notion of survivance as the assertion of "an active sense of presence"[80] in the face of deracination and linguicide,[81] educational linguist Leisy Wyman proposed *linguistic survivance* as a way past the binary of "speakers" and "nonspeakers" in discussions of language shift and revitalization.[82] Analyzing everyday verbal behavior in terms of linguistic survivance, by contrast, "illuminat[es] the ways that individuals and communities use specific languages, but also second languages, language varieties, and specific features, as well as bilingualism and translanguaging," or language mixing, to sustain cultural identities and practices in environments that are often hostile.[83] We recognize that it is not appropriate to apply a term developed to characterize Native North American experiences unthinkingly to Indigenous immigrants from Latin America. Nevertheless, the discourse around linguistic survivance is useful for expanding the horizon of what "counts" as language maintenance for Indigenous communities in diaspora, in that it emphasizes that Indigenous languages may continue to play a crucial role even if they are supplanted by colonial languages, to some degree, in everyday interaction.[84]

Literature from Native North America testifies to the diverse ways that communities have engaged in linguistic survivance, even in the absence of widespread conversational language use. Arikara activists, for example, compose songs that simultaneously reinvigorate the language and attempt to connect with spiritual powers.[85] Hopi youth resist reductive definitions of speakerhood, choosing to situate language use within Hopi cultural practices and Hopi values instead.[86] Finally, Lenape language teachers work to expand "authentic" participation in the Lenape speech community beyond traditional heritage learners.[87] Other scholars have examined the phenomenon of "language use without proficiency" in both Indigenous and immigrant communities, looking into the creation of "metalinguistic communities"—groups organized around language-based identities, but not necessarily with proficient speakers—through symbolic uses of language that "[point] towards broader communities of belonging."[88] Such strategies fit into a larger framework of linguistic survivance or "language reclamation" insofar as they "[aim] to remedy . . . ideologies . . . that impose a narrow notion of speech community" on minority language speakers or their descendants.[89]

For our purposes, the point is that linguistic survivance has different meanings for different speakers and speech communities and manifests in a range of linguistic practices beyond everyday conversational usage. Scholars of language and migration are attending more closely to the presence of speakers of Latin American Indigenous languages in the United States. Some have documented dynamics of linguistic survivance at the community level, examining how migration and transnational family life have contributed both to language maintenance and loss, while others have examined how Indigenous-origin students and parents position themselves in Spanish-English bilingual classrooms and other school spaces.⁹⁰ The emerging body of literature on Mayan speakers in US educational settings shows that even young Maya students develop "a consciousness and practice of becoming-with in diasporic location" through critical engagement with Spanish, English, and Mayan languages.⁹¹ Other work attests to the continued vibrance of Mayan codes in the US as community languages among Mayan-speaking immigrants and non-Maya, to a limited extent.⁹² Even immigrant and second-generation youth with limited Mayan proficiency have found contact with traditional cultural practices and Mayan languages to be a source of strength and resilience in challenging diasporic circumstances.⁹³

Much of the analysis in the following chapters focuses on Maya youth's appropriation of Spanish and English as "colonial codes of power" as a form of *preparación* for *adaptación* to life in Los Angeles, where *sobrevivencia* (and future-making in a broader sense) depend greatly on youth's access to discourse communities associated with colonial languages.⁹⁴ Still, we also try to account for youth's shifting Mayan language ideologies and practices as an essential part of their multilingual *adaptación* to life in Los Angeles as Indigenous immigrants seeking *sobrevivencia*. As is true of Native North American Indigenous speech communities, Mayan speakers in Los Angeles "are attempting to find a form of multilingual adaptation in which the heritage language continues to perform a valuable role while conceding . . . a dominant one" to Spanish and English, in different social domains and with respect to different interlocutors and dimensions of survival in diaspora.⁹⁵

Research with Unaccompanied Maya Youth Migrants

Research for this book includes six years of ethnographic observation (2012–2018), including four years of weekly fieldsite visits and two years of "episodic fieldwork"; it also includes in-depth interviews with thirty-six "L1 Mayan" (first-language speakers, primarily K'iche') Guatemalan youth workers who arrived in Los Angeles as unaccompanied minors between 2003 and 2013.⁹⁶ Our use of L1 speakers (first-language speakers) should not be taken to reify a native-speaker ideal in second-language acquisition nor to understate the fluid, flexible, and non-dichotomous nature of bilinguals' practices.⁹⁷ Here, and throughout the book, "L1 speakers" serves as useful shorthand for capturing the difference that Mayan speakers perceived between their own proficiency as sequential Mayan-Spanish-English bilinguals and the proficiency of others who had grown up speaking English and/or Spanish and were positioned very differently in the context of the labor market in Los Angeles. Some data also come from field observations and informal conversations with participants between 2018 and 2024.

Among interviewees, nine of the thirty-six participants (25 percent) were women. Men were over-sampled due to their more consistent participation in public settings where observations and interview recruitment were conducted, likely stemming from gender ideologies and occupational structures that confine Maya women to private spaces.[98] While perhaps unavoidable, the gender imbalance in the sample does necessarily limit the scope of our findings, as we have more data on Maya men's experiences with language during incorporation. These data come from a more extensive study on the migration and incorporation experiences of Central American and Mexican young adults who arrived in the US as minors and grew up without parents or legal status. Most of the youth workers in the study worked in the garment industry. Garment factory workers were committed to between twelve- and sixteen-hour workdays. Gender constraints on women's time and gendered social expectations that women's socializing takes place in private settings, namely in the household, greatly limited women garment workers' participation in public settings where recruitment for this research took place and, more importantly, where social ties were formed and community life was lived. Finally, all youth profiled in this book lived in the Pico-Union and Westlake/MacArthur Park area near downtown Los Angeles. This socialization context is important in that youth's local context, which is densely populated by Central American and Mexican diasporic communities, is nested within a diverse, multiethnic Los Angeles where interactions with non-immigrant and non-Latina/o groups were assured.

Ethnographic data presented throughout this book come primarily from that collected with participants in the support group, Voces de Esperanza, hereafter Voces. The goal of Voces was to promote self-help and community connectedness among unaccompanied Guatemalan Maya youth in Pico-Union and Westlake/MacArthur Park, Los Angeles, though non-Indigenous Guatemalans and non-Guatemalans occasionally participated in the group meetings. Voces was led by two group coordinators, Jorge and Wilfredo, non-Indigenous Mexican and Salvadoran immigrants, respectively (and non-Indigenous language speakers). The group gathered on Friday nights for two hours each week to answer one simple question: "How was your week?" The group had about forty members, but meetings drew between one and two dozen attendees weekly. Participants, aged eighteen to thirty-one, migrated to the United States as unaccompanied minors and grew up both unaccompanied and undocumented. As such, they were encouraged by Jorge and Wilfredo to *desarrollar* (develop) in seven areas—physical, intellectual, moral, emotional, spiritual, social, and sexual—and to keep this process in mind as they answered the opening question. Wilfredo, especially, emerged as a pivotal figure—a master of ceremonies for the participants' rite of passage, perhaps—who urged the youth to *"tomar nuevos caminos"* (take new paths) to achieve stability and remedy the pressures and emotional difficulties of immigrant life, rather than becoming trapped in permanent liminality.[99] Group participants spoke Spanish in the larger group setting, especially as neither Jorge nor Wilfredo spoke a Mayan language. Still, participants occasionally spoke their Mayan language to one another during personal conversations.

Many youth arrived at Voces after experiencing several years of material and emotional *retraso* (setback) in religious communities that required youth to donate their limited time and resources to maintain good standing.[100] Charismatic leaders within these religious communities, including pastors, expressed that youth's social and economic marginalization was evidence of their weak faith and exploited the youth's feelings of shame to encourage service and tithing. Such experiences made interactions with supportive figures like Wilfredo, Jorge, and others even more impactful in Maya youth's transitions from disorientation through preparation and adaptation in Los Angeles.

Stephanie, the first author, was invited to Voces by Jorge in 2012 and participated in weekly meetings thereafter. Though a first-language Spanish-language speaker, Stephanie lost much of her Spanish-language fluency during her K-12 education and began fieldwork with limited Spanish-language abilities, which proved beneficial in building rapport as she asserted her interest in learning from and alongside Maya youth participants. Being of similar age to research participants during data collection provided some common ground for cultural interests. Finally, Stephanie's community participation was facilitated because she is the daughter of Salvadoran immigrants, familiar with the Pico-Union and Westlake/MacArthur Park neighborhoods, and could hold informal conversations in Spanish about the local neighborhood and cultural events with the young people. Stephanie recruited interviewees through Voces and other community spaces and events and employed a snowball sampling strategy with interviewees to reach the total study sample. Brendan, the second author, is a linguistic anthropologist and a second-language (L2) Spanish speaker. He became involved with the project in 2019 when Stephanie invited him to collaborate on the analysis of data pertaining to language socialization and language maintenance among study participants.

All research was conducted in Spanish, and the interviews were transcribed and analyzed in Spanish.[101] For purposes of space and readability, we have translated data excerpts in the book into English. We include the original Spanish words and utterances where necessary, most especially when the English translation does not neatly capture the full meaning of the Spanish terms or phrases participants used. Furthermore, we rely on Spanish-language terms strategically to remind readers (and ourselves) that the analysis presented here draws directly from the young people's experiences in their spoken language at the point of interaction with the researcher and one another and in their own words.

Stephanie interviewed unaccompanied Maya youth who were Mayan language L1 speakers, some with and others without the ability to read and write their Mayan language. Most Maya participants were speakers of K'iche' (thirty-two), the most widely spoken Eastern Mayan language, but our group also included one speaker of Mam, two speakers of the Western Mayan language Q'anjob'al, and one of the Western Mayan languages Akateko.[102] Among participants, Spanish learning was limited to those who had some formal schooling in Guatemala (typically no more than three years) or who had worked alongside parents in agriculture or as vendors at local markets where they might have encountered Spanish speakers. Youth who did not attend school and who worked in the household alongside female caregivers had grown up as Mayan-language monolinguals, reflecting their caregivers' monolingualism.[103] Hence, many migrated to the US with limited Spanish-language proficiency and gained proficiency during migration and throughout their time in the Spanish-speaking Latin American immigrant community in the United States. By the time observations and interviews were conducted for this study, all participants had gained enough proficiency in Spanish to facilitate communication with the researcher.

It might be said that English became the participants' third language, but to represent unaccompanied minors' language learning in sequential terms understates the complexity of their language socialization. Instead, youth's linguistic preparation and adaptation, we will show, occurs within a multilingual ecology where individual pathways to language development take unexpected turns, as youth make choices about how to invest themselves in Spanish and English learning and Mayan maintenance in response to the variable circumstances of their work, community, and family lives.[104]

Overview of the Book

Everyday Futures examines the migration and coming of age of Guatemalan Maya youth who were full-time low-wage workers in Los Angeles, California, and the role of language in their incorporation process, which we theorize as future-making. Chapter 1 documents that the stigmatization of Indigenous identity and language "traveled" from Guatemala to Latin American immigrant communities in the United States, prolonging Maya youth's initial disorientation and complicating their distinctive journeys toward incorporation. The chapter provides an overview of the history of anti-Indigenous discrimination and violence in Guatemala and explores the youth's relationships to their Maya identities before migration, as well as their encounters with racism upon arriving in Los Angeles. We analyze how Maya youth experienced quotidian dislocations while growing up in Guatemala, where centuries-long anti-Indigenous racism shapes patterns of political underrepresentation, economic disinvestment, infrastructural underdevelopment, cultural misrecognition, and disrespect. This racism, among other forces, has contributed to disproportionate experiences of poverty and violence within and across contemporary Indigenous communities. Chronic, compounding, and immutable dislocations resulted in the displacement of the Maya youth participants of this research from Guatemalan society. Many then experienced renewed dislocations through overt discrimination from non-Indigenous Latinas/os in Los Angeles and had to combat *timidez y miedo* (shyness and fear) and low self-esteem stemming from internalized inferiority and concerns about physical violence. This was profoundly disorienting for the young people who had hoped to find a reprieve from violence in the United States. In both countries, Maya youth coped with disorientation by employing discourse strategies they had used in prior similar situations—for example, concealing or cloaking their identities as speakers of K'iche' and other Mayan languages and, thus, their identities as Indigenous people. Continued experiences of discrimination in the Los Angeles community and workspaces reinforced the racialized stigma attached to Indigenous identity and Mayan languages.

In Chapter 2, through an analysis of talk about Spanish and English learning (and Mayan maintenance, to a lesser extent), we illuminate the central place of language in the youth's imagined futures in the US. The young people identified numerous adaptation-related goals for which effective linguistic *preparación* was crucial: pursuing greater employability and easier work, cultivating family and community belonging, and preparing for long-term resettlement and *sobrevivencia*, or survival, in the host society and in the absence of parental guidance and formal education. Through *preparación*, Maya youth could agentially move from feelings of disorientation to being ready to "adapt" within and across nested social communities to achieve *sobrevivencia* in an imagined future. We analyze the forms of *preparación*, like *desahogo* or emotional unburdening, that took place in collective settings, along with others, like language learning, that youth generally pursued individually.

Chapter 3 shows how Maya youth apply and contest social constructs surrounding language proficiency—specifically, the use of "percentage talk"—to assess their preparedness for particular adaptive moves and assert Maya identity in contrast to binary (Spanish or English) or all-or-nothing (American or foreign) conceptions of incorporation. The youth's tricultural *adaptación* and contestation of an all-or-nothing (0 percent versus 100 percent) ideology of proficiency showed their nuanced understanding of the role of language in immigrant incorporation and their finegrained sense of how much language was "enough" to achieve particular goals. This chapter documents that the youth measured the potential for *adaptación* through the social construction of language proficiency—that is, construing current proficiency as a percentage of idealized full proficiency—as a discursive strategy for assessing their language ability and level of *adaptación* relative to native English and Spanish speakers, other Indigenous Latin Americans, and their past selves. In doing so, the young people wrestled with social stratification and inequality in the US and Guatemala and imagined themselves as future members of Spanish- and English-oriented discourse communities in the United States. While outwardly individualistic, in that it referred to individuals' beliefs about how their own language proficiency equipped them for adaptation, percentage talk also allowed youth to gauge their developing ability to support the language socialization and social incorporation of other, more recently arrived Mayan speakers in Los Angeles.

Chapter 4 demonstrates how Maya youth saved space for their Indigeneity within their Los Angeles-based future-making practices. We explore how youth reframed stigmatizing ideologies about Mayan languages and reconsidered the role these languages might play in the future immigrant community. This reflection was enabled by the youth's participation in coethnic small group settings that valorized Indigeneity. It was also related to the young people's growing embeddedness in Los Angeles's multicultural society as they overcame their isolation and became aware that other immigrant communities had thrived without abandoning their heritage languages or traditional cultural practices.

As an analytical category beyond the dichotomy of assimilation or transnationalism, the concept of future-making is well suited for examining the role of language learning and maintenance in the stages the youth participants described as *preparación* and *adaptación*. Like homemaking, future-making focuses attention on "migrants' interactions with specific local structures of opportunities" and "the minute *work* of adaptation on the immigrant side."[105] Future-making also illuminates the day-to-day interactions and practices that contribute to compounding "stability and predictability" over time as the inverse of the compounding dislocations that may drive migration in the context of changes in the life course and youth's concrete living circumstances.

The Conclusion returns to the guiding incorporation and language diversity and survivance frameworks presented in this Introduction. We also summarize the primary findings of the book, contrasting them with what we know about, first, non-Indigenous Latin American immigrant youth's experiences of language and education during incorporation, and second, the experiences of school-aged Indigenous Latin American-origin children and their families. We also reflect on how the findings from this study invite us to think differently about the process of incorporation, Indigenous identities in diaspora, and the nature of language socialization. The Conclusion presents recent examples of the "scaling up" in the visibility of Mayan and other Latin American Indigenous languages in the United States, such as increased advocacy for and access to interpretation services. We end with recommendations for policy leaders and program advocates interested in the mobility and well-being of unaccompanied Indigenous youth in the United States.

ONE

Becoming the Maya Youth Diaspora

Lucy was twenty-seven when she sat down for an interview with Stephanie in Pico-Union. Lucy was born in San Andrés Xecul in Totonicapán, Guatemala. She was seven when she left school and began working in the corn fields to help her parents make ends meet. Lucy then migrated to Los Angeles to seek new opportunities as an unaccompanied fifteen-year-old. At the time of the interview, Lucy was a garment worker. She worked seventy-two hours per week, from 7 am to 7 pm Monday through Saturday, at piece-rate wages, making somewhere between $300 per week when there was "*bastante trabajo*" (lots of work) and $150 "*cuando no hay nada*" (when there is nothing). These wages were meant to cover her share of rent and other expenses and remittances home, averaging about $100 every two months. Lucy had a boyfriend, also an unaccompanied Maya migrant, whom she met in the garment factory where she worked, but he spent his free time with friends while Lucy spent most of her time at home.[1] She felt alone most days. "Did you think it would be like this?" Stephanie asked. "*No sé*," Lucy responded, "I don't know. I think life is very difficult here."

Lucy noted that language posed a distinct challenge in the everyday encounters of Maya migrants. Lucy grew up as a K'iche' speaker. She learned some Spanish in Guatemala but became proficient in Los Angeles. Indeed, migrating from the Guatemalan Highlands, where Indigenous communities are concentrated and Mayan languages are predominantly spoken, to the US, where most Latina/o immigrants speak Spanish, made navigating even the most mundane tasks in Los Angeles, like buying groceries or clothing in stores, challenging. "I notice that (Maya) people want something," Lucy elaborated, "and the (sales)people at the stores don't understand them because they [Maya people] don't speak Spanish."

Lucy sketched the contours of what applied linguists have termed a "language ecology," or a social landscape within which Maya immigrants must "mediate complex encounters among interlocutors with different language capacities and cultural imaginations, who have different social and political memories, and who don't necessarily share a common understanding of the social reality they are living in."[2] Immigrants' ability to navigate the distinct linguistic ecology they are in fundamentally shapes their life chances, as language helps to determine their access to social networks, work and housing opportunities, and participation in public life.

Lucy explained that speaking *only* a Mayan language could make life in Los Angeles "difficult," but speaking both Mayan and Spanish was "good":

> It's so different, but it's easier for someone who speaks Spanish and dialect because . . . let's say that I only speak a dialect, but what you need here the most is Spanish because that's what people speak. So, let's say that you come here and you speak a dialect; you won't understand what people are saying, or you won't know how to ask for something. But if you know how to speak Spanish and your dialect, that's good.

Despite naming multilingual Mayan and Spanish language proficiency as "good," Lucy's explanation revealed the normalized colonial logic that Mayan languages are not universally perceived as valuable. Lucy referred to Mayan languages as "dialects" (*dialectos*), a practice that marks them as lesser or inferior relative to Spanish, revealing her understanding that—even if she saw K'iche' as legitimate—others did not.³ In Guatemala, as elsewhere in Latin America, treating Indigenous people as less than human has historically gone together with denigrating Indigenous languages as mere "dialects" as opposed to languages, "not human communication systems, but a set of animalesque noises."⁴ Maintaining these "archives of meaning" is one way that sociologist Julian Go observes that the "colonial past shapes the present" by "bequeath[ing] to us an entire discursive formation or *culture* replete with meanings that persist and continue to be drawn upon today, lodged in popular imaginaries, discourses, arts, culture, and even nationalism."⁵ Navigating this archive of meaning across the Mayan-Spanish language ecology was not new to Lucy. In fact, she explained, "It's the same way over there (in Guatemala). It's hard for people who only speak dialect. And then people get here, and it's the same thing."

This chapter shows how ethnoracial and linguistic discrimination, first in Guatemala, resulted in Maya youths' *dislocation* in two senses: (1) *to* the bottom of multiple societal hierarchies, and (2) *from* the institutions and social roles usually occupied by adolescents, that is, from schools into workplaces, and from students to workers, respectively. We trace unaccompanied Maya youth migrants' pre- and early post-migration encounters with ethnoracial and linguistic hierarchies, using the concepts of *dislocation, displacement*, and *disorientation* to analyze how their experiences of marginalization sometimes changed, and sometimes remained the same, across sites and over time.

Eventually such compounding quotidian dislocations led to youth's displacement from their origin society entirely, as they realized that the best hope for their and their families' survival was for them to migrate, alone, to the United States. Once there, as unaccompanied youth workers proficient in neither English nor Spanish, however, Maya youth quickly became disoriented as they discovered not only that they were similarly dislocated in the US, but also that the anti-Indigenous discrimination many hoped they had left behind was reproduced—and in some ways—even exacerbated in immigrant communities.

Prior to migrating, many Guatemalan Indigenous youth believe that migration to the US will provide a reprieve from the dislocations and discrimination experienced in their society of origin. But, broadly speaking, this is not the case. The myriad dislocations that Maya youth suffer in Guatemala are often not just replicated but magnified in the US as ethnoracial and linguistic hierarchies from the origin country "travel" across borders with youth and converge with existing hierarchies in the destination country, causing a profound sense of disorientation.[6] This reality underlies Lucy's only seemingly contradictory declarations that the US was "so different" but also "the same" as Guatemala. Maya youth must grapple with conditions that seem both completely strange and unexpectedly familiar. In attending to youth's accounts of origin country dislocations and displacement, and destination country dislocations and disorientation, we explore their understanding of their social roles and responsibilities across societies and show how they dealt with conflicts and contradictions in their sense of self and imagined futures.

Understanding how Guatemalan Maya youth learn to navigate complex ethnoracial and linguistic ecologies during diasporic future-making in Los Angeles first requires understanding the distinctive challenges they face in their country of origin. We begin with a brief discussion of the broad and historical structural conditions that shape Maya youth's encounters with, and attempts to counter, ethnoracial and linguistic discrimination in Guatemalan society. We then turn to an analysis of how anti-Indigenous racism and linguistic discrimination produced dislocations and, ultimately, displacement, impelling Maya youth to migrate. Next, we examine how migration provided (or did not provide) refuge from the dislocations youth experienced in Guatemala once they arrived in Los Angeles. Throughout, we highlight the themes of *timidez y miedo* (shyness and fear), forms of embodied distress that youth identified with ongoing exposure to dislocation, displacement, and disorientation.

Maya Dislocation and Displacement in Historical Context

Guatemala's history, and indeed the history of Indigenous Guatemalan youth migration, is one of "forced displacement and oppression from colonialism, plantation labor, foreign intervention, armed conflict."[7] The colonization of Central America, which introduced the notion of race and racial hierarchies to Indigenous communities, began with Spain in the sixteenth century. The terminology of racial classification varied across the Spanish colonial empire, but in Guatemala, non-Indigenous people have historically referred to themselves as Ladino.[8] Those identified as *Indio* and their descendants were considered backwards, culturally deficient, and lazy, while Europeans and their descendants (Ladinos, whose distinct ethnoracial characteristics are blurred except for their identity as non-Indigenous[9]) were considered modern, civilized, and wealthy.[10] These characterizations were used to justify the domination of Indigenous people, alongside the dispossession of their land and exploitation of their labor, and continue to shape the treatment of Indigenous groups today.

Beginning in the sixteenth century, colonialism ushered plantation labor into the Guatemalan economy, allowing for foreign economic and political intervention. Central America was drawn into the world economy in the nineteenth century following its constituent nations' independence through coffee production and export expansion. The Spanish established haciendas across Guatemala's southern region, a land fertile for coffee plantations and one where most inhabitants were Maya. Already holding power within colonial Central America, the Catholic Church became a stronghold in capitalist production and export and relied most heavily on the Indigenous population for labor. Any lands held by the Indigenous population that the Church desired for coffee production were promptly expropriated by the Church, stirring conflict between communities whose land was being redistributed by the government without their consent. Tension between the Guatemalan government and Indigenous communities grew as workers resisted leaving their land. To take control, the government imposed a system of enforced labor and debt peonage that brought workers from the highlands, another region densely populated by Indigenous Guatemalans, to the southern region's coffee plantations. Seasonal migration eventually expanded into Mexico, where workers sought coffee plantation farm work. Others migrated to the United States.

By the twentieth century, German companies bought significant proportions of commercial estates and took "significant control over the coffee industry" until World War II, when the United States expropriated land from Germany amidst financial instability.[11] Upon US intervention, domestic banana farming of Guatemala (alongside Honduras and Costa

Rica) was reorganized as mass banana production through enclaves along the Caribbean coast. Here, the United Fruit Company of the US dominated. Seasonal out-migration from Guatemala continued, as did migration from El Salvador and Honduras into Guatemala to capitalize on the expanding privatization of agricultural markets. Industrialization and market interventions were not without resistance, and banana production and export became central to low-wage labor and labor organization in the 1920s. The administrations of democratically elected presidents Juan Jose Arevalo and Jacobo Árbenz between 1944 and 1954 brought with them the promise of restoring rights and property to the majority landless poor and Indigenous population. Known as the Eternal Spring or Democratic Spring, this era was characterized by efforts to increase the minimum wage, improve education, and institute agrarian reform by purchasing land from foreign companies for redistribution to Guatemalans.[12] Indeed, an agrarian reform law introduced in 1952 was meant to redistribute up to 1.5 million acres of land to 100,000 Guatemalan families.[13]

Most threatened among landowners was the United Fruit Company (known today as Chiquita), which armed an anticommunist campaign against Guatemala and called on President Eisenhower and the US to intervene on its behalf. In 1952, President Eisenhower drew on the power of the newly formed Central Intelligence Agency to launch a covert operation to remove Guatemalan President Árbenz. This began by recruiting an opposition force, which it found in Guatemalan military officer Carlos Castillo Armas.[14] By 1954, and with the support of the US government and CIA, Castillo Armas launched an invasion that ultimately incited the onset of the Guatemalan Civil War.[15] Education scholar Michelle J. Bellino summarizes US intervention as "[m]ired in the Cold War fears that communism could gain influence across the region, but also highly motivated to protect US economic interest in Latin America."[16] Bellino elaborates that the US plan to remove President Árbenz from power "was designed to support elites and mitigate the growing popular interest in expanding social and economic rights to Guatemala's poor."[17] Intensifying political and economic repression motivated greater resistance, especially from students, teachers, labor unions, and others who demanded the right to land and labor, free of coercion and control. In Guatemala, as in all conflict-ridden Central America during the Cold War period, some members of the Catholic Church espoused a liberation theology in opposition to violence against and oppression of the poor.[18] Castillo Armas was assassinated in 1957 by a presidential guard in the presidential palace in Guatemala City. Miguel Ydigoras Fuentes succeeded him in power.[19]

For thirty-six years, between 1960 and 1996, armed conflict plagued the whole of Guatemalan society as the government deployed military forces to protect the interests of US corporations and Guatemalan elites. In urban areas, the focus of the early Civil War years, military death squads targeted political leaders, organizers, and activists.[20] In rural areas where Indigenous Guatemalans most densely populated the contentiously held lands, Indigenous communities, including youth, were labeled the "internal enemy."[21] These areas became the focus of the second phase of the war beginning in the 1970s, during which the military launched a scorched earth policy in the highlands: people, including women and children, were tortured and "disappeared"; families were massacred and entire bloodlines were erased; Indigenous villages were decimated; and cultural symbols were desecrated.[22] In total, 1.5 million refugees fled their homes, 200,000 people fled the country, and 150,000 people were killed or disappeared. Among them were Indigenous children and youth framed as enemies. In a United Nations–sponsored Guatemalan Commission for Historical Clarification Report, investigators concluded that:

> [A] large number of children were also among the direct victims of arbitrary persecution, forced disappearance, torture, rape, and other violations of their fundamental rights. . . . [The conflict] left a large number of children orphaned or abandoned, especially among the Maya population, who saw their families destroyed and the possibility of living a normal childhood within the norms of their culture, lost.[23]

Additionally, 600 villages were destroyed. Intending to eliminate Indigenous communities, the military targeted "Maya community and spiritual leaders, as well as cultural markers central to Indigenous identity, making public displays of their desecration."[24] At least 100,000 women were raped. In a Truth Commission report on the genocide, the US Institute of Peace estimated that 83 percent of these atrocities were committed against Indigenous Maya, who were targeted because of their identity.[25] It is estimated that the government committed 93 percent of all human rights violations during the armed conflict.

Violence remains rampant in Guatemala despite the signing of the 1996 Peace Accords, and the US continues to have much to do with this. Central American teens fleeing with their parents to the United States during the civil wars in their origin countries formed protective cliques in their destination communities. In Los Angeles, two cliques became violently organized and, following the deportation of some of their members, expanded into Central America, primarily to El Salvador and Guatemala. As global economic expansion and climate change continue to devastate familial and community subsistence farming, children and youth who are targeted by gangs are susceptible to the lure of earnings, however harmfully acquired, and the feeling of belonging. Indigenous youth, especially boys, are violently recruited into gangs and assaulted when they resist.[26] Meanwhile, the state continues to enact violence on Indigenous elders and leaders who resist what Maya communities refer to as the Fourth Invasion, or the expansion of private extractive hydroelectric mega projects in Indigenous communities.[27]

Research on changes in the Guatemalan census suggests that the binary racial taxonomy (*indígena-ladino*) that held for much of the country's history has become less rigid at an institutional and bureaucratic level, even as entrenched stereotypes about Indigeneity and European descent continue to shape the life chances of these youth. In the 2002 census, the umbrella *indígena* category was expanded to accommodate diverse ethnic affiliations (Maya, Xinka, and Garífuna), and *ladino* and *indígena* were no longer assumed to be mutually exclusive (i.e., an individual could claim both identities). Social anthropologist Gemma Celigueta linked these changes to a broader trend of *mayanización* or *indigenización* following the 1996 Peace Accords, or greater visibility of Maya identity and, perhaps, willingness to identify as Maya or pan-Indigenous.[28] Our participants' accounts of persistent anti-*Indio* discrimination and violence imply that these changes have yet to filter down to youth's day-to-day interactions, but we acknowledge them, nonetheless.

In the aftermath of civil war and genocide, everyday life in Guatemala is characterized by dislocation. A long line of research has established that Indigenous Guatemalan adults are subjected to social, political, and economic violence and marginalization. Men, revered as heads of household in patriarchal societies, are blocked from land and labor market opportunities. Men's dislocation from roles that uphold patriarchy, hegemonic masculinity, and claims to manhood can result in violence against women. Women, whose traditional gender roles as homemaker and caretaker tend to relegate them to the private sphere, are subjected to quotidian violence ranging from domestic abuse to femicide.[29] That women are barred from public office and civic life suppresses their ability to secure representation of their rights in public and policy spheres. When chronic, compounding, and immutable, these dislocations can lead to displacement through migration.

Maya Youth's Dislocations in Guatemala

A developing line of research focused on the growing-up experiences of youth in Guatemala shows that children are also subject to dislocation. It is estimated that about 60 percent of the Guatemalan population is under the age of thirty, and 40 percent is under the age of fifteen.[30] That is, 40 percent of young people are navigating adolescence, a life stage between childhood and adulthood normatively considered a time for young people to learn their social roles and responsibilities, establish a sense of self, and begin to set goals and plan for the future.[31] Western democratic societies embed these processes within schools, institutions that educate, socialize, and cultivate civic actors to fully participate in society in the transition to adulthood. Yet a high percentage of Guatemalan adolescent youth are out of school, and levels of educational attainment are comparatively low as well. In rural regions, where poverty is concentrated and where Indigenous communities live, youth average only four years of formal education.[32]

Even in schools, the formation of youth as civic actors is made more difficult by many adults' reluctance to reckon with the legacy of the genocidal war between the Guatemalan military and left-wing revolutionaries linked to Indigenous communities.[33] The lack of transparency around aspects of the civil war, particularly the incidence of government-abetted atrocities against the Maya, and institutional eagerness to "move on" from the past has sometimes resulted in a historical amnesia that makes it challenging for youth to function as well-informed civic actors.[34] The young people's position in Guatemalan society is also threatened by the proliferation of gangs, especially Mara Salvatrucha 13, colloquially known as MS-13, and Barrio 18 (18th Street), two gangs that formed in Los Angeles and were imported to Central America through US deportation policy.[35] Youth are excessively criminalized because of the dominant presence of these gangs and are frequently suspected of gang activity. Along with the inattention to the lasting effects of the civil war, this has contributed to a tendency to blame youth "delinquency" for Guatemala's present-day problems. The presentist framing of "delinquency" as an individual-level moral phenomenon, as opposed to a pattern of behavior stemming from structural factors in Guatemalan society, further marginalizes youth who have inherited a lack of opportunity in a deeply hierarchical situation.[36]

Maya Youth's Displacement from Guatemala

Armed conflict, systemic violence, and structurally produced inequality have driven Guatemalan youth to a state of "migranthood," which anthropologist Lauren Heidbrink has described as a life stage in Guatemala wherein children engage in migration as an act of care to counter ongoing structural violence.[37] On one hand, the absence of opportunities to realize their goals causes some youth to experience "waithood," a sort of life stage transition paralysis wherein young people "struggle to meet cultural expectations that facilitate their transition to social adulthood."[38] On the other hand, families' precarious social, political, and economic positions thrust young people into what are typically assumed to be adult roles and responsibilities at an early age.[39] The displacement of parents and other adult workers from increasingly privatized industries obliges children to enter the workforce early, taking on the role of breadwinner to support their families. Children have long been active contributors to family and community care networks. Still, migration offers the promise of allowing youth to address the deprivation that plagues their families and communities actively.

Youth from Maya and other Indigenous communities experience the most severe dislocation and displacement from Guatemalan society. Within Guatemala, Maya and other Indigenous communities experience the distinct consequences of a national legacy of anti-Indigenous colonialism and imperialism as social, political, and economic marginalization; land dispossession; extreme poverty; and ethnoracial violence. The devaluation of Indigenous individual and community life has fed decades of underdevelopment in infrastructure and disinvestment in education, safety, and public health. In the Western highlands region, where Indigenous communities are densely concentrated, the poverty rate approximates 76 percent, with 27 percent of families living in extreme poverty.[40] Among Indigenous youth, internal, regional, and transnational migration offer a chance to provide families with material and emotional resources to *aguantar* (endure) life in Guatemala and strengthen family and community collectivism.[41] Potential migrant youth also understand migration as an escape valve that can free them from oppressive systems of power, even those within their own homes.[42] Migration is imagined as moving them closer to their futures as educated and employed adults, free from the imminent threat of poverty or violence, and capable of caring for themselves and their families.

Scholars describe Maya migration from Guatemala since the 1970s as unfolding across three distinct phases. First, in the late 1970s, there was pioneer migration led by those seeking employment opportunities in the United States. Second, in the 1980s, there was war refugee migration by those fleeing genocide, which was facilitated by networks with pioneer migrants. And, third, from the late 1980s to the present, there has been migration of single young men and women following existing networks in pursuit of mobility out of enduring poverty.[43] Over the last several decades of Maya migration, family and community structures have become more complex as family mobility and community development have become increasingly individualized and more reliant on out-migration and transnational networks.[44] Anthropologist Briana Nichols notes that, for youth growing up in Guatemala, "few institutions exist to facilitate a future at home and leaving seems inevitable."[45]

Today, migrants include youth with no prior internal or regional migration experiences, as Indigenous Guatemalan families are reliant on the young people for their collective economic survival. Already actively contributing to their households' material and emotional economies, Indigenous youth thus engage in youth-led transnational migration as an act of care.[46] The above-mentioned rise of unaccompanied minor migration suggests children and youth represent a distinct migration era. Just as the displacement and migration patterns of Indigenous unaccompanied Guatemalan youth are shaped by Guatemala's history of colonialism, plantation labor, economic and political intervention, and armed conflict, so too is their arrival to and incorporation into the United States. Understanding *how* is especially important today as Indigenous refugees' and asylum seekers' migration from Central America to the United States has increased steadily since 2012 and intensified since 2021.

Maya youth are joining the Maya diaspora in the United States, which is concentrated in traditional urban destinations for Mexican immigrant and/or Mexican-descent communities.[47] Established migration networks and proximity to the low-skilled, low-wage industries of downtown Los Angeles draw many unaccompanied Guatemalan youth—both with and without migration networks.[48] Though Guatemalans began migrating to the US during the 1950s, Maya refugee migration to Los Angeles became notable in the 1970s and 1980s as political and economic hostility in the region intensified.[49] Today, nearly 2 million Guatemalans live in the US, 1 million of whom are immigrants.[50] Twenty-seven percent of Guatemalans live in California, and Los Angeles is home to the largest Guatemalan community outside of Guatemala, concentrated in the Pico-Union and Westlake/MacArthur Park neighborhoods west of downtown Los Angeles.[51] The Guatemalan population in Los Angeles is diverse. While an estimated 43 percent of Guatemalans in Guatemala identify as Indigenous, between 50 and 60 percent of Guatemalans in Los Angeles are Maya.[52] Indigenous Maya communities in the US, including today's unaccompanied youth, are not legally recognized as refugees and navigate settlement in the US without formal protections and support.

Confronting Compounding Quotidian Dislocations

Maya youth in the study often told stories of compounding quotidian dislocations that ultimately led to their displacement through migration. For example, on one occasion in 2012, Stephanie was invited to a Pico-Union McDonald's, where Wilfredo was talking with a young Maya man named Jonny. Jonny grew up in Chivarreto in Totonicapán, Guatemala. To acquaint Stephanie with Jonny, Wilfredo asked Jonny several questions about himself and his background, including questions about his life in Guatemala. The three got onto the topic of home country education and the myriad ways educational trajectories can be cut short for Maya youth. Jonny's school-going ended when, at the age of thirteen, his father abandoned him and his family, prompting Jonny to assume a breadwinner role. Jonny recalled the series of events that night:

> When I started studying in my *aldea* of Chivarreto, I got up to the fourth grade, but I still didn't know how to read or write. I transferred to a municipality known as San Carlos, where there are only *güeros* (light-skinned people), only white people. From there, I remember that even though I was in the fourth grade in my *aldea*, I was moved down to first grade. I had to start over. I remember there was a teacher, an older man, that had me go to the chalkboard. I remember I couldn't say a-e-i-o-u but I learned. Then I went to second, third, fourth, I was never held back. I got to fifth grade when I was thirteen years old, but then my dad abandoned us. I am the oldest, so my mom went to sign me up for sixth grade, but it was sixty (quetzals) per year. My mom told me that I couldn't start the new school year. I wasn't going to be able to continue because she also had my siblings, and she was not going to be able to take care of us all. From then on, I started working to support my brothers and sisters.

When Stephanie asked Jonny to clarify how old he was when he was dislocated from his role as student to that of worker, Jonny remembered that he "always worked in the fields" while enrolled in primary school, where, as a K'iche' speaker, he initially struggled to succeed in a system that was designed for Spanish-speaking *güeros*. Before his father left, like thousands of young people in Guatemala, Jonny worked to earn small sums that would supplement his parents' earnings. But when Jonny's father abandoned the family, Jonny's mother inherited the full responsibility of supporting six children aged thirteen and younger. Being the eldest, Jonny then became the male head of household, which meant prioritizing short-term survival over long-term social mobility: work over school. "I stopped going to school when I was thirteen years old," Jonny reiterated. "That's when I started, in the fields, and then I went to work in San Carlos Sija. From San Carlos, I went to the capital [Guatemala City]."

After confirming that a year of schooling cost sixty quetzals, Wilfredo asked Jonny, "Sixty quetzals is like $9 per year to go to school, and your mom didn't have that so you couldn't continue?" "No [she did not have that]," Jonny confirmed. "Did you feel responsible for others because you're the older brother?" Stephanie asked. Without hesitation, Wilfredo stepped in, "Yes, because their father left them." Jonny decided to migrate to Los Angeles at fifteen.

Migration decisions are rarely abrupt unless made facing acute violence and persecution.[53] Instead, they are thoughtfully considered and often represent a final effort to pursue *sobrevivencia* in a new society when all origin-country options are exhausted. In many cases, youth's displacement narratives began with dislocation from their social position as students in school, potentially engaged in some work, into the position of full-time low-wage workers in extractive industries. Eventually, the youth felt entirely dislocated from opportunities for wage and occupational mobility in Guatemala, and these feelings of desperation and hopelessness incited curiosity about opportunities elsewhere.

The reproduction of ethnoracial and linguistic hierarchies was one young people were warned about by family members prior to their migration. These tendencies were sometimes reinforced by messages from parents and relatives in Guatemala, who encouraged youth to isolate themselves to avoid contact with White people (in particular) and limit the risk of exposure to immigration enforcement. For example, Aarón said that his parents and grandparents warned him not to trust the public transportation system "because Immigration [and Customs Enforcement] might find out where you are" and that "if you see a White person, they will kill you, so you cannot associate with people outside of your own group." Because this warning is commonly given to youth growing up in Guatemala, adolescent and teenage migrants, like adult migrants, carry "racial baggage."[54] This concept, introduced by sociologist Sylvia Zamora, refers to the "racial ideas and practices [that] travel across geopolitical borders to influence the racial thinking and practices of individuals 'here and there' and in the process, generate new experiences of racial difference, belonging, and citizenship for those who migrate."[55] Racial baggage affects Indigenous youth's long-term incorporation and coming of age by dictating and delimiting the nature of their social ties, which are in many cases already strained by legal, social, and economic precarity.[56]

Poverty and the Dislocation from Childhood
Like Jonny, Caterina's familial poverty dislocated her from student to worker. Caterina was seventeen when she migrated from San Francisco el Alto, also in Totonicapán. She stopped attending school just after completing her primary education and began working alongside her mother and grandmother in the fields. Also, like Jonny, Caterina's story of leaving school was one of dashed aspirations for social and economic mobility due to intersecting family and structural circumstances in a society where education was unattainable for many.

Stephanie and Caterina met in Los Angeles when Caterina was nineteen, at which time she remembered her mom as supportive but constrained in her ability to help Caterina reach her goal of becoming a doctor. "My mom was helping me when I was in primary school," Caterina detailed. "She would pay for my school and everything, but after that, when I went to secondary school, she didn't help me anymore. And my dad never wanted to help me." Caterina's father was not around while she was growing up, but she knew who he was and where to find him. She had approached him for financial support to continue going to school several times, but he refused. "I lived with my mom, and I would tell my dad that I wanted to study but that it wasn't an option for me," Caterina explained.

> Sometimes I would go to him to ask him for money to help me pay for school, but he would get angry with me. He refused to help me. I

decided I would work. I started working so that I could save money and maybe eventually return to school. But as it turns out, that would not be the case.

Caterina soon realized she could not earn enough to meet her family's basic needs and save enough to return to school. Caterina would "help her [mom] in the fields, and make food for the workers and everything," but she wanted more.

Caterina was dislocated from educational opportunity, wage mobility, and, ultimately, her dreams of becoming a doctor. She believed migration could offer an alternative future. "When I told [my mother] I wanted to leave, she said, 'No, don't go. I know it's not fair that you must work, but don't leave.'" Caterina contemplated her mother's request but resolved to migrate anyway: "I want to get ahead," she confessed to her mother:

> My dream is to be a doctor to help impoverished children in Guatemala that can't study or afford their basic needs. I told her, "I want to go." A part of me didn't want to come here [Los Angeles]. I didn't want to leave my mom alone but another part of me did want to come here because I had no way of getting ahead. So, I told my mom, "I'm going to go. I'm very sorry, but I want to study. I don't have that possibility here."

Caterina felt trapped between the urgency of the present and her longing for an imagined future. She reiterated the tension she faced, explaining,

> Even though I was working, I still didn't have enough money. It was too much to pay for school and all of the supplies I needed. And yeah, my mother always told me she didn't want me to leave, but I didn't have any other choice. I had to come here.

Caterina understood her migration as the last straw—her final attempt to get by and get ahead. In a sense, Caterina's situation was the inverse of the "transnational care constellations" education scholar Gabrielle Oliveira describes in that, rather than a mother migrating and leaving children in the care of older relatives, it was the child who had to migrate with the same goal of securing a better future for herself and her family.[57]

Caterina made her migration decision on the day her "brother and sister told [her] to go to Los Angeles." She recalled that her siblings, who were already living in Los Angeles, promised "they would help me but that I would have to continue working to take care of myself." Already taking care of herself in Guatemala, Caterina agreed to the terms of her migration to Los Angeles: "I said, 'Yes, that's fine.' I had been living with my grandmother for three months at that time but when my siblings called to tell me that, I left. My brother said my cousins were coming here, so I left with them two days later." Caterina summed up her story of dislocation and displacement by saying: "I came here [Los Angeles] because I didn't have the possibility of studying."

Caterina, like Jonny, spoke matter-of-factly about the dislocation that led to her decision to migrate, reflecting the extent to which structural violence for Indigenous people in Guatemala has become "so commonplace as to become invisible."[58] As a disproportionate burden of poverty falls on Indigenous families and communities, youth are prompted to leave school and enter the labor market to make ends meet.

Ridicule and Peer-Group Dislocation

Maya youth revere education as a pathway to mobility and well-being in Guatemala, yet evidence demonstrates that schools are also the primary sites where these young people confront the race- and gender-specific nature of Guatemala's idealized national identity.[59] Aarón was twenty-six years old when he and Stephanie met. He had been living in the US for ten years by that time. Having grown up with both of his parents, unlike Jonny and Caterina, Aarón described leaving school by his own volition after concluding that learning Spanish would not be useful in his hometown of San Antonio Sija, Totonicapán, where K'iche' is the most widely spoken language. He attributed a feeling of disconnection between his school and home realities to a lack of interest and motivation: "I would go somewhere else to study Spanish, to learn Spanish, but then we would come back to our town [where Spanish was not spoken]. So, I did that until I was thirteen."

Probing, however, revealed that anti-Indigenous racism and the dislocation of Maya youth in Guatemalan society also played a role in Aarón's displacement from school. A keen observer of language and social life,

Aarón theorized that what made Spanish seem "hard" was not the language itself, but the fact that Maya youth were exposed to it in an environment of intense discrimination. "Discrimination of what?" Stephanie asked.

> Well, of, well, okay. . . . Since I am Maya, I don't speak Spanish. So, where I would go to study, we could say that it was 100 percent *hispanos* [Hispanics, meaning from Spain]. They come from Sevilla, Spain. They got here some, I don't know, 500 or 400 years ago. These people are totally White. We know about Americans, their stature, their physical appearance, all of that. It's the same over there. They look the same. They're tall, blue-eyed, White people. So, we, the Maya people, the majority of us are of short stature, and they are tall. Growing up, I noticed *cómo se burlaban* [how they ridiculed us]. I wasn't subjected to this ridicule much, but I noticed how much my friends were discriminated against because they had a darker skin tone than I did. But sometimes they would tell me too. *Tuve miedo* [I was scared] because they noticed, "Ohh, you're also from *that* town." And I would say, "no." Imagine that? I mean, I am from San Antonio Sija. That's about fifteen minutes from San Carlos Sija. It takes like, fifteen minutes to get from San Antonio Sija to San Carlos Sija in a car. It's really close. But I started to see just how much discrimination there was.

Aarón's account of *hispanos* in nearby San Carlos Sija, where he attended school, presented a starkly segregated picture of Guatemalan society, in which even "500 years" of coexistence had not weakened the social divisions between "short, darker" Maya people and "totally White" or Ladino Guatemalans of Spanish ancestry. In this representation, Maya and *hispano* realities are in "really close" proximity, yet entirely separate. Bellino similarly recalls a bus trip with one of her Maya participants, during which she saw a sign reading "Language: Español" outside a so-called Ladino town, only a few turns away from the Maya-speaking village to which they were headed.[60] Aarón invoked *miedo*, or fear, to describe the feeling of being ridiculed by non-Indigenous people. He also described the *hispano* town of San Carlos Sija as a place where he "started to see" the extent of discrimination. In other words, he began to develop a critical awareness of how language and race overlapped in others' construal of the inferiority of Maya people:

> When I started to see that discrimination, I would ask myself, "Why are we *Indios*? Why do they treat us like this? And why do we speak a dialect, but they speak Spanish?" So that really started to affect my self-esteem. I felt rejected. I felt humiliated. I started to notice that *todos los jóvenes crecían con miedo porque nos discriminaban mucho* [all of the teenagers were growing up in fear because they discriminated against us a lot]. People say, "Hey, you don't know anything," like, among teenagers, among students. That's what happened in *secundaria* [the equivalent of junior high school, typically students aged twelve to fifteen].

Reading between the lines of Aarón's comments, the scope of his critique becomes clear: "Why are we *Indios*?" is a very different question than the self-evident "Why are we Maya?" (see, e.g., Andrés's remarks on Maya identity in the Introduction). Asking why Maya students are considered *Indios* who "don't know anything" and are mistreated at school spoke to Aarón's humiliation and damaged self-esteem; it also represented an incipient process of inquiry about the structural conditions that led *Indio* to become a relevant category in Guatemala (and, later, in the United States). Likewise, asking "Why do we speak a 'dialect'?" stood in contrast to Aarón's commonsense description of his language background earlier ("Since I am Maya, I don't speak Spanish"). As in Lucy's juxtaposition of "dialect" and "Spanish" at the beginning of this chapter, it begs the question of how some languages get relegated to the status of dialects and, like their speakers, associated with rurality, ignorance, and so forth. Aaron's reliance on the imperfect aspect in the Spanish version of his narrative underscored Maya youth's pervasive, long-term exposure to racial and linguistic discrimination—*se burlaban, nos discriminaban, los jóvenes crecían con miedo:* "they always made fun of us," "they always discriminated against us," "the [Maya] youth were growing up with *miedo.*"

Aarón also commented that the promise of Spanish as a route to social mobility was false, since learning Spanish on its own did not necessarily diminish discrimination against Indigenous youth:

> There were so many problems. I realized that speaking Spanish is not that hard; it's just that there is *tanta discriminación* [so much discrimination]. So, you learn the language, but there is still discrimination. That's what caused me to lose my motivation to study, too.

In essence, Aarón realized that learning Spanish did not equate to greater social incorporation in Guatemala. Instead, he would have gone out of his way to learn a new language only to face the same roadblock of "so much discrimination."

Aarón's experience supports Nichols's assertion that "the Guatemalan public educational system was built on racialized social and epistemic exclusion," in which "anti-Mayan racialized exclusions are an example of enduring coloniality."[61] Per Nichols, Maya youth in Guatemalan schools "must navigate local histories of discrimination, disenfranchisement, and structural violence as they intersect with perceptions of possible futures." Aarón mentioned his peers' ridicule, but some youth in the study described instances of being targeted for verbal and physical harassment by their teachers. One participant, Brayant, said that, at school and in society at large, "*si el niño es indígena, lo menosprecian*" (if a child is Indigenous, they are belittled). They might be called slow or incapable of learning in front of their peers. Frustrated teachers might shove a desk or hit students over the head for their failure to respond coherently to class activities or assignments. Brayant saw the challenge in learning not in Maya students' capacity to learn but with the teachers' approach of speaking only Spanish to the class, which left little room for Maya students to "absorb" the appropriate meaning and uses of the language, especially if the students were the only ones in the home to (attempt to) speak the language. Teachers, Brayant clarified, did not speak Mayan languages. "Everything was in Spanish," Brayant said. "At school, they spoke to us in Spanish, but it's not like . . . Well, yeah, if the teachers spoke to us in Spanish, but I was speaking K'iche' at home, there was no way for me to absorb what we were learning. I wasn't being *entrenado* [trained] to speak Spanish."

Aarón was dislocated from his peer group and school and Brayant felt dislocated from the classroom and the learning process during their critical transition from adolescence to young adulthood, when one's self-concept and sense of place are developing. Describing Maya youth's compounding dislocations before the ultimate displacement of unaccompanied transnational migration, Aarón said:

> So, I think those are the issues we deal with: problems at home, problems at school with discrimination, and feeling alone because there's no one to motivate or protect you. Then I realized: "No, I needed to come here [Los Angeles]." That's what motivated me. That is what made me come here.

Aarón was displaced from Guatemala at sixteen.

Feelings of Inevitable and Inescapable Dislocation
Maya youth who were pushed out of schools and into the public sphere were not buffered from the ridicule, discrimination, and low self-esteem that Aarón experienced at school. The notion that Indigenous people, including youth, not only *knew* less but *were* less than Spanish-speaking Ladinos was pervasive. In the public sphere, youth were also talked down to by adults. This was often the topic of conversation during Stephanie's early visits to Voces de Esperanza, where she met Ximena for the first time in November 2012. When the two met, Ximena had been attending Voces for just a few weeks.

Typically the only single woman in the group, Ximena was often the unwilling center of attention among at least a dozen teenaged boys and young adult men, which made her even more reserved. Stephanie had not heard much from Ximena directly during the first month of their overlapping meeting attendance, but one November evening, Ximena spoke candidly about herself and her background. Ximena began by sharing that, in a two-hour conversation with group coordinator Wilfredo earlier that week, she began reflecting on her life story and her adolescence. When the Friday night group meeting occurred, Wilfredo encouraged her to tell the group what she had shared during their one-on-one meeting.

Ximena hailed from San Pedro Soloma in Huehuetenango, Guatemala. Prior to arriving in Los Angeles, Ximena had only ever traveled to San Carlos Sija, about five hours away in Quetzaltenango, Guatemala. She was excited to visit another town, but her excitement turned to dread when she and her mother experienced ridicule for speaking their Mayan language, Q'anjob'al, in public. Echoing Aarón's comments above, she explained the behavior of San Carlos Sija residents this way:

> The people from San Carlos Sija are descendants of Spain. They have light skin and blue eyes. When people from [San Pedro Soloma] visited and interacted with them, the people of San Carlos Sija would say, "You are *Indios*, you should learn Spanish."

Ximena spoke to the widespread racist practice among non-Indigenous Central Americans and Mexicans of referring to Maya and other Indigenous groups with the derogatory term *Indio*, or "Indian." This "historical racist moniker [is used to] denote someone who is inferior."[62]

Indigenous cultural identity is also embodied through dress. Indigenous communities maintain their traditional *traje*, including embroidered shirts for men and women, which women pair with elaborately colored textiles worn as skirts and shawls. Young people learn at an early age that both phenotype and traditional clothing mark them as different and presumably inferior within the dominant non-Indigenous Guatemalan society.

Leopoldo explained a recent confrontation with the persistence of this reality for children in Guatemala even as he lived in Los Angeles, which reinforced his preexisting beliefs that discrimination dislocated him and others like him. In an interview in a noisy Pico-Union coffee shop, Leopoldo said that the people who most discriminate against Indigenous communities "are from the city," people like those Ximena encountered. Leopoldo described having evidence that these were not singular experiences but systematically embedded anti-Indigenous beliefs that non-Indigenous people learn at early ages.

Describing an experiment conducted in Guatemala similar to the 1947 Doll Test (in which four dolls, identical except for their complexion, were presented to Black children to understand the psychological effects of racism and segregation), Leopoldo shared that the video of the experiment showed that:

> Parents will sometimes ask boys or girls . . . the kids will have dolls; one has a *corte* [a traditional Maya women's skirt], and the other has

a dress. So, the parents will ask them in an interview, like a study, where they ask the kids, "Which one do you like?" [The child says,] "This one." [The adult asks,] "Why that one?" [The child responds,] "Well, this one is pretty, and that one is ugly." [The adult then asks,] "Why is that ugly?" [The child says,] "Look at it, it has a *corte*." [The adult asks,] "Why is that ugly?" [The child says,] "Well, I don't know where those people are from." So, to me, that's discrimination. They [non-Indigenous people] are teaching the kids, "No, not them, they're not the same. And I don't even understand what they're saying!" So, there is a lot of discrimination in cities against the Maya and K'iche' people.

Even as Leopoldo elaborated on the discrimination of Maya people's way of dress, his concluding expression ("And I don't even understand what they're saying!") reveals the insidious nature of discrimination against Indigenous languages. Like Aarón and Ximena, Leopoldo associated the ascribed inferiority of Maya people with their phenotype (skin and eye color) and their culture, both as a way of dress and language. Discrimination of dark features and non-Spanish languages produced violence, and this violence produced what Ximena described as a lifelong fear. "*Nacemos con miedo*," she shared, "*y más cuando hablamos*" (We are born with fear, and even more so when we speak).

Maya youth are first dislocated by being placed outside the national identity of Guatemalan (as non-Indigenous and Ladino) and then physically displaced from that nation-state. Ximena explained that these dislocations and displacements were latent throughout Maya people's lives but were made salient and exacerbated through the simple acts of living in one's body and speaking one's native language. Research on other Maya-origin youth (in the US and Mexico) supports Ximena's and Leopoldo's contention, as Mayan language use has been linked to youth's perceptions of anti-Indigenous discrimination and their resulting levels of distress.[63]

Extreme poverty and anti-Indigenous racism stemming from colonial and imperial interventions in Guatemala have forced Maya youth to negotiate quotidian dislocations and longer-term displacement. Migration is understood as an escape from the "the unresolved past, the unstable present, and the unfulfilled future" that Guatemalan youth share, but that Maya youth feel especially, as their intersecting ethnoracial, linguistic, and class, as well as their identities as youth, put them at an even greater disadvantage.[64] In many cases, Maya youth imagined that their futures in the US would be free of the acute violence and poverty they experienced in Guatemala. Few found this to be the case; instead, they continued to experience prolonged and recurrent dislocations as immigrants.

The Disorientation of Enduring Anti-Indigenous Racism in the US

In the absence of an adult caregiver, unaccompanied migrant youth are especially reliant on non-parental family ties and coethnic community ties for their survival and incorporation in the US. As in Guatemala, Maya youth are embedded in a nested social and language ecology upon arrival in the US.[65] First, they encounter the predominantly Spanish-speaking Latina/o immigrant community, followed by the predominantly English-speaking American mainstream. But unlike in Guatemala, many are unaccompanied by a parent or adult caregiver for the first time. This flies in the face of what most people assume about immigration—namely, that newly arrived immigrants can rely on family and coethnic ties for survival and to achieve incorporation. Children are assumed to grow up in parent- or adult-led households in which caregivers act as liaisons for community participation. Unfortunately, research shows that the impoverished family and community ties they encounter are often fragmented, at best, and opportunistic, exploitative, and toxic, at worst.[66]

Given their low levels of human and financial capital in Guatemala and their undocumented status in the US, Indigenous immigrants tend to experience high levels of familial and community impoverishment in diaspora.[67] Recall that Guatemalans made up an estimated 11 percent of the unauthorized population in Los Angeles County in 2019, totaling over 100,000 people.[68] About 50 to 60 percent of the Guatemalan population is Indigenous. Furthermore, given their more nascent immigration history (arriving to Westlake, Pico-Union, and MacArthur Park neighborhoods of Los Angeles at higher rates in the 1990s) relative to Mexican migrants, many Guatemalan Maya youth, especially teenage boys, may be the first in their families to migrate and to do so unaccompanied. Unaccompanied immigrant youth with long-settled relatives tend to arrive at the doorsteps of undocumented immigrants who, in many cases, are unable or unwilling to take on the financial and legal risk of welcoming an undocumented newcomer into their homes.[69] In this way, life has been reconfigured for many who did not anticipate having to be fully independent at a young age. Young people are thrust into low-wage work in Los Angeles to afford housing, food, clothing, and the repayment of their migration debt.

Alberto recalled the difficulty of being on his own: "When I got here, I needed to get a job, but I couldn't. It was really difficult for me. I came here and I was . . . how do I say it? I don't know . . . It's just that the laws are different here." Growing up as an unaccompanied and undocumented immigrant teen is a disorienting experience as young people navigate social, political, economic, and cultural systems and norms independently. At fifteen, Alberto was the first in his family to migrate. Lacking the social networks that he could rely on to secure housing and employment, Alberto did not anticipate that the US *sistema* (system) included child labor laws that would inhibit his ability to find work. In Guatemala, "you can work at whatever age, but it's not the same here. So, it was difficult for me because I needed to work. But I finally resolved the situation. I found work."[70]

Only a few days after his arrival, Alberto began working as a piece-rate garment worker, a typical first job for Maya youth in Los Angeles. Once employed, "the issue then became the language." Alberto elaborated:

> I needed to communicate with people one way or another. I needed to be able to ask people questions. Or, like, sometimes, they would ask me questions. I got here when I was fifteen, so people would see me and think that I was from here. They would see a little kid still, and they probably thought I went to school or, I don't know. But they would speak English. I would go to stores, and people would speak English. When they would speak English, I would freeze and ask myself, "Oh, what did they just say?" And, yeah, it made me feel *incómodo* [uncomfortable] because, I mean, you don't know how to respond, and I didn't even speak Spanish. That was really difficult for me when I arrived here.

Being a minor seeking employment and a non-English speaker were key factors in Alberto's disorientation after arriving in Los Angeles. Alberto's stage of adolescent "migranthood" was apparently at odds with what people in the US expected of a fifteen-year-old, meaning that they saw him as "a little kid still." Moreover, not understanding English speakers, and not knowing how to respond, caused him discomfort. Alberto's clarification that he "didn't even speak Spanish," implied that speaking Spanish would at least have allowed him to communicate with his coworkers and employers.[71]

Aarón shared similar reflections on the compounded pressures of learning a new language and navigating dislocation that felt both familiar and unfamiliar. On the one hand, he was forced into adult roles and spaces in the US as he had been in Guatemala, but now there was the added disorientation of experiencing this dislocation in a society that—at least normatively—assigned rights, roles, and responsibilities based on age. When Aarón first arrived in Los Angeles, he said that he felt mature: "*Me sentí grande* [I felt grown-up] when I got here," he said:

> At the time, I started looking for work. I looked for work in landscaping and in construction, and, you know, people would give me jobs. When I started to work, I forgot all about school. Five years went by really quickly. I was working and working.

"After those five years," at twenty-one years old, Aarón "started to feel bad" about himself. "I started to feel really depressed":

> I asked myself why and thought it was because I did not accept myself. I did not understand why the world, why people, did not understand me. I felt like people rejected me. They rejected me over there; they rejected me over here. So, I couldn't find help. I fell into depression. I didn't see anything positive. Everything felt negative. But yeah, I would ask myself, "Why is everyone else okay but I'm not okay?" And you know what I would always tell myself? "It's because I am *Indio*." That's how I understood it, you know?

The more socially isolated Aarón's rigorous work schedule made him, the less emotionally well he felt.[72] Aarón explained that he felt disoriented—or confused—by the fact that his rejection "over there" in Guatemala had been extended to "over here" in Los Angeles. His explanation testified to the extreme disorientation of youth for whom migration to the US was imagined as a reprieve but ended up reproducing their social dislocation and resultant low self-esteem from Guatemala. He had already so internalized the narrative that his Indigeneity was the source of his social and emotional distress that, upon experiencing continued dislocation in the US, it seemed clear to him that the problem was, again, his Maya identity—something he could not escape.

Aarón's excitement about feeling mature for his age, because he successfully arrived in Los Angeles and found a job, soon lost its luster. He noticed others were also mature and had a leg up: They spoke English. In Aarón's words, "The people who were already here *también ya estaban grandes* [were also already mature]. They knew more English than I did. So, I got here and felt worse. I felt even more discrimination. I said, 'Wow, why is it like this? I do not understand.' I truly did not understand." To be sure, this sense of disorientation is common among many unaccompanied immigrant youth during the incorporation process, unfamiliar as they are with many facets of life in the United States, ranging from how to use public transportation to the social position of children in US society.[73] But unaccompanied Maya youth experience a distinct and heightened form of disorientation due to the hybrid hegemonies, continued dislocation, and displacement caused by anti-Indigenous discrimination.

Timidez y Miedo: Shyness and Fear

Maya youth overwhelmingly spoke of their initial settlement experiences in terms of *timidez y miedo* (shyness and fear). Aarón described that some of this related to feelings of abandonment. Aarón migrated at sixteen and, at age twenty-five, confessed that, over the course of nine years in Los Angeles, he came to believe that *"La verdad es que hemos sido abandonados"* (The truth is that we've been abandoned). Unaccompanied Maya youth first felt abandoned by long-settled relatives and compatriots who were unwilling or unable to receive them upon arrival in Los Angeles and/or guide them through their settlement. Some young people turned to local churches, which provided a shared community space and spiritually uplifting messages around faith and hope for the future. Yet many youth, including Aarón, expressed that their Indigeneity was not valued there, which eventually prompted them to form and participate in groups like Voces.[74]

Because parents and other adult family members who remained in Guatemala had not migrated and were therefore unfamiliar with Los Angeles life, they were often powerless to assist Maya youth tangibly in their settlement and integration. Rather than employing a dual frame of reference to compare their experiences to those left behind in Guatemala, Maya youth's assessments of relative disadvantage and opportunity emerged with reference to numerous others: immigrant youth whose parents had accompanied them, Spanish-speaking Guatemalans, Indigenous migrants who had been in the US for longer and *"ya conocen más"* (already know more), US-citizen youth, and so forth.[75] These comparative frames shifted over the course of the young people's journeys through the liminal state as they became more *adaptados* and reevaluated their own experiences as a result, as in the shifting evaluations of language proficiency discussed in Chapter 3.

Aside from feeling *abandonados,* youth attributed their *timidez* and *miedo* to discrimination from non-Indigenous Latinas/os and others. Some youth recognized that their *timidez* stemmed, in part, from the colonial processes of oppression and stigmatization of Indigenous identity, language, and religion. Youth were exposed to these processes in Guatemalan schools and society and found that they persisted in the United States. Fernando commented on the role of colonial religion in socializing Indigenous people into a sense of inferiority:

> One of the things you suffer the most from as a Guatemalan and especially a Maya is the *timidez* because they always treated you like you're not as important, you're stupid or only good for labor. [Stephanie: Why is that a Maya thing?] I think it starts from colonization, from the Spaniards, it's like [switches to English] all what, all what you are doing is, is devil [switches to Spanish], all that's from the

devil, the practice of the ceremonies, it's all from the devil. So that has to be eliminated—[the Spaniards] couldn't do it, but here comes Guatemalan Protestantism and they keep it going, it's that way of thinking that [the Protestants] call witchcraft.

Like Fernando, other youth understood that their feelings of *timidez y miedo* following migration were not simply the products of isolated incidents of discrimination. Rather, these feelings and experiences were part of a centuries-old pattern of racism and marginalization dating to the Spanish conquest of Latin America. Thus, shyness and fear were also tied to a more general sense of rejection that transcended home and host societies on account of being Indigenous, which some internalized as self-rejection. Along with religion, youth were attuned to the role of schooling and language education in reproducing entrenched racial ideologies and maintaining Indigenous people in an inferior position, as in Aarón's comments on how the profoundly racialized differences between "totally White" Ladino and "darker" Maya bodies in Guatemala shaped his schooling experiences.

Ximena elaborated on this during the Voces de Esperanza meeting where she first opened up to the group about why she migrated to Los Angeles as an unaccompanied child in November 2012. The *incomodidad* (discomfort) and low self-esteem that Alberto and Aarón named, respectively, added to preexisting *timidez y miedo*, which Ximena suggested stemmed from interactions with Spanish-speaking Guatemalans beginning in childhood in Guatemala. After detailing how the people of San Carlos Sija would refer to her and her family with the derogatory term *Indios*, she went on to say that life in the United States was "worse" in part because people "come to the US, and find people speak English so that is a double discrimination." To Ximena, it felt like people "make fun of them, so you learn to hide your language" because *"la gente te dice, 'son Indios, no valen nada'"* (people say, "they're Indian, they're worthless"). Stephanie asked Ximena, "Do you ever speak Q'anjob'al in Los Angeles? Is there somewhere that you feel like you can speak it here?" Ximena reiterated: "When I went to San Carlos Sija, I did not speak Spanish well and then they discriminated against you. 'No!'" she shouted, ventriloquizing the abusive remembered critic of her non-native Spanish, "'You're saying it wrong!' So, when I am around people who do not speak Q'anjob'al, I'd rather stay quiet."

Maya youth's exposure to anti-Indigenous racism intensifies their feelings of marginality in society, where racism and internalized inferiority can make youth appear shy and scared, uncomfortable and insecure, and quiet. The explicit racism that Ximena experienced made her distrustful and leery of speaking Mayan languages within earshot of non-Maya people. Stephanie realized that her first impression of Ximena had been mistaken. Rather than being a shy and reserved person by nature, Ximena had been silenced.

Wilfredo turned to the group and responded to Ximena's introduction by saying, "*Tienen que superar y reparar su autoestima. Hay que perder el miedo*" (You must overcome and repair your self-esteem. You must lose your fear). Before speaking to the whole group, Wilfredo had leaned over in his chair to offer Stephanie some context: "Language is something that we [the group coordinators] need to focus on in Los Angeles because they are here, but they are not here. If we help them with language, we are giving their security back to them." "They are here, but they are not here" was a powerful way to express the extent of the young people's dislocation: Not only had they been dislocated (from school and childhood, and then from Guatemala), but they had not even really "arrived" in Los Angeles in the sense of having begun the adaptation process.

The youth quickly understood that language was essential to their material and emotional *sobrevivencia*. One way to *superar* (overcome) and *reparar* (repair) was through language learning. Many youth pointed to the need for more formal education, including opportunities for language learning, among their fellow Maya immigrants. When, for example, Stephanie asked Caterina if she still wanted to attend school in the US despite her siblings' assertion that she would need to work to support herself, Caterina said, "Yes, because it will help me not to work as hard as my siblings. I can learn new things, and not suffer so much because people do not get paid well, and things like that." "What work do your siblings do?" Stephanie asked. Caterina replied:

My brother is in the garment industry. My sister works in a . . . I honestly don't know what to call it. I think she is in sales. So, that's what really motivates me to keep studying because I see how hard it is for them. I see how not having an education has affected them. They cannot speak English well. It's difficult for them. I see how important studying is. That really helps me to not only learn new things, but also helps me in the future. It will help me get a better job and not suffer so much.

Caterina sees "how hard it is" for her older siblings, despite having been in the US for years before Caterina's arrival, because they do not have an education—and, more specifically, because they don't speak English. In this way, Maya youth come to see learning the English language, a "colonial code of power," as nonetheless necessary to decrease fear, discomfort, low-esteem, and even poverty—all of which are tied to material and emotional suffering.[76] This association is further concretized in the workplace, where the youth encounter many of the most overt forms of anti-Indigenous discrimination.

Confronting Anti-Indigeneity in the Workplace

As the young people enter wage labor in Los Angeles, their ascribed status as "little kids" and their Indigenous appearance and verbal behavior can make them easy targets for workplace abuse. For many, work is where they learned that the experience of being Maya in Los Angeles has many parallels with being Maya in Guatemala. All of the participants became full-time workers upon settling in Los Angeles, concentrated in the garment industry (n = 23, 64 percent), but also other jobs such as hospitality (as line cooks and dishwashers; n = 6, 17 percent), domestic workers (n = 2, 5 percent), auto repair, warehouse packing, and homemaking. One participant was unemployed at the time of the interview but oscillated between landscaping and garment work in a practice that migration scholar Jacqueline Hagan and colleagues (2015) refer to as "*brincando*" or "job jumping."

The youth's negative experiences in the workplace are representative of the ways that many organizations reproduce broader social systems of power and disempowerment. One's organizational participation is determined by the "inequality regimes" that govern the broader society in which organizations are embedded.⁷⁷ These regimes reinforce ethnorace, class, and gender hierarchies and "determine power differences within organizational class levels."⁷⁸ In this way, the workplaces that unaccompanied minors enter, which are the organizations in which they spend most of their waking hours, replicate ethnoracial dynamics. Given that they are unaccompanied youth workers, immigrant Maya youth come of age in a workplace context that feeds off these hierarchies and capitalizes on youth's displacement. Thus, the youth in the study often found themselves in exploitative and even abusive work situations where being identified as young and Indigenous intensified their vulnerability.

The participants consistently received several messages in the workplace: that they were unskilled and undesirable—and therefore exploitable—and that they were excluded from the larger Latina/o community. Andrés was among the many participants who singled out work as a place where ignorance and intolerance were regularly on display:

> Being Maya is a little hard because people don't understand what your culture is. They discriminate against you a lot, "Don't have anything to do with him, he's an *Indio*" . . . I've found people, especially Mexicans, "You don't speak Spanish well, you're an *Indio*," or "You have a poor [person's] dialect." That's how they talk . . . . Like at work: "You don't speak this, and you don't speak that, and you shouldn't be here, you should be in *Indio*-land or in the mountains taking care of animals." That's what they tell you.

In this troubling description, Andrés nimbly linked incomprehension or erasure of Maya immigrants and culture ("people don't understand") to negative attitudes toward Mayan languages, especially among Spanish speakers, and then to stereotypes that equated Maya/Indigenous people with animals: as rural, backwards, inarticulate, and only suitable for manual labor. These are familiar themes from other research on Indigenous Latin Americans' experiences in the United States.⁷⁹ In Andrés's voicing of the workplace bully, "You should be . . . in the mountains taking care of animals" carries an echo of Lucy's comments (at the beginning of this chapter) about the devaluing of Mayan languages as "dialects" and a tendency to see them and their speakers as "animalesque," less than fully human and fit only for demeaning jobs.⁸⁰

Fernando, a K'iche'-speaking garment worker who migrated at fourteen and was twenty-eight at the time of his interview, told a story that was strikingly similar to the one told by Andrés. When asked if he felt like he belonged in Los Angeles, Fernando said that he did not, even though he had lived there for fourteen years:

> No, I don't feel it, because . . . many people see you differently . . . maybe because of the color of your skin or because of your stature or maybe it's other things. They see you differently from themselves because maybe you don't speak the same language or you are doing a job that they wouldn't do. Maybe it's a job where you get dirtier or in the sun more or something like that. That's why I don't feel like I belong in this country.

Referring first to the phenotypic characteristics of Indigenous people generally but Maya people specifically, Fernando noted that people might see him differently "because of the color of your skin or because of your stature." He linked these stereotypically Indigenous features to Maya youth's labor, suggesting that one might be identifiable as Indigenous or an immigrant because of having "a job where you get dirtier or in the sun more."

Fernando went a step further than Andrés in suggesting that Maya phenotype and language had undergone a process of *rhematization* in the context of diasporic wage labor. In linguistic anthropology, "rhematization" refers to "a shift of focus" in how signs represent their objects "from indexical to iconic"; in this case, signs that first indexed or pointed to "Guatemalan" or "Indigenous"—darker skin, speaking a *dialect*—became *icons,* signs bearing a visual or auditory resemblance to the people they represented, coming to reflect both the "dirtiness" of jobs open to Maya workers (and, by implication, the underlying "dirtiness" or subhuman nature of the people themselves).⁸¹

Fernando attributed these trials to *"una programación* [a brainwashing] *donde,* 'Ey, you're a dog,'" that "we [Maya] bring over here," connecting his *timidez* at work and in other public spaces to the border-spanning racialization of Maya vis-à-vis Ladino, or European-descended, Guatemalans and other non-Indigenous Latin Americans. "You're a dog," like Andrés's imagined slur about animals, placed Fernando squarely outside the community of non-Indigenous Latina/o immigrants (in placing him outside the human community). He went on, "I feel really, really, really timid, lots of fear about that—to say, well, I'm Maya, and I can do things like a Ladino. You feel really put down in that sense." Fernando and other youth workers were aware, like Andrés, that the demonization of Indigenous people and practices did not begin in Los Angeles. Nevertheless, Maya youth at work in Los Angeles were socialized through repeated discriminatory remarks to "know their place," or to recognize that they had not yet escaped the stigma of Indigenous identity.

Conclusion

Maya youth experience compounding quotidian dislocations in Guatemala, which undergird their displacement from Guatemala through migration. Though anticipating reprieve from overt ethnoracial discrimination and exclusion, Maya young people experience renewed dislocations and feel a disorientation as they continue to wrestle with feelings of *timidez y miedo*, low self-esteem, and barriers to opportunities for mobility, inclusion, and well-being in the United States. Importantly, dislocation, in both origin and destination countries, has two different but interrelated dimensions. First, Maya youth are dislocated *to* the bottom of multiple hierarchies. Second, they are dislocated *from* the roles and spaces normally occupied by youth. That is, they take on the social roles and responsibilities typically attributed to adults and become workers while still teens. Our use of "diaspora" refers to dislocated Maya youth's subsequent *displacement* from Guatemala and to the United States in the context of the larger-scale dispersion of the Maya population, during and following the genocidal conflict that officially concluded with the Peace Accords of 1996.[82]

While scholars have attributed the youth's ability to weather discrimination to the capital—material, cultural, social, and emotional—that parents, extended families, coethnic communities, and supportive adults in schools provide, unaccompanied Maya young people are bereft of these interventions. Thus, they experience disorientation in adult spaces, where protective and socializing resources are largely absent. The next chapter turns to how youth navigate the disorientation of their distinct social position and the structure of opportunities before them to highlight youth's strategies to secure their long-term *sobrevivencia*.

TWO

Preparing for the Future

On a gloomy evening in June 2014, Stephanie, Wilfredo, and Jorge met at a Pico-Union McDonald's to discuss the need for group participants to seek out resources beyond those Voces de Esperanza could provide. While the three spoke, two Voces participants, Enrique and Omar, walked through the double glass doors. They scanned the lobby and spotted Wilfredo from across the room, throwing their hands up to greet him with broad smiles. Jorge and Stephanie waved back as Wilfredo called the pair to join them. As Enrique and Omar walked over and shuffled into their seats, Wilfredo began to tell Stephanie of a time that Enrique explained to him and Jorge that there is no direct K'iche' equivalent to the word *ayuda* (help) but that *jóvenes* are instructed to *escuchar el consejo del anciano, del mayor* (listen to the advice of elders, those older than them).

Enrique, who entered nearly every conversation with a nod and an *"ajá"* (right!), elaborated, saying that his parents had never given him advice directly but would instruct him to listen to their stories because their past experiences revealed essential lessons about life. Omar added that *"en Guate[mala], el jóven no tiene peso en sus palabras"* (in Guate[mala], a young person's words do not carry weight). Adults are presumed to possess unique wisdom and life lessons that can be imparted to someone younger through storytelling. That is why, Enrique said:

> Over there, there is no word for "help." There is no concept of help. No one is telling you to get help or thinking that they can get help for what they are going through. [Drawing on the lessons of elders' stories] they simply face their challenges on their own.

Stephanie wondered how unaccompanied youth managed this in the absence of parents and other adult caregivers, and whether their relationship to asking for help had changed with time in the US. Enrique nodded as Omar responded:

> We are learning this, yes, because here [Los Angeles], we talk to one another. We hear other people's stories. When you learn from other people, you realize that there is not one person with all the answers. *Y aunque sea más pequeño, uno puede aprender algo de otro* [and even if someone is younger, you can learn something from one another].

Stephanie probed more deeply: Did learning this affect youth's relationships with their parents still living in Guatemala? Omar described that relationships changed between children in the US and their parents in Guatemala because children felt, for the first time, that they possessed lived experiences their parents did not. Omar, for example, told his mother stories about life in Los Angeles and felt wise. He also now felt comfortable sharing his opinions on their family issues. Omar was also a bit more autonomous in his relationship with his parents because he chose when to call home; he never called during a slow work week, when he felt sick, or when he was upset with his parents. He did not want them to worry.

Stephanie speculated that youth might experience this as a transformation of developmental stages within their life course, as the weight of elders' words was replaced by the weight of stories from longer-settled, more experienced immigrant youth. "Does that make you feel like adults?" she asked. *"Eso es cosa individual,"* Omar said. It's an individual thing. "Yeah, this is individual," Enrique agreed. "A person feels like an adult when they feel mature, but that's individual," Omar said. "Yes, some people feel like adults because they have their own jobs and are able to pay for their own things. *Maduran porque ganan el dinero* [they mature because they earn money]," Enrique added, shedding light on the relationship between material and emotional stability in unaccompanied youth's subjective understanding of successful incorporation and coming of age.[1]

According to Enrique, he did not feel like an adult when he arrived in the United States. In an image that recalled Andrés's emotional distress and isolation (in the Introduction), he remembered sitting alone in his apartment in anxious anticipation of seeing his mother walk through the door. It felt "weird," he said, that "I was at home, and she wasn't there with me." As the days went by, Enrique would look at the clock in his bedroom every so often and think, "Is she coming? Is she coming?" Finally, he came to "accept that she was at home [Guatemala] and she wasn't coming [to Los Angeles]."

The group turned quiet as they imagined Enrique's early days. Stephanie glanced at Wilfredo, who was shaking his head, then at Jorge, who was looking down at his hands resting on his lap. Omar added that thinking about home, "keeping home in mind," can be distressing while unaccompanied youth workers are coming of age and "dealing with life here [in the US]." "People will tell you that they are constantly thinking about what is going on over there [Guatemala]," Omar said. Enrique added, "Thinking about home is what makes you feel like a kid. When you think about home, you don't grow up." Enrique implied that keeping one's mind fixed on Guatemala prevented youth from doing the hard work of *preparación*—that is, of accepting that their lives were now centered in the United States and making decisions about how to invest their time and energy with that in mind. Taken as a whole, this interaction also highlighted the distinctive role that Voces played in helping Indigenous youth counter disorientation with *preparación:* rather than simply connecting youth with material resources, the group exposed them to *consejos* from longer-settled youth and mentors, or those who counted as elders in the diasporic context.

Together, Enrique and Omar articulated a distinct Maya youth culture born in diaspora. The previous chapter showed that unaccompanied

Maya youth were disoriented by the persistence of anti-Indigenous discrimination that they thought they would leave behind in Guatemala, which they acutely experienced in low-wage workplaces, a social sphere typically reserved for adults. The conversation described above reveals that young people were also disoriented by their changing roles and responsibilities, unfamiliar US norms and values, and the new dynamics of their relationships to self, family, and community. They experienced socioemotional and material disorientations as newly arrived migrants transitioning into a new social and cultural milieu and adolescents transitioning to adulthood. And, whereas in Guatemala, young people might be embedded in familiar and trusting families and communities and a culture in which parents and other elders might transfer knowledge to them, unaccompanied youth workers are independent in the US. What's more, left-behind parents had few *consejos* to aid young people living in a country that the parents had never visited or lived in. Unaccompanied youth were reliant on themselves and community members to achieve *sobrevivencia*.

As Enrique and Omar suggested above, accepting the circumstances of their displacement and disorientation, including the need for forms of *ayuda* that were previously unknown, rather than longing for Guatemala, was a key step in *madurando* or coming of age in the US. This process of identifying needs and forms of *ayuda* is a process they referred to as *preparación*. This chapter explores *preparación* as a distinct phase of incorporation between disorientation and adaptation for Maya youth in diaspora in which they strategically pursue forms of socialization to ideologies, practices, institutions, and social roles to "prepare themselves" to secure long-term *sobrevivencia*. Maya youth participants sought various forms of *preparación*—including spiritual, social, emotional, and financial—sometimes through mentorship and community participation and other times on their own.

Preparación, in other words, was a form of education. Unlike the education that other immigrant youth may receive in institutions or from parents and older family members, it involved an individualized process of seeking knowledge and *ayuda* elsewhere. The opening vignette elucidates that *preparación* can occur through day-to-day interactions with peers or mentors. *Preparación* can also occur through agentic and strategic engagement in collective learning communities, like Voces de Esperanza or adult English-language schools, in ways that are aligned with youth's imagined futures as workers, community members, and transnational migrants.

Through *preparación*, Maya youth could move from feelings of disorientation, like those Enrique and Omar discussed, to adaptive activity within and across nested social communities that moved them incrementally closer to the *sobrevivencia* they imagined. *Preparación* was a site of youth agency and self-realization, through which youth came to see themselves not as victims or dependents on agencies or the state, but as emergent adults who were responsible for cultivating their own strengths.[2] Still, understanding how these migrant youth used informal and non-school spaces to further their preparation for thriving in diaspora may also be useful to practitioners and service providers, since youth's assessments of their own needs and spaces of possibility can orient human service agencies, community-based organizations, and school systems to points of intervention.

After outlining the significance of *preparación* for unaccompanied Maya youth workers in the absence of parents and outside of K–12 schools, we show how Voces de Esperanza offered a collective space for socialization for Maya youth growing up outside of parent-led households and without access to the teachers, mentors, and peers that schools offer.[3] Socioemotional *preparación* took place through exposure to ideas and practices like expressing one's worries and grief, exploring personal skills and interests, and accepting oneself, particularly when other, more traditional organizations—namely, faith-based organizations—failed to support unaccompanied Maya young people in doing so.

We focus especially on the strategic pursuit of English and Spanish skills and knowledge in Maya youth's *preparación*. Given youth's intersectional marginalization, and especially the disparagement of their Indigenous identity within the Latina/o community in which they were most immediately embedded and on which they relied, youth's imagined futures were predicated on the possibility of belonging to distinct discourse communities through targeted investment in language learning.[4] Youth explored these discourse communities in light of their ideologies of language learning—that is, their beliefs about the desirability and feasibility of learning different languages—and their understanding of their own and others' language proficiency.[5] Though English and Spanish took precedence in early resettlement, youth's linguistic maneuvering, in the context of broader dynamics of *preparación*, ultimately came to encompass their ideologies of Mayan language maintenance and use for the greater good of the diasporic community. (We address that specific dimension of incorporation in Chapters 3 and 4.)

This chapter ends by demonstrating Maya youth's attunement to the language ecology that characterized their position within Los Angeles society. We show how Maya youth's *preparación* included obtaining greater proficiency in multiple languages to communicate with people in their workplaces, neighborhoods, and the broader Los Angeles landscape to secure better treatment and reduce their *timidez y miedo* in everyday life. Participants connected the need for *preparación* in Spanish to their adaptation within Spanish-dominant Latina/o community life. By contrast, moving beyond the Latina/o community to neighborhood contexts and networks shared with English speakers, such as workplaces and community spaces, required English-language *preparación*. All the while, retaining transnational family ties and advocating for less "prepared" coethnics in Los Angeles required that Mayan-speaking youth maintain their Indigenous languages.

The Significance of *Preparación* for Unaccompanied Maya Youth Workers

Preparación was one step in the study participants' future-making process and, like the other steps, was contoured by their intersectional identities. Maya youth used the term *preparación* to refer to their efforts to learn and navigate ideologies, practices, institutions, and their positions as unaccompanied and undocumented Indigenous low-wage workers while coming of age in US society.

Preparación was critical for Maya youth in ways that differed starkly from immigrant children living in parent-led households and non-Indigenous migrant youth. Non-Indigenous immigrant children and the children of immigrants growing up in parent-led households might be buffered from full-time work and the need to be financially independent and were generally able to attend US public schools.[6] If young people in parent-led families work, it is typically to supplement local household income, as was the case for youth who worked while in Guatemala (see Chapter 1).[7] They might also learn youth culture and practice English and other features of English-dominant society at home or in school.[8]

Meanwhile, non-Indigenous youth would be somewhat shielded from the overt racism and ridicule of their language and cultural practices that Indigenous youth faced within Latina/o and non-immigrant communities. Focused on how parents and coethnic communities function as buffers from racial discrimination through the promotion of cultural retention and cultivation of cultural pride, social scientists have insufficiently explored how migrant youth navigate racism and discrimination without the presence of supportive adult figures.[9] The unaccompanied, undocumented Maya youth workers in this study had limited access to adults who could provide support in times of need.[10] Of the thirty-six Maya participants, twelve participants (33 percent) had a non-parent relative living in the United States, including (a combined) ten older siblings, one older cousin, and one aunt and uncle. But their undocumented and low-income statuses constrained long-settled relatives' ability to provide material support.[11] In many cases, material constraints incited feelings of disillusionment and betrayal among newly arrived children who hoped to be well-received. This could fracture relationships between children and their long-settled relatives, blocking access to meaningful social support.[12]

Without household-level support, many young people became oriented to various organizations in their local community and attempted to participate in these and leverage their resources to combat their isolation, loneliness, and angst.[13] Within these organizations, seventeen participants (47 percent) reported having a community figure they looked to for guidance, including religious and recreational group leaders, support group coordinators, or job center training mentors. Another seven participants (19 percent) did not identify any sources of support, did not participate in community organizations or activities, and reported feeling alone and isolated from their local communities. Young people without interpersonal and organizational connections tended to speak longingly about their left-behind families and retained transnational community ties over the years.

The Maya youth in this study saw *preparación* as a prerequisite for *adaptación* to everyday life in the US and their ultimate goal of *sobrevivencia*. As such, *preparación* was not passive, aimless, or occurring by chance, but an intentional process through which youth aligned opportunities for socialization, linguistic and otherwise, to their imagined futures as workers, local and transnational community members, and Los Angeles residents who could call the city home. As Enrique and Omar suggested above, these were migrant young people considering what it meant to "grow up" independently—in a material and an emotional sense—and far from home. *Preparación* was a way for Maya youth to gain some control over their situations, and language, though not the only element of the process, was arguably the focal point of *preparación* as the most visible and essential form of symbolic capital that youth sought.

Linguistically, identifying flexible processes of *preparación* as a prerequisite for the effective *adaptación* of Maya youth is important, in part, because Indigenous language speakers often come to view their languages as problems.[14] Indigenous languages are associated with a lack of economic opportunity in Latin America and the United States and the whole history of racial and cultural stigmatization discussed earlier. Furthermore, Indigenous speakers' competence in colonial languages (e.g., Spanish and English) is often viewed through a deficit lens, or in terms of what proficiency speakers lack in other languages. *Preparación* entailed beginning to confront and oppose these stigmatizing language ideologies through everyday discourse practices. As part of the process of *preparación*, participants came to understand the importance of using at least three languages to navigate an array of social spaces in the US. And, in their *preparación*, they strategically considered how they might leverage their developing language proficiency to adapt to new situations more readily and secure *sobrevivencia* in terms of economic self-sufficiency and overall well-being.

In the following sections, we highlight the key contexts where Maya youth pursued *preparación*, the most salient forms of *preparación* they sought out, and the adaptive ends to which they turned the lessons of *preparación*. Our analysis draws attention to the social domains and roles that youth were oriented to as most central in shaping their prospects for mobility and well-being in Los Angeles, as well as the material and emotional constraints they encountered in attaining these. Thus, before discussing participants' efforts to prepare themselves linguistically for social and financial mobility, we consider the forms of socioemotional *preparación* that allowed youth to deal with experiences of *retraso*, or "setbacks," and *timidez y miedo*, which affected them emotionally.

Pursuing Socioemotional *Preparación* Through Voces de Esperanza

At the time of the study, Voces de Esperanza was a community space in which Maya young people engaged in socioemotional *preparación*. Over the years of fieldwork, Stephanie noticed that many youth arrived at Voces after friends recommended that they meet Wilfredo, Jorge, and others who attended the group each week. But the original Voces members began gathering regularly because of the emotional and material setbacks they experienced while participating in other organizations in their neighborhoods, namely the Catholic Church, from which many came to feel alienated because of discrimination against Indigenous people.[15]

In explaining the role that Voces played in their *preparación*, in contrast to the church, Maya youth reported that the messages of "waiting on God" and "trusting God's timing" caused setbacks in their adaptation to life in Los Angeles and threatened their *sobrevivencia*. This happened when young people who were told to be patient did not feel they were actively preparing themselves to navigate their lives as unaccompanied and undocumented Indigenous youth workers. In addition to being alienated from the church through overt discrimination, they also felt alienated from the practice of patience and resignation that the church urged and that they found to be at odds with the pressing need to prepare themselves actively to meet the challenges of immigrant life. These paired temporalities—"God's time" and time of their present suffering—created tension for Indigenous youth, who chafed at their treatment in (mostly) non-Indigenous church settings and came to resent others' guidance to wait for God's providence instead of actively working to better their situations.¹⁶

Voces de Esperanza became a place where young people spent time with Maya peers and did not feel marginalized. It was also a place where they observed how other youth and their mentors were engaging in *preparación* and could model their behaviors after them, as opposed to being told to bide their time and trust in providence. Aarón clearly articulated this when he said:

> I was lost in church around 2008 when I met Wilfredo and Jorge. That's what I realized: that they were studying. They were in church, but they were also studying. I said, "What's going to happen with me? I am going to study." That's when I started to work part-time. I went to study ESL [English as a Second Language] and then I finished ESL and went to another program. An intensive English program. I did that for a year and just barely finished. So, I am barely waking up. Later, I realized, "Wow, look at all the things that have happened."
>
> I thought I was the only one, and then I realized that there are a ton of *jóvenes* from my culture and from my country, and I said, "Wow, this is very painful. Why do we have to suffer so much?" And I thought I was the only one. But there are so many *jóvenes* that are here that aren't studying, and they only live to work. I had started studying and realized we don't have any leaders. We don't have anybody. So, I think that was maybe what caused me pain, but it also motivated me to tell people, "Hey, let's read, let's go to Voces de Esperanza, let's go to church." And we go. Everything has its time. That's what I've been doing now.

For many youth, coming to Voces coincided with the realization that one could prepare oneself to suffer less, in effect, even if one continued attending church (as Aarón did). When he met Wilfredo and Jorge, Aarón realized that waiting for an intervention from God was not his only option; he also had to pursue his socialization proactively. As he did, he noticed how few precedents for this type of *preparación* existed among unaccompanied Maya youth. Many youth "[weren't] studying and only live[d] to work" according to Aarón. This implied that it was possible to "get by" in the US without seeking out *preparación,* but that doing so would not end in the holistic form of *sobrevivencia* that Aarón envisioned but in further "suffering." Working part-time to accommodate English classes, as Aarón decided to do, was an example of how youth might sacrifice greater earnings in the present in order to prepare themselves (in this case, through language learning) for greater success in the future. It is also striking that Aarón contrasted "studying" with going to church, in the sense that, while church might have a place for some youth, churchgoing was not a practice that was likely to result in increased *preparación* and had to be complemented with "study"—not just language learning, but the therapeutic "study" of youth's experiences in the group setting of Voces.

Many youth told similar stories about what motivated them to attend Voces de Esperanza and eagerly invited their neighbors and coworkers—all unaccompanied Maya youth—to attend the group on Friday nights. Stephanie first began attending Voces de Esperanza in 2012. The group met on a Starbucks patio for two hours on Friday nights between 7 pm and 9 pm. Beginning with Wilfredo and one or two youth around a table, others slowly trickled in, listening as each participant answered the question: "How was your week?"

Over the years, the gathering grew, and as more young people joined in 2014 and 2015, some formalities started to develop. By then, Voces met in a cooperative housing complex in Pico-Union. The formalities included the need for a greeter, since the housing complex door required a door code, which the attendees were not given for the residents' security. There was also the introduction of a group welcome. Written by Wilfredo, this welcome was read aloud by a Voces participant at the start of each gathering. The welcome went as follows:

> *Voces de Esperanza es un programa alternativo de formación humana, sanación interior, crecimiento espiritual, sanación de las adicciones cualesquiera que estas sean. Trabajando con honestidad, mente abierta, y voluntad, este grupo surge ante la urgente necesidad de muchos jóvenes, familias, y miembros de distintas comunidades del sur de California, particularmente en el área de Pico-Union/MacArthur Park. Voces de Esperanza, programa alternativo, trabaja con personas afectadas por cualquier herida que quieran*

ser autosuficiente por su comunidad. Nuestro método es la honestidad, mente abierta, y la voluntad. Bienvenidos a Voces de Esperanza.

Voces de Esperanza is an alternative group for personal formation, internal healing, spiritual growth, and healing from addictions, whatever one's addictions may be. Through honesty, open-mindedness, and free will, this group is born out of the urgent need of many teens, families, and community members across Southern California, particularly in the Pico-Union/MacArthur Park area. Voces de Esperanza, an alternative program, works with people who are affected by their wounds that want to be self-sufficient for [the sake of] their community. We practice honesty, open-mindedness, and free will. Welcome to Voces de Esperanza.

Informed as to the group's intention, youth who participated in Voces did so in pursuit of socioemotional *preparación*. Consistent participation in Voces de Esperanza allowed Maya youth to undergo socioemotional *preparación* through practices like "unburdening" from overwhelming emotions so that they might take action in their lives, as well as mentors encouraging youth to exchange *timidez y miedo* (shyness and fear) for cultural and linguistic pride.

Unburdening and Taking Action
Unburdening or *desahogo* (literally, undrowning or vomiting up) was an essential practice in realizing the Voces de Esperanza mission of formation, healing, and growth noted in the group's welcome. Each week, young people would arrive to share experiences and *preocupaciones* (worries). One night, a participant shared that he felt sick and had to leave work earlier that week, which meant lower earnings and financial distress for himself and his left-behind family. Another worried that his teenage cousin was growing *desesperado* (desperate) because he had an unrequited crush on a girl at work. "*Estoy preocupado por el bicho*" (I'm worried about the kid), he said, perhaps alluding to how desperation could lead to erratic behavior. Another saw that his older brother was losing himself in alcohol in Los Angeles and could no longer send remittances to his wife and child. "[His wife] keeps calling me from Guatemala," he said. "I have

a nephew there, so she keeps calling me, asking me to send her money for him to go to school. I'm not worried about my brother because he made the decision to drink [alcohol]. I worry more about the child." Another was worried about his niece who attempted to take her life *"porque está enamorada"* (because she is in love).

Each of these *preocupaciones* gave insight into the complex relationship dynamics youth were navigating across borders, their sense of responsibility for themselves and others, and their vigilance of the present and the future. Throughout the week, they were largely alone and focused on work and making ends meet. On Friday nights, they could unburden alongside other unaccompanied Maya youth. Some of the worries they had to unburden were not specific to their status (as unaccompanied, undocumented Indigenous youth) but were life-stage ordeals of late adolescence and young adulthood, such as the desperation occasioned by unrequited love. Understanding the nature of Maya youth's *preparación*, then, also entails understanding how the anguish of widely shared rites of passage was intensified due to youth's structural marginalization in Guatemala and the United States, and how youth experienced these realities simultaneously—that is, being young and in love *as well as* being targeted for racist abuse and treated as exploitable labor. The "breached initiations" of youth's dislocation and displacement from traditional adolescence did not suddenly render their typically "young" concerns irrelevant.[17]

After the evening's attendees shared their *preocupaciones*, Jorge addressed the group:

> I want to thank you all for being here this week. We are all dealing with our own issues, but you have made time to come to this group. It's important to make space for things like this. We benefit from sharing with others, from *desahogo*, and from hearing from our peers.[18]

He went on to say that he wanted to discuss the topic of peer pressure with the group that evening, focusing on the constant worry youth feel as they think about what others are doing and what others will say about them and the peer pressure of having to be and look a certain way, which might weigh particularly heavily on adolescents and teens.[19] "For example," Jorge said, "sometimes we feel pressure to buy name brands. If we want new shoes, we say they must be Converse or they need to be Jordans." That's name brand peer pressure, he continued, but there's also peer pressure related to money, to debts that need to be paid, or expenses that need to be met. "Does anyone feel that pressure?" Jorge asked.

The room was quiet, but Jorge continued. "You," he said, with his arm extended and finger pointing to the young man who had shared that his sister-in-law was calling and asking for money for her son's education. "What you shared with us is economic pressure." There were other pressures still, he assured the youth. Jorge mentioned the pressure to live in the nicest apartment with the best view. "These are pressures we live with day in and day out. Many people here are only trying to survive, so you aren't thinking about the pressures of 'what will they say?' or of having the newest things, but that is the culture here." Jorge explained the concept of consumerism to the group. "That's the culture here. Everything is consumption, consumption." He mentioned iPhones and other devices as being alluring to teenagers.

He then talked about young people being pressured to try drugs and alcohol and how they can lose their way if they feel the pressure of a group of friends. "Has anyone experienced something like this?" Jorge asked. The room was still quiet, until Edwin offered a story about being invited to a party that he did not enjoy because everyone around him was drinking alcohol, but he refused. After that night, Edwin's friends stopped inviting him out, which meant he now spent more time alone. The overwhelming feeling of loneliness was a new worry for him. But he assured the group that he knew he had to create distance from his former friend group to protect himself and that he needed to make new friends. It's why he was attending Voces. Wilfredo interjected to return to the topic of economic pressures from families still living in Guatemala, as he often warned the youth that they carried the burden of unrealistic expectations of those who only knew of life in the US through Facebook photos. In doing so, he broached what must have been a sensitive topic for many youth: balancing their day-to-day survival and steps toward long-term *sobrevivencia* in the US with the survival and well-being of their families in Guatemala, which had been the impetus for migration. "Speaking of pressures," Wilfredo began, "we have a lot of economic pressures here. *Vayan preparándose*" (begin preparing yourselves). "We are not the saviors of the world," he said, "but our families think that we are here picking up money."

Wilfredo leaned over the front of his chair and began sweeping his arms as if brushing dollar bills from the floor. "People don't understand how difficult it is to earn a dollar here. And I am sorry to say this, but there is a lot of pressure coming from over there [Guatemala] as well. You get the pressure of, 'give me, give me, give me,' and sometimes you are left with nothing. Don't let yourself be pressured too much. We must adapt." The way to *salir de preocupaciones,* or find one's way out of the labyrinth of worries, was to continue to prepare oneself so that one could adapt—in other words, to take action to improve one's own situation and, ultimately, to position oneself to do good for others.

Jorge nodded in agreement and began encouraging the *jóvenes* to seek out resources in their neighborhoods to make ends meet. They did not have to stay in a place of *preocupaciones*; they could take action. He gave the example of the community garden across the street as "a good place for people to build self-confidence," which Jorge thought was essential for "taking action." He explained that it was common for people to say that they did not need to take action because they were waiting on God, but that God had also given each of us a mind to use to develop resources so that we can take action in our own lives. If we have confidence and take action, Jorge shared, we "will be better off." Jorge then went on to say that another part of growing up is learning how to function within society:

> You are part of this society. What is a society? Society is everything. And you are not the only one in this society. Learn how to function in this society. If you only have $15 per week, think about how you can spend your money best. If you don't know what to eat or how to cook, the [community] garden is there. Buy onions and beans and start learning how to cook. Look for resources to better function in this society.

On this occasion, Jorge's direct talk to youth touched on the issue that Omar and Enrique raised: growing up in Los Angeles meant accepting that they were now "a part of this society," rather than allowing their sense of self to remain tethered solely to Guatemala. This does not mean that Jorge wanted youth to forget who they were or where they came from. He wanted them to understand that *madurando* in the United States would involve *preparación*, defined as "look[ing] for resources to better function in this society." Even if getting vegetables from the community garden and learning to cook were not expected milestones for adolescent males in Guatemala, life in Los Angeles was a different story.

In sum, within the Voces group, grounded in shared values of honesty, open-mindedness, and free will, young people vented their anxieties (*preocupaciones*) and received *consejos* from Wilfredo and Jorge, who were happy to give advice but never expected youth to take a specific action. This approach was congruent with the narrative approach to immigrant socialization that Enrique and Omar identified as distinct from the privileged "wisdom of elders" in Guatemala. It also resembled other contexts where adult immigrants organize themselves to tell stories that reflect the shared reality to which they all need to adapt.[20]

The coordinators aimed only to motivate youth to take action. In this way, Voces de Esperanza was a place of socioemotional *preparación*, or, as one participant put it, a place for *"entrenamiento de la mente,"* a place for youth to train their minds and learn to think about their *preocupaciones* differently, not only as burdens but as opportunities for action. In reviewing handouts from Voces meetings alongside the fieldnotes, a clear theme emerges of empowering youth by encouraging them to focus on what they could control and not on circumstances outside their control. "Training the mind" was, in part, a matter of giving youth tools to reframe their perspectives on difficult situations in a more optimistic, action-oriented way. A handout (in Spanish) entitled "Do you take things personally?" (which urged youth not to do so, because "it can get to be a problem that damages self-esteem") summed up the theme of the Voces session: "You can't change the actions of others, but you can change your own reaction." Many of the handouts and accompanying discussions struck similar chords: One elaborated on the different parts of the Serenity Prayer, which is best known for its use in twelve-step programs and asks God for serenity to accept things that are out of one's control and courage to change what one can.

Activities sometimes presented youth with opposing statements and invited them explicitly to change their self-talk in ways that the coordinators believed would promote positive thinking. For example, one handout juxtaposed hypothetical statements from disaffected and exhausted youth with Bible verses intended to strengthen them: "YOU SAY . . . I'm always worried. GOD SAYS . . . Put all your worries on me." The bottom of the handout affirmed the mission of Voces: *"Liberar al Oprimido, despertar al dormido y Levantar al Caido"* (to liberate the oppressed, wake the sleeping, and lift up the fallen).

Being able to wade through overwhelming feelings of worry, loneliness, hopelessness, or fear, among other distressing emotions, was a critical phase of *preparación* that preceded more advanced attempts to adapt to life in Los Angeles. The next section explores how youth used the practice of *desahogo,* or unburdening, to bond over common challenges and draw on what they had learned at Voces for their responses.

Transforming Timidez y Miedo *into Cultural and Linguistic Pride*

The bullying, harassment, or violence the young people encountered in the workplace and in public spaces because of their Indigenous features, short stature, darker skin, and accented Spanish was a frequent topic of conversation. One Friday evening, Omar opened the group meeting by reading the Voces de Esperanza welcome statement from a laminated sheet of paper. Omar had invited a guest that night, so he added a bit more to the end of the introduction, saying that Voces was a place where *jóvenes* were encouraged to overcome addictions, heal emotions, and "find out what the good and bad is in your life."

When it was his turn, Andrés shared vaguely that he had faced a difficult moment of ridicule at work that week. Despite this, he said, throughout the week, he was comforted by remembering one of Wilfredo's mantras: *"Eres lo peor"* (you're the worst). While it sounds self-deprecating, Wilfredo often shared this phrase with the group with the intention of teaching the *jóvenes* that he did not assume himself to be the best at anything. This meant it was just as easy for him to ask for help as it was to receive criticism, maintaining a neutral mindset that was not ego driven. Wilfredo frequently said, "If someone tells you that you're the worst [at something], say, 'Okay, pray for me.' Okay, so if someone tells you that you're the best at something, say, 'Okay, great, pray for me.'" In keeping with the stated commitment of Voces to *crecimiento espiritual,* or spiritual growth, *"eres lo peor"* took on the flavor of "turn the other cheek," a biblical exhortation not to respond to mistreatment. The saying, however, was Wilfredo's trick in managing his emotions as he interacted with others who might be harsh or unkind throughout the day. When Andrés thought of *"eres lo peor,"* it encouraged him. *"Me dio ánimo"* (it gave him energy), he said—"and I am realizing that whether [I'm facing] highs and lows, I am trying to overcome them. I am looking for positive things to do to be a better person."

During group meetings, it was often the case that each person had one turn to share about their week before an open discussion. With one to two dozen participants in any given meeting, this left just enough time at the end for Wilfredo and Jorge to give *consejos* to the *jóvenes,* as in the example above. On this night, however, Omar spoke up again, perhaps motivated by Andrés's mention of harassment, to share that he had been jumped by a *marrero* (gang member) when he was getting off the bus near his apartment at 12:30 am after a church event. He shared with the group that he felt more shocked than afraid that night, perhaps to save face with the other young men and women in the room. When Omar was done sharing, Bryson interjected, saying this had happened to him one night on his way to school. The person who jumped Bryson managed to get away with his backpack. Marianna shared that she was also once assaulted while using a pay phone. A man passing by on a bike swiped Marianna's bag from her shoulder. Unlike her male companions, who were overcome by their shock and failed to act, Marianna ran after the man. She laughed as she told the group that she took off one of her shoes and threw it at the man as he biked away, and eventually ended up recovering her belongings and the bike. The group roared with laughter at the ironic turn of events.

Always a step ahead and wanting to equip the *jóvenes* with tools to navigate everyday life in Los Angeles, Jorge asked, "Do you ever call the police when these things happen?" No, the group responded in unison. They did not think to call the police. Plus, people got away too quickly, so they did not have time to gather details to report the incidents. Perhaps linking both Andrés's "difficult moment" at work and the other stories of assaults to the young people's frequent talk of racially motivated violence against them and Jorge's idea of calling the police, Wilfredo began to encourage them to find ways to adapt. "*Vayan adaptándose poco a poco*" (begin adapting little by little). "Do what you need to do." In this case, whether to call the police might be an individual decision, but a reflexive attitude that isolation was the safest course would not likely benefit youth over the long haul.

What Wilfredo wanted to make sure the *jóvenes* did *not* do was to internalize the violence and isolate out of fear. Referring to the hybrid hegemonies that followed Indigenous youth across borders, he continued, "People will tell you, 'You're not worth anything,' and we bring that from our home countries, too. That affects our self-esteem a lot. People from other countries say they speak their language, and they aren't afraid. But coming from Guatemala, [the language] causes insecurity." Wilfredo encouraged youth not to be overcome by insecurity but to hold tightly to their culture because "your culture is what identifies you as a unique person."

As linguistic anthropologist Leisy Wyman writes of elders in a very different Indigenous language ecology, Wilfredo and Jorge did not present themselves as authority figures, but their "strong talk" was meant to send a clear message about which forms of behavior would and would not benefit Maya youth in their drive for *sobrevivencia*.[21] Wilfredo singled out cultural shame and internalized colonial attitudes toward Indigenous languages as culprits in the long-term struggle to adapt and survive. At the same time, he asserted that Mayan language and culture need not be in tension with the need for *preparación*. In other words, he wanted youth to recognize that incorporation did not mean assimilation and that actively preparing oneself to function successfully in the new society of Los Angeles did not require youth to silence themselves. Wilfredo asserted that the Maya youth present that night were just as entitled to express themselves and their cultures as others were:

> If you walk near Rampart and Sixth [two Los Angeles streets], you will see that everyone there is speaking their language. But you can also get ahead with *preparación*. I have seen many [immigrant] people get further than native-born [people] because they know they have the same capacity but come to this country to get ahead. We can work and get money, but that's not enough. Learn English, get a GED or a high school diploma. People think success is something you're

born with, but really, it's a struggle. You can [achieve success] if you accept yourself and prepare yourself. The key is to know who you are. Every person can get ahead. Think of how that will help others.

As the meeting came to a close, Jorge shared that he wanted to get people together in the garden in the coming weeks because "things are growing." He reminded everyone of an activity they did where they wrote their fears down on papers and tore them up into small pieces. He said that they "planted fear, and corn grew." He mentioned that other fruits and vegetables were growing, including berries and beans. Jorge thought the more beneficial opportunity was for the *jóvenes* to spend time outdoors, learning to grow foods and, in turn, growing themselves. Voces participants were receptive to these *consejos* and appreciated what they interpreted as care for them in the absence of their kin caregivers. They demonstrated their receptivity by not only taking up the framework of *preparación* and *adaptación* broadly, as in this chapter and the next show, but also by making an honest effort to adopt the *consejos*—in this case, by showing up to the community garden on Saturday evenings and Sunday afternoons for weeks and months after Jorge's invitation.[22]

Socioemotional *preparación* often required developing interpersonal and organizational ties that youth could call upon to mitigate the distressing nature of being unaccompanied and undocumented Indigenous youth who nonetheless sought to move from disorientation to successful adaptation to their social roles in US society. Socioemotional *preparación* bolstered youth's prospects for *sobrevivencia* in diaspora. But, as Wilfredo and Jorge made clear time and again, additional forms of *preparación* were essential for youth's *sobrevivencia* as they came of age. And since Voces meetings were only two hours per week, most of these efforts would be taken individually, independent of the group and its coordinators, but hopefully, with the *consejos* in mind.

Linguistic *Preparación* and Hope for Imagined Futures

Despite youth's shared interests in improving their spoken Spanish or learning the English language, Voces de Esperanza was not a language-learning group. Youth would have to find independent ways of language learning if their ideas of *preparación* included linguistic *preparación*. Just as among unaccompanied Maya youth, dutiful expressions of the value of English are common among recent immigrants to the US. Transnational literacy scholar Doris Warriner has argued that these expressions do not always correspond to the "real" value of English—as a symbolic resource in itself—for English learners.[23] As Warriner asserted,

> [T]he . . . ability to understand and speak English must be supplemented with the communicative competence and cultural capital needed to know where to get information, how to ask for it, and what to do with that information.[24]

In other words, language learning can be one dimension of *preparación*, but language alone may not be sufficient for someone to deem themselves adequately "prepared" to adapt to a certain context. Maya youth in the study generally tied English learning not to abstract notions of survival but to specific, well-defined workplace and community-oriented goals, a reflection of their orientation to life as unaccompanied and undocumented migrant youth workers.

While unaccompanied, undocumented youth workers usually cannot enroll in the US K–12 educational system, some study participants eventually enrolled in adult English schools that offered classes for a few hours each day, Monday through Thursday. To qualify, some falsified their age and entered these after-work classes as minors; others waited until they were young adults. In all, sixteen Maya youth were enrolled in this alternative form of education at the time of their interview. Another two had been previously enrolled in school but were no longer enrolled and had no plans to return.

Attending adult English-language schools, even delayed or sporadically, to gain proficiency for workplace and community interactions made clear that the participants perceived a relationship between language learning and social mobility en route to their imagined futures. Below, we outline three key areas in which talk about *preparación* through language learning (and, to a lesser extent, language maintenance) was intimately connected to the youth's preferred futures for themselves and other Maya: greater employability and easier work, family and community belonging, and successful long-term (re)settlement.[25] Speaking Spanish in Guatemala and both Spanish and English in the United States served, at the least, as protective mechanisms. Beyond that, youth viewed language as a tool for promoting increased feelings of place and community belonging.

Alberto's story exemplifies how young people confronted obstacles to pursue language learning as part of *preparación*. He had first attempted to enroll in adult English language schools as a minor but was rejected by administrators who told him to "enroll in the daytime school for kids ... It's not that I didn't want to. It's just that I couldn't. I had to take care of myself." As was true for many youth, the immediate demands of day-to-day survival meant delaying longer-term investments in *preparación* for meaningful *sobrevivencia*.[26] Focused on working to support himself and his left-behind family, Alberto had to hold off on schooling for some time. He was enrolled in an English-language night class at the time of his interview and explained that he saw English education as important "to find a better job" as well as to "communicate with others" from different parts of the city or the world. Alberto lamented that he "didn't go for a long time" but still expressed pride that he had eventually figured out how to prepare himself in English, saying, "It's never too late"—the flipside, maybe, of the advice many youth received: to trust God and wait.

A Future of Employability and Easier Work
Without parents to support them financially and act as community liaisons or buffers from social and economic poverty, work was the primary site that Indigenous Maya youth had to learn to navigate in the United States. Adding to its importance was the role of youth as financial provider for many of their left-behind families. Unaccompanied Maya youth viewed linguistic *preparación* as directly related to their employability in the US and, beyond merely finding a job, as key to gaining access to *easier* work. Linguistic *preparación*, then, was a prerequisite for financial stability in the short term and socioeconomic mobility in the long term. Among factory workers, language needs included speaking Spanish to non-Indigenous Latin American coworkers and English with non-Latina/o or non–Spanish-speaking coworkers.

Youth were aware that stereotypes of Indigenous Latin Americans as backward and uneducated shaped their employment prospects and workplace experiences. Andrés described how being Maya was "a bit difficult because people do not understand your culture. They discriminate against you. They want nothing to do with you because you are *Indio*." He said that he had encountered non-Indigenous people (Mexicans in particular) who said things like, "You don't speak Spanish well; you are an *Indio*," or "You have a poor [person's] dialect," which affected him negatively. This account reinforces the point that stigmatizing language ideologies attach both to Maya youth's Indigenous languages (e.g., "You have a poor dialect") and their second language-inflected Spanish (e.g., "You don't speak Spanish well [because] you are an *Indio*"). In the garment factories where many youth worked, this disparagement translated into racialized exclusion from non-Indigenous coworkers. As non-Indigenous language speakers deployed crude stereotypes of Indigenous Latin Americans as uneducated, rural folk fit only for agricultural labor, they acted as gatekeepers of real and perceived opportunities for employment and mobility, and the youth's language behavior was often taken to index their level of incorporation and suitability for better-paying, easier jobs. Spanish and English language proficiency were therefore perceived as necessary for youth to avoid being pigeonholed as unskilled manual laborers in a global city like Los Angeles.

The relationship between language and youth's employability is shaped by the industry that employs them and, for some, goes together with job security. For example, Marianna was able to find employment as a domestic worker at the age of sixteen with limited Spanish and English proficiency. However, she quickly learned that retaining her job and securing safe and fair work conditions would require clearer communication with her employer and the two children she looked after. Since she was unable to attend a traditional high school, Marianna began sharpening her spoken Spanish skills in her church youth group on weekends and learning English through the subtitles of the television programs the children watched during the week. Marianna recalled that as the years passed and the young children entered school, they would enthusiastically share their worksheets with her, allowing her English proficiency to progress alongside their own. In Marianna's case, her *preparación* in Spanish and English proceeded nearly in tandem with her adaptation to her workplace, as she first found the job and only then realized that keeping the job and solidifying her position within the household would require a higher level of L2 proficiency in English. Over time, her confidence in communicating in English grew, and she was able to speak to her employer, the mother of the children, in English. As her Spanish proficiency improved, she was increasingly able to bond with other Maya youth and the coordinators at Voces, as when she shared the story of the attempted theft.

In addition to providing employability and greater job security, youth believed that having the language skills they needed to adapt would ultimately improve their ability to find less tedious, physically demanding, and repetitive work and to counter exploitation and violence in the workplace. In keeping with the future-oriented nature of *preparación*, the young people also thought strategically about which languages to prioritize and why. Andrés speculated that speaking English in the garment industry would allow him to communicate with factory owners and enable him to move from being a double-needle sewer (making hundreds of garments per hour for a few hundred dollars per week) to a sample maker (making one single project for a flat rate)—an opportunity for job and wage security.

Another garment worker named Felipe associated learning English with easier work because he saw that English-speaking employers appreciated when an employee could communicate with them. When asked what kind of work he saw himself doing in the future, he responded that he wanted to "find a job that's easier where I can speak English, people will understand me, and it will be easier. I don't know what I could get now if I didn't speak English." Felipe's disadvantages of being an underage worker and the youngest in the workplace were offset by his ability to use English in limited ways with his employer—a skill not shared by most of his older coworkers. He explained, "The bosses like when you can talk with them. . . . That's why [my boss] told me that he was very happy. . . . The boss was Korean, but no other worker could talk to him because they were all from Mexico or around there."

Language is important for negotiating inclusion in the workplace but is also essential for mitigating the threat of exclusion, especially through the violence of verbal harassment, wage theft, or underpayment. Gonzalo elaborated on these pressures through his experiences of labor exploitation and wage theft, linking a stereotypical image of Guatemalans as passive and uncomplaining to the history of anti-Indigenous discrimination in Guatemala:

> They don't pay in the garment industry; they pay less, well, they pay for what you do. Sometimes, the Koreans take advantage of you, but as Guatemalans, we don't speak up because, like I said, like Latinos or like Guatemalans, we come with fear [of discrimination], we don't speak up. Well, in my case, I am a very quiet person. I don't speak. If someone is yelling at me, I only listen. I didn't know how to defend myself, and they took advantage of me, well, of us [Guatemalans]. Then, one day, I saw I earned $200 for the week. For the week. I said, "No, that can't be." I said, "I am getting out of the garment industry, I am going to look for another job . . . with the little bit of experience I had."

Alluding to the influence of hybrid hegemonies at work, Gonzalo identified the importance of language and voice in advocating for one's position within the workplace and securing new jobs when existing ones prove problematic. After all, as educational linguists have observed, there is a difference between being able to speak a certain language and "activating one's voice" in that language in order to counter exploitation, especially when one's voice has historically been suppressed by the kinds of ideologies Gonzalo mentioned.[27]

A Future of Family and Community Belonging

The isolation of being Indigenous within a largely non-Indigenous immigrant community may be even more acute for youth who arrive without supportive older family members. Once in Los Angeles, Aarón described the attitudes of non-Indigenous Latinas/os toward him as "worse or the same as when I was [in Guatemala]." That the experience of discrimination was subjectively worse for Aarón in the United States was probably because of his unaccompanied status, as the pain of discriminatory experiences was compounded by the loneliness of being an unaccompanied minor who "didn't have affection, the love of my grandparents or my mother, I didn't have it, and then [the] discrimination. I felt lonely."

Over time, however, Aarón and other youth began honing their critical awareness of the pervasive, systemic nature of anti-Indigenous discrimination. In this context, Aarón's view of linguistic *preparación* was connected to a preferred future where language learning would allow him to overcome linguistic and social isolation in Los Angeles so that he could participate actively in his local community. In Aarón's view, with this *preparación*, his progress toward adaptation would become evident when he was able to interact with others without fear of "rejection" or "humiliation."

Overcoming discrimination and loneliness requires that youth traverse linguistic barriers to community integration in the host country as they simultaneously deal with the reverberating effects of racial and linguistic discrimination from their countries of origin. The correlation between language and community integration and sense of self is seen through interaction and Mayan speakers' embodied behavior in public, or their body idiom.[28] Aarón noticed this in his improved ability to engage with other Spanish speakers from diverse national origins:

> That's why now, since I am also learning Spanish, I don't have a problem speaking Spanish with another culture from Mexico, South America, Central America, or Spanish speakers from Europe. I don't have a problem speaking with them.... That's not me anymore. I have a ton of friends from different cultures, and I feel good.

Language strengthens youth's ability to relate to others, build community, and overcome the double isolation associated with being Indigenous and being an unaccompanied newcomer in the United States.

Youth's imagined futures were not linked only to issues of employability, belonging, and so forth, on an individual level, but included the futures of their families. As transnational youth are often the first in their families to migrate, left-behind family members rely on unaccompanied Maya youth for social as well as financial resources. Aarón, for example, hoped that linguistic *preparación* in Spanish could also be the first step toward adaptation for his brothers still living in Guatemala. Maya youth in Los Angeles saw language learning as a means to mitigate their own post-arrival suffering in the United States, but they also recognized that, if their family members were better prepared with regard to language, they might avoid the worst of the suffering, whether they opted to remain in Guatemala or migrated to the United States.

Aarón paired his experiences of discrimination and loneliness in Guatemala with those of linguistic *preparación* and adaptation as modes of community and self-esteem building in the US as lessons he could share with his left-behind family. In doing so, he tried to relay the value of Spanish proficiency to his family in Guatemala, instructing them, "'If you want [to succeed] you need to adapt to everything, learn these things, language first,' I tell them." Teaching his brothers Spanish and emphasizing the importance of linguistic *preparación* allowed Aarón to put the hard-earned lessons from his own experience to use. While he regretted that he had suffered for so long because of failing to "adapt," he aspired to help his brothers understand how preparing for linguistic and cultural flexibility would benefit their own adaptation:

> For me, adapting to this country is learning the language, like I am doing with my brothers. That is the first thing. Why did I suffer here for five years? Because I didn't, I didn't adapt to the language. That was it, that's why I suffered so much. Over there [Guatemala], I suffered a lot because I didn't adapt to the other language, other cultures, for example, Spanish, and then when I got here, it was the same thing. I didn't adapt. I felt the discrimination.

Much to his gratification, he reported that, at the time of the interview, his brothers "now . . . [knew] Spanish."

There is a striking contrast between participants' low self-esteem and feelings of rejection because of being Maya and a K'iche' speaker in Guatemala, and their feelings of empowerment through *preparación* in the United States, which some were determined to pass on to family members in Guatemala. Linguistic *preparación* could involve hiding one's Mayan language proficiency or adopting features of Mexican Spanish, as we discuss later, but it also involved an active process of *choosing* to prepare oneself linguistically in certain ways with specific outcomes in mind. These outcomes included imagined futures for oneself, one's family, and one's community, where adaptation, following *preparación*, had the potential to transform migrant youth's social and economic position in the US.

As Maya youth overcame barriers to improved self-esteem, family support and community belonging, they began to see themselves as potential resources for others. Learning Spanish and English to varying degrees of proficiency endowed youth with cultural capital that they could use to mentor or guide newer arrivals. This was especially visible in 2015–2016, following the highly publicized "surge" of unaccompanied youth and women from Central America arriving in the United States, when many of the Voces-involved youth began thinking in more collective terms about their roles in the community.

Omar, for one, saw his language-learning trajectory as closely related to his ability to broker community ties for other Indigenous Maya newcomers in Los Angeles. He reflected that during his first few years in the US, he "didn't understand life . . . life was just entertainment, I didn't think of doing anything. I didn't think about studying. I did think about learning English, but only to communicate with girls." As in others' accounts, Omar contrasted "studying" (as a future-oriented element of *preparación*) with his initial focus on "entertainment" in the pre-preparation survival mode.

With time, however, he said that he came to "think differently." Beyond the individual benefits of finding enjoyment in entertainment or communicating with love interests, he became motivated to "learn English [so] I can help people because, sometimes, say I have *paisanos* [fellow Guatemalans] that don't even speak Spanish well and English either, so then I can help with anything they need because it is necessary for someone to prepare themselves. That's what I am seeing. It is necessary." Omar recognized that K'iche'-Spanish bilingualism would help him support others' *preparación* ("because it is necessary for someone to prepare themselves"). He also anticipated that proficiency in spoken English would contribute to this goal. Omar's imagined future was therefore interwoven with the future he imagined for the Indigenous Maya community in a predominantly non-Indigenous Latina/o Los Angeles.

Future-Making and Sobrevivencia

Many youth interviewed for the larger study indicated having the intention of living and working in the US for less than five years and eventually returning to their home country to see their families again.[29] Despite their professed desire to return to Guatemala, migrant youth workers often find that the structure of the labor market, low wages, and their undocumented status, along with political and economic uncertainties in their home countries, keep them in the US as they transition out of their adolescent years and into young adulthood. Over time, youth's imagined futures shift from being origin-country oriented to destination-country oriented.[30] Hence, their everyday efforts of *preparación* likewise become directed toward an imagined future of long-term residence in the United States.

Maneuvering with language can make the difference between getting by and getting ahead as unaccompanied Maya youth come of age. This disjuncture is evident in youth's descriptions of the importance of language as a mechanism for *sobrevivencia*. Beyond employability and better day-to-day work experiences, Maya youth workers' long-term resettlement requires them to think strategically about remaining competitive in a neoliberal and globalized labor market that seeks to extract the greatest amount of labor at the lowest cost from the most vulnerable workers.

Juan realized this after attaining the coveted job of being a sample maker—the same job for which Felipe, quoted above, wanted to prepare himself. When asked what allowed him to enter and maintain this position, Juan pointed to his ability to "speak a little bit of English." In the next chapter, we detail the social construction of language proficiency among Maya youth and pay particular attention to evaluative discourse through which youth compared their proficiency to others'.[31] Here, we note that the young people leveraged finely attuned language proficiency assessments in their attempts to gain a leg up in the competitive and exploitative Los Angeles labor market. Juan's knowledge of the English language, and his attitude toward it, gave him an advantage relative to other predominantly Spanish- or Mayan-speaking workers.

As sociolinguist Elise M. DuBord has noted, immigrant workers' understanding of their own and others' language proficiency allows them to leverage their bilingualism strategically in work contexts where such bilingualism is relatively rare.[32] Despite not speaking English "100 percent," Juan engaged in strategic linguistic risk-taking. He said, "Sometimes I talk low, but, I mean, I take a risk. I am not afraid.... There are many people who are in high school here, but they don't take the risk to look for another job. So, what I have to do is go for it.... What is helping me is speaking English at work." Juan's statement implied that, even if one had made strides toward *preparación* in the sense of gaining knowledge and skills, it was still necessary to put that *preparación* into practice by actively working to adapt oneself to new contexts. He juxtaposed the image of someone who studied but was unwilling to "take the risk" (e.g., to look for a better job) with the image of himself, who was willing to "go for it" by putting his English *preparación* to use as he adapted to the labor market.

As Felipe ruminated about the extent to which he felt comfortable moving about Los Angeles and his future in the US, he explained that speaking English had "really helped me to survive." He underscored the importance of language to his adaptation in the US by comparing his interactions with English speakers in public when he first arrived in Los Angeles to those at the time of our interview. Initially, he did not understand what others were saying when they spoke English to him, but he said, "Now, when someone asks me something, because the words people ask on the street are very basic, and you can answer them." Fairly limited English proficiency was sufficient for "surviving" (in the usual sense of the word) these "basic" street conversations, but youth knew that greater English proficiency was necessary in different contexts, including the workplace where, Felipe affirmed, "it's different because there you really need more [English-language ability]."

Sobrevivencia could also refer quite literally to youth's physical health and to youth's desire to keep themselves healthy in a situation where they had relatively few resources to address health concerns, some of which were work-related. Enrique was among the many participants who worried about physical illness, injury, or the possibility of a health emergency. He worried that his inability to speak English well would impede his ability to seek assistance if "something happens." When asked where the English language would help him, he responded:

At school, at work, on the street. It would help me. If something happens at work, for example, say I get into an accident, how would I report it if I can't speak English? If a doctor speaks English and asks me what pains I have, and I don't know . . . that's why I have to learn, *para sobrevivir* [to survive].

It is important to be clear about what Enrique meant by *"para sobrevivir"*: He was not necessarily worried that he would suffer an injury or illness that was literally fatal, but that he would not be in good health over the long term if he lacked the ability to report health problems in sufficient detail. Specifically, Enrique worried that he would be unable to communicate his injury to factory floor supervisors or factory owners or discuss symptoms of illness with medical professionals.

As youth imagined their long-term futures in the United States, English language proficiency became more salient as it was perceived as a deciding factor in their well-being as unaccompanied and unauthorized migrant workers. Enrique's description of needing English to report work injuries also fits with a broader discourse of the young people's youth's needing English (and, to a lesser degree, Spanish) to advocate for themselves in the workplace—not just in case of injury but also to report wage theft, ingratiate themselves to bosses, move into more desirable jobs, and defend themselves from discrimination.

Finally, beyond Spanish and English learning in the context of Indigenous Maya youth's imagined futures, it is important to acknowledge that *preparación* also entailed beginning to imagine a place for Mayan languages in Los Angeles and reconsidering how youth's stigmatized Mayan-language competence might be reframed and reconsidered in immigrant settings. Youth workers expressed ambivalent language ideologies around Mayan languages, sometimes asserting that Mayan languages had "set them back" with respect to Spanish and English, and at other times professing pride in Maya identity and thanking God for the continued presence of the Indigenous language.[33] Some, like Andrés, reflected on the prevalence of Mayan-Spanish translanguaging or syncretism in ways that suggested concern for how transnational migration might be contributing to language shift: "And sometimes in K'iche', '*Oh disculpa*' [Spanish: 'oh sorry']—we don't say what it is in K'iche' anymore.

It's been combined, so that's why I say that I speak 90 percent [of K'iche'], not all of it; there are also words that I don't know anymore."

We will continue to explore Mayan-language ideologies and maintenance in the chapters that follow. The main takeaway we observe is that some youth began to interpret changes in Mayan languages as an ongoing loss of the language or a move away from its fluid use in everyday interactions with other Maya. *Preparación* with respect to Mayan languages, then, was a matter of first recognizing that patterns of use and communicative competence could change on an individual ("there are words that I don't know anymore") as well as a community level ("we don't say what it is in K'iche' anymore"). Then, as we will show, concerns about the maintenance of Mayan languages in diaspora could lead to questioning the language ideologies that had long painted them as inferior and fueled the displacement of their speakers from Guatemala.

Conclusion

Unaccompanied, undocumented Maya youth workers arrive in the United States to the disorienting reality that their intersectional identities present multiple material and emotional barriers to incorporation. Moving from disorientation to having the ability to adapt effectively to new circumstances requires youth to engage actively and strategically in interpersonal and organizational relationships that support *preparación*: exposure to the ideologies, norms and values, institutions, and languages of the new society in ways that facilitate youth's ability to navigate them. *Preparación* supports adaptation and *sobrevivencia* in an imagined future as youth envision becoming upwardly mobile workers, loyal and supportive family and community members, and long-settled immigrants who have successfully made the transition to adulthood.

The participants' talk about *preparación* as essential for *sobrevivencia* demonstrates their keen understanding of their multiply-disadvantaged position within hybrid hegemonies as legal, cultural, and social outsiders who must proactively access knowledge and resources and patch them together to make ends meet. They imagined futures that encompassed their roles as workers, as members of transnational households and communities—sometimes operating as liaisons for compatriots, parents, and/or siblings in the country of origin—and as young people transitioning into adulthood while separated from their families. It is evident that there is not a single process of *preparación* (or a single form of successful *adaptación,* for that matter) that can be identified for Maya youth; rather, the specific form of these processes depends on youth's nested contexts of incorporation, including (but not limited to) their ties to coethnic community members, their interactions outside of their ethnic enclave, and their occupation and occupational aspirations.[34]

The concept of *preparación* illuminates how Maya youth, as Indigenous teenage migrants growing up without parents and legal status, experience the incorporation process differently from those of their non-Indigenous, locally parented, and school-going counterparts. Not only must they pursue incorporation in vastly different roles and contexts and without direct support from family members, but their incorporation processes are characterized by a distinct temporality, space, and pace. The forms of *preparación* we described in this chapter, linguistic and otherwise, are necessary to replace institutional structures that are normalized in narratives of incorporation and may be taken for granted by other youth (older family members, K-12 schools, churches, and so on). Youth strategically engage in interpersonal and organizational relationships that bolster their *preparación* as unaccompanied teenagers, Indigenous migrants, and undocumented workers who participate in local and transnational communities. This requires them to interact independently with institutions typically thought to be reserved for adults and to actively negotiate the terms of their involvement within these institutions.

The processes of language socialization we outline and analyze here might be perceived as an erasure of Indigenous languages as expressions of "resilient indigeneity."[35] We see it instead as a process whereby Maya youth move from disorientation to adaptation through emotional and cultural *preparación*. The remaining chapters examine how youth measure their linguistic adaptation and how language proficiency, including the retention and strengthening of Mayan language proficiency, becomes a mechanism for cultural pride that enables an inclusive mode of future-making.

THREE

Measuring Adaptation

Enrique aspired to leave the garment industry and work in retail, even entertaining the possibility of owning his own restaurant someday. He knew he would need English for these endeavors and had been going to adult English as a Second Language (ESL) classes for about three years; still, he said, he did not always stay for the full duration of the class: "Sometimes . . . I didn't last a year but [I did] six months, three months," which caused him to have to repeat levels. Even when he was able to attend class, he was often so exhausted after work that he found it difficult to focus: "*Me cuesta concentrarme*" (It takes a lot for me to concentrate).

Enrique offered that he was in ESL level 3B at the time, explaining that there were six numbered levels and that students proceeded through the A, B, and C sections of each. Enrique felt like he was learning the language "but not a lot," and that he struggled to understand English speakers who spoke quickly; when pressed for specifics, he pivoted from talk about levels (e.g., 3B) to percentage talk: "Now, I think around 50 percent for reading . . . and some 20, 30 percent [of understanding what I read]. . . . On speaking, like 20 [percent], I think, I'm behind on speaking." In terms typical of schooled literacies—that is, those expected, valued, and practiced in mainstream educational settings in the US—Enrique seemed to contrast his "higher" reading fluency with his "lower" comprehension, then compared both favorably to his spoken English.[1] The discourse of being "behind"—on a particular way of using language, as here, or because of being an L1 Mayan speaker, as other participants asserted—begs the question: "Behind" relative to whom?

In the previous chapter, we analyzed unaccompanied Maya youth's conceptualizations of incorporation as including the phase of *preparación* to make *adaptación* possible. In other words, we showed that youth saw it as necessary to prepare themselves in specific ways to adjust materially and emotionally within and across social domains of the destination society. Youth sought *preparación* in the forms of knowledge, expertise, relationships, and support networks in different spheres of immigrant life to succeed in achieving material and emotional *adaptación*. Above, Enrique illuminated youth's self-assessment and self-positioning with respect to linguistic *preparación* as a measure of readiness for *adaptación*—not in general terms, but to consider whether he was well suited to a particular social role and context, in this case, as a worker pursuing job mobility. He also demonstrated how the dialogic and social construal of language proficiency can fit into the broader project of examining "migrants' interactions with specific local structures of opportunities" in future-making.[2]

Heeding Enrique's example, this chapter explores the social construction of language proficiency among Maya youth as one dimension of the broader process of *adaptación* that youth projected with their talk of *preparación*. Other research has shown that Mayan-speaking immigrants claim proficiency in Mayan, Spanish, or English strategically, in context-sensitive ways that reflect the historical marginalization of Mayan languages as "lesser" and a corresponding desire to "pass" as non-Indigenous to mitigate discrimination in immigrant settings.[3] Here, we explore how youth used their perceptions of their own and others' language proficiency (i.e., in Spanish, English, and Mayan) to evaluate their degree of incorporation in the Latina/o immigrant community and US society more broadly. Talk about language proficiency, in other words, was used to gauge how well *preparado* and *adaptado* different individuals were, according to study participants.

We focus our analysis on a particular discursive strategy that unaccompanied Maya youth used in assessing people's preparedness to adapt to life as immigrants in the United States: "percentage talk," or explicit talk about language proficiency couched in percentages. Such talk allowed the young people to reflect on the usefulness and limitations of their uneven communicative repertoires in relation to specific others in the US and Guatemala.[4] Percentage talk also allowed them to wrestle with social stratification and inequality in the US and Guatemala and to imagine themselves as future members of Spanish- and English-oriented discourse communities in the US. Participants consistently described proficiency in terms of the percentage of "total proficiency" that they perceived as necessary to reach their imagined futures—as workers, transnational family and community members, and potential long-term US residents who would nonetheless display "resilient indigeneity" in maintaining Mayan language and cultural practice in diaspora.[5] Because of this, percentage talk around Mayan languages, while less frequent than that around Spanish and English, is still important to consider as part of youth's overall picture of their language ecologies.

Unaccompanied Indigenous youth formed perceptions of proficiency within distinct interactional contexts, co-constructing their perceptions of language proficiency relative to their perceptions of interactants' proficiency. We focus our analysis here on how the youth gauged their own level of linguistic *preparación* for certain milestones on the journey of *adaptación* (e.g., getting a new job, talking somewhat comfortably with non-Indigenous Latinas/os, being able to advocate for other Maya) compared to the perceived proficiency of others, such as non-Indigenous and L1 (first language) Spanish-speaking Latinas/os, the bilingual interviewer, and English-speaking bosses. Adaptability was central to youth's individual *sobrevivencia* and that of the Indigenous immigrant community as a whole. Youth's talk about perceived proficiency framed linguistic adaptation as a natural extension of this.

We conclude by analyzing how youth's ideologies of language learning and beliefs about language proficiency shaped their imagined futures. These imagined futures are predicated on the possibility of belonging to discourse communities, which youth explored with reference to their ideologies of language learning—that is, their beliefs about the desirability and feasibility of learning different languages—and their understanding of their own and others' language proficiency. This suggests that Maya youth's *sobrevivencia* during their transition to adulthood required that they maintain a sense of ethnolinguistic community in diaspora.[6]

Percentage talk co-opted Western ideologies of individual learning and language assessment, including the notion that language proficiency could be quantified and measured in isolation from social contexts. Over time, however, youth's individualized talk about perceived proficiency allowed them to assess their ability to support the linguistic *preparación* and eventual *adaptación* of other L1 Mayan speakers in their local community. Thus, prompted to think in both individualistic and collectivistic ways, unaccompanied Maya youth workers harnessed individualistic understandings of language proficiency with assessments for the collective good. While we emphasize youth's maneuvering around Spanish and English in this chapter, we look more closely at how the same question is applied to K'iche' and other Mayan languages in diaspora later in the book.

The Social Construction of Perceived Proficiency

Studies of second-language acquisition have often treated proficiency as a measurable property of individual speakers. However, several researchers emphasize the social construction of perceived proficiency, or how interlocutors judge one another's linguistic competence and position themselves and others accordingly.[7] In this view, language proficiency is better understood not as a static or measurable property of individuals but as a social object that speakers collaboratively produce through their perceptions of others' competence. Constructions of perceived proficiency appear to be a pervasive feature of conversational interaction; even very young emergent bilinguals engage in such evaluations of others' competence.[8] Applied linguist Melinda Martin-Beltrán observed that perceived proficiency is constructed both "at the interpersonal and institutional levels"—that is, it emerges from the interactional dynamics between individual speakers and through institutionally sanctioned definitions and understandings of language proficiency.[9]

Since perceived proficiency is mutually constructed within communities of speakers, it is not just consequential in the short term of face-to-face interaction. Instead, when language learners co-construct one another's proficiency, they articulate imagined futures, including future possibilities for belonging to distinct discourse communities.[10] Talking about perceived proficiency allows speakers to imagine themselves (or others) as belonging (or not) to communities of speakers. The social co-construction of perceived proficiency also influences participants' language learning *ideologies*—that is, their beliefs about the utility or necessity of learning either Spanish or English to varying degrees of proficiency, for pragmatic ends.[11] Language ideologies—briefly, "cultural ... system[s] of ideas about social and linguistic relationships"[12]—are profoundly intertwined with all processes of language socialization and play a significant role in how language learners "appropriat[e] and approximat[e]" elements of others' voices "for [their] own purposes."[13]

Speakers like the unaccompanied Maya youth workers in our study, who come of age in a dynamic, globalizing context, must mobilize resources from uneven communicative repertoires to interact with others whose repertoires differ considerably.[14] While the Maya youth are not immune from the bias toward "balanced bilingualism," or being able to use elements of one's named languages in similar ways, their percentage talk suggests a rather sophisticated view of translingual practice in immigrant communities.[15] To be clear, we are not suggesting that balanced bilingualism is a bad thing—only that it is not the only standard for "successful" language use within an approach that acknowledges the unevenness of speakers' repertoires. The fact that youth described language proficiency in terms of percentages provides evidence that the young people took a dynamic view of bilingualism,[16] focusing on how their positioning on the immigrant "languaging continuum"[17]—the spectrum of proficiency in all three languages—equipped or did not equip them to meet their communicative needs.

Perceived Linguistic Proficiency and the Functions of Percentage Talk

Percentage talk was a common strategy used to assess linguistic *preparación* in Maya youth's accounts of their language experiences in diaspora. By "percentage talk," we mean talk that construed a speaker's knowledge of a language in terms of a certain percentage of "full knowledge" of the language. What participants precisely meant by "full knowledge" differed from person to person, as we will see. Still, percentage talk occurred consistently across participants, even though the accounts analyzed here come from one-on-one interactions.

Talking about percentages of linguistic knowledge presumed *perceived* proficiency to be *measured* proficiency. In other words, Maya youth's percentage talk appeared to be recursive with ideologies of proficiency from Western schooling, in which an individual's knowledge is assumed to be quantifiable and able to be measured in standardized ways.[18] This is striking for several reasons. For one, study participants had relatively little access to formal education either in Guatemala or in the United States, which raises the issue of how they might have been exposed to such ideologies.[19] It is possible that some participants encountered similar beliefs about language proficiency and assessment in adult ESL classes in the US or among English-learner peers. It has also been argued that beliefs about assessment among Maya immigrants in the US stem from Maya parents' contact with teachers and schools; clearly, many of the participants in this study must have developed their beliefs about proficiency and language learning in other contexts.[20] Some youth, on the other hand, did attend English classes, though their attendance could be intermittent and was contingent on work and other life circumstances. These participants' accounts of in-school language learning support the idea that the young people borrowed school-like discourses to assess their own proficiency.

Percentage talk served several interrelated discourse functions that worked to facilitate comparison and contrast among different speakers or types of speakers. Youth evaluated their own proficiency relative to the interviewer's (in English and Spanish) and that of non-Indigenous Latin American immigrants (in Spanish; secondarily in English). They also compared their levels of linguistic *preparación* to the perceived English, Spanish, and Mayan competence of other Indigenous Latin Americans, including their left-behind family members, and to their past selves—that is, they contrasted their linguistic repertoires at the time of the interview with those they possessed as children in Guatemala or as recently arrived unaccompanied migrants in the United States. Assessments of perceived proficiency at a given moment in time, therefore, pointed backward to less capable former selves (in terms of their ability to function in the US), as well as forward to futures that were connected to greater levels of proficiency in Spanish and English, whether for the participants themselves or for their families and fellow immigrants. At times, this future-oriented gaze was accompanied by concerns of diminishing Mayan proficiency and a desire to regain it. Attending closely to the construal of proficiency within these contexts—that is, relative to native English and Spanish speakers, other Indigenous Latin Americans, and the speakers' past and future selves—shows how the participants imagined their trajectories of language socialization, their community membership, and the parameters of their aspirations for the future.

Most obviously, perhaps, given their marginal social and economic position in the US, youth evaluated their own English and Spanish proficiency with respect to L1 speakers of those languages and to gauge their present level of *adaptación* and prospects for the future. Participants saw English and Spanish as central to the process of *adaptación* to life in multiple diverse communities in the United States. Aarón, for example, succinctly said, "For me, adapting to this country means working with the language." *Adaptación*, for Aarón, "is trying to figure out how to live with others." Notably, Aarón distinguished *adaptación* as "working with the language" from the process that youth called *preparación,* which they generally thought to involve gaining the knowledge required to "work with" the language in workplace and other community settings. While Maya youth assessed their proficiency across multiple dimensions of Spanish and English—speaking, understanding, and reading/writing—they connected the fundamental economic and social dimensions of *sobrevivencia* mainly to proficiency in spoken Spanish and English. Having some degree of spoken proficiency would allow them to *defenderse* ("defend themselves" or look after themselves) in situations involving wage theft, according to Gonzalo, or work-related medical issues, according to Enrique.

Adaptación *to an English-Speaking Language Community*

While the participants perceived clear differences between their English and that of L1 English speakers, this did not entail an all-or-nothing view of language learning and use, nor did it mean that the participants' goal was native-like proficiency in Spanish or English. Even incremental advances in perceived proficiency could dramatically improve one's work circumstances. For example, Andrés used percentage talk to illustrate the gap between his English proficiency and that of "people like you who speak English" as a first language (i.e., the interviewer) and to put forth what he saw as a realistic view of his prospects:

> I have the dream right now, I mean, of mastering—maybe not 100 percent, like people like you, the ones who talk like you all who speak English—but I have the dream of at least speaking the basics so that I can work in a job that isn't so backbreaking, not so much like a slave, an exhausting twelve-hour job where my mind gets tired out from all the noise for twelve hours and I get home tired, and I have to go study.

Andrés's vivid description of his appalling work conditions underscored the social and linguistic distance between Stephanie's English proficiency and his own. It also revealed that percentage talk could be used to contest the idea that L1 Mayan speakers could not improve their economic situation without aspiring to native-like proficiency in English or Spanish. Andrés acknowledged that, given his current exhausting job, he was unlikely to be able to study enough to speak "100 percent," like the interviewer. Nonetheless, he suggested that an advanced level of English proficiency was unnecessary to achieve his immediate goals. "Speaking the basics" might be enough to get a job that was, literally, *no tan esclavo* (not so much like a slave). Ultimately, it might allow him to learn more English, since he would not be as exhausted after work.

Andrés's comments about his lack of English proficiency compared to the interviewer could be read as self-deprecating. We argue, however, that they point to an emergent language ideology that Andrés shared with many of his coethnics in the Maya diaspora in Los Angeles. Acquiring competence in English and/or Spanish—and evaluating one's progress toward doing so—was not an end in itself. English or Spanish competence only mattered as an element of *preparación* and insofar as it promoted *adaptación* in the short term and *sobrevivencia* over the long term. According to this ideology, the discursive contrast with Stephanie's English underscored the difference Andrés perceived between the kind of English he *needed* ("not 100 percent, like people like you") and the kind of English she spoke. Andrés, like other Maya youth, had a plan in mind—an imagined future—and language learning was one form of *preparación* through which he worked to realize that plan.

Beyond employability and better day-to-day work experiences, Maya youth workers' goal of *sobrevivencia* required them to think strategically about how to remain competitive in a neoliberal and globalized labor market that seeks to extract the greatest amount of labor at the lowest cost from the most vulnerable workers.[21] Maneuvering with language can make the difference between getting *by* and getting *ahead* as unaccompanied Maya youth come of age. Andrés's comments pointed to this economic reality: Spoken Spanish or English proficiency is *not* necessary for employment in the secondary labor market, yet it is critical for achieving mobility *within* low-wage occupations.[22] For Maya youth, it meant also ensuring they would be able to enact a greater sense of agency at work and within the labor market in the future.

Jerónimo was a native Mayan-language speaker who, because his parents were able to keep him in school until the age of fifteen, considered himself a proficient Spanish speaker. He described the language as "fresh" in his mind when he arrived in Los Angeles at that age. Jerónimo loquaciously detailed in Spanish that he had been in his current position at a business selling aftermarket parts for sports cars for just over a year by the time of his interview in 2016, a job he described as "the best job I've had in my thirteen years in the US." As he described it, the opportunity came about through a chance conversation about work with a fellow Guatemalan, who encouraged him to apply for work at the other man's job after "screening" Jerónimo's English proficiency:

> He says to me, "Do you speak English?" "Honestly, I only speak a little bit," I tell him, "Not so much." But he told me, "If you speak a little bit and you understand more or less, there, where I'm working, they'll hire somebody even if he only speaks a little English." I said, "Well, whatever it is, that's fine, I'll go and at least see what it is."

While Jerónimo did not engage in percentage talk, exactly, his discourse echoed Enrique's in the opening vignette, referring to the relative amounts of English a person might speak or understand and on account of which they would be positioned differently in the Los Angeles labor market.

Moreover, having "a little bit" of English and understanding "more or less," as Jerónimo thought he did, led to increased exposure to the language and, over the long term, promoted a higher level of English proficiency. Jerónimo's job afforded him further opportunities to practice his English since he used the language with the Koreans who worked there, although there were also Spanish-speaking Latina/o employees. In addition to its usefulness at work, Jerónimo, like many youth, saw a degree of English proficiency as a necessity for alleviating the suffering he experienced during his post-arrival disorientation: "Look, I don't like English, but when I came to this country, I suffered." He offered a story about one of his early LA experiences that made him realize he needed to learn at least some English; when he got confused about the bus fare, a Spanish speaker came to his rescue, but not before Jerónimo was utterly humiliated. "Believe me that I was almost crying on that bus. I wanted to go running out of there—even better, *flying!*"

Jerónimo's experience was striking because his English development took place almost against his wishes. Perhaps being more invested in "standard" Guatemalan Spanish than many Maya youth in this study because of his unique length of formal Spanish-language schooling in Guatemala, Jerónimo confessed that he disliked speaking English and only used it when it was absolutely necessary. He was not one of the youth who aspired to higher proficiency in the language and lamented that his Spanish was becoming peppered with English discourse markers like "so" and "I mean." This aspect of Jerónimo's relationship with English—that he recognized he needed it but disliked it and used it as little as possible—is worthy of comment because it highlights the *intentional* and *strategic* nature of youth's language learning and understanding of proficiency. It also implies that investment in speaking Spanish "well"—in addition to, or instead of, attaining a high level of English proficiency and/or maintaining Mayan proficiency—was another ideological option for Indigenous youth who were often at a linguistic disadvantage in the United States.

The initial question Jerónimo's coworker posed to him was representative of Maya youth's strategic decision-making around language and assessments of proficiency: How much of which language is enough, and for what? Jerónimo made clear that learning English (or Spanish) was not just something that happened to youth as they "assimilated" to life in the US, nor were youth pursuing language learning for abstract reasons. Rather, Maya young people deliberately sought linguistic capital in the "codes of power"[23] to pursue opportunities within the "specific local structures" of the LA labor market and/or to shield themselves from the worst effects of disorientation and discrimination.[24]

An example of this was the difference that youth workers noted between piece-rate workers and sample makers in garment factories. While piece-rate workers typically line factory floors, there are only a handful of sample makers in each factory. Additionally, whereas piece-rate workers can only earn as much money as their cumulative work allows, sample makers are promised an hourly rate for more detailed and specialized work. The role of sample maker was coveted among participants in the garment industry because of its social prestige within the factories and because of the potential for higher, more secure wages.

Juan, who worked as a sample maker and was not enrolled in English-language school, identified spoken English proficiency as the route to mobility within the garment industry. Like Andrés, Juan used percentage talk to characterize the degree of proficiency necessary for specialized, better-paying work. In an interview, Juan detailed an interaction that had transpired between his supervisor and himself that same morning:

> For example, they gave me a blouse today. [His supervisor instructed him,] "You sew this blouse today. And this, I want it to be this style." And they show you.

Juan described the project as a "puzzle," where "sometimes you get stressed." He continued, "What helps me is that I speak a little bit of English. Not 100 percent, but I understand it." Juan acquired the coveted sample-maker position in no small part because of his ability to speak directly to his floor supervisor in such interactions. In doing so, he not only escaped the challenges facing piece-rate workers but was able to mitigate some of the stress associated with the demanding craft of sample making.[25]

Despite speaking less than "100 percent" of English, Juan felt a sense of pride as he drew on his English resources to secure his position as a sample maker and to complete his work. His pride was bolstered when he compared himself to immigrants who "[are] in school, but do not take the risk of looking for another job." What good is English, in other words, if you don't use it to improve your economic situation and your future prospects? Juan's percentage talk came across not as a deficit discourse (i.e., a way of putting himself down) but as an indicator of his savviness: He knew exactly how much proficiency was needed to achieve specific, work-related goals from a position of disadvantage. Like Jerónimo and Andrés, Juan understood that "100 percent" proficiency was not necessary for employability, nor was formal language learning. Just enough English proficiency combined with other individual traits, such as his willingness to "take the risk," was essential. Like the bilingual day laborers in the US–Mexico borderlands in Elise M. DuBord's study, Juan was quick to recognize the economic edge that a relatively low percentage of proficiency could confer.[26]

Spanish-Language Proficiency and Latina/o Community Adaptación

To measure their readiness to adapt, Maya youth also compared their proficiency in Spanish to that of L1 Spanish speakers. Unlike comparisons with English speakers, these comparisons often relied on fears that Maya youth would be identifiable as native speakers of Indigenous languages and, therefore, singled out for anti-*Indio* racism and discrimination by other Latinas/os.[27]

The ideologies of Spanish learning and proficiency were intertwined with colonial ideologies about Mayan languages, which sometimes resulted in ambivalent or contradictory attitudes toward proficiency. For example, in describing school, Felipe, a car washer, said, "School is nice because you can meet new friends. I like it because I feel really happy. I am studying three languages. Sometimes I regret having the [K'iche'] language that I have." When asked why, he responded:

> Because I don't speak Spanish well, I feel worried that someone will hear me and think I don't speak it well. . . . Some people tell me not to be embarrassed because I can speak three languages [laughs] and

they can only speak Spanish and English. I speak Spanish, English, and my *dialecto* [K'iche']. "You're the best!" they say.

Felipe contrasted his "regret" at speaking K'iche' with his non-Indigenous peers' contention that he was "the best" because of being trilingual. He was acutely aware of others' surveillance of his language and how non-native Spanish features could index Indigeneity, commenting that he felt "worried" and "embarrassed." When asked directly whether he felt ashamed of being Maya or speaking K'iche', he responded, "I think so, that I'm ashamed. I don't like it. Because I'm not like the people who speak Spanish." The discourse of regret was also associated with a language ideology among the participants that Mayan languages were valuable and to be cherished, on one hand, and responsible for "setting them back" with respect to Spanish and English learning, on the other. Juan put it succinctly: "Thank God that we have another language, but I think it held me back a little."

In the absence of adults who could offer youth consistent guidance in navigating anti-Indigenous racism and language discrimination, Maya young people adapted by making situational decisions about how to protect themselves, physically, as explored in the previous chapter, but also emotionally. This often prompted them to learn Spanish as quickly as they could. Carlos, for instance, shared similar feelings of shame and embarrassment at being identifiable as a Mayan speaker upon arriving in the United States: "I was a little ashamed of speaking K'iche' when I arrived, so I was like, 'No, then I have to learn Spanish,'" and he did. Likewise, Gonzalo, a florist in the Los Angeles Flower Market, linked this feeling of shame or embarrassment to an internalized sense of inferiority among Indigenous migrants, owing to the fear they brought with them from Guatemala as described in Chapter 1: "We arrive with that fear.... We feel like we're less than the people who are born here, we feel lesser, why? Because we're afraid, we're ashamed of speaking K'iche'." One way Gonzalo could mitigate this feeling of being lesser was by speaking Spanish. In this way, language learning gave youth leverage to independently manage their emotions and self-esteem in their transition to adulthood.

Adaptación Through Mayan-Language Proficiency

As mentioned above, metacommentary about Maya youth's L2 Spanish proficiency often went together with talk about their proficiency in K'iche' or other Mayan languages. Participants sometimes opposed being *adaptado* to being *atrasado* (behind or held back) and connected being held back on account of Mayan languages to an ideology of semilingualism among non-Indigenous Latinas/os.[28] Youth described that others sometimes interpreted their relative lack of Spanish proficiency as evidence that they did not have fully developed competence in any language. Comments directing youth back to *"Indio*-land" connected speaking Mayan languages to beliefs that Indigenous languages were *dialectos*—less-than-full languages—and to stereotypes of rural backwardness and ignorance. Insofar as Maya youth saw being linguistically *atrasado* as the opposite of *adaptado*, these discourses associated Mayan proficiency with difficulty in responding to the contingencies of immigrant life.

Percentage talk was a double-edged sword in the context of circulating ideologies about semilingualism and deficit-based responses to Maya youths' language. At times, we have argued, it served the function of allowing youth to gauge their level of *adaptación* and progress toward material and emotional goals. At other times, percentage talk, which invited youths to measure their perceived proficiency against that of others, led them to conclude that they were coming up short in all three languages. Andrés, who attested to others' beliefs about Mayan semilingualism, said that he could read "about 70 percent" and speak "about 80 percent" of Spanish; English, by contrast, was more limited: "I'm getting there a little bit with English. Maybe I've got around 7 percent and I'm lacking the 93 percent." English was unsurprisingly presented as a work in progress. But strikingly, Andrés, an L1 K'iche' speaker, did not claim to speak "100 percent" of K'iche'. Rather, he represented his K'iche' proficiency as the flipside of his English proficiency, commenting that he had either never acquired, or had started to lose, around 10 percent of "full" competence in K'iche'. We quote his comments at length, as they demonstrate the complex functions and ideologies involved in Maya youth's percentage talk:

> Maybe I write around 40 percent [in K'iche'] but I speak around 90 percent. I'm missing the other 10 percent because there are things

like, like, let's see, for example, sometimes [in Spanish] instead of *disculpa* [Spanish: sorry] we combine it [in English] "Sorry." So, we already combine Spanish and English, so that's where we are with K'iche'. That's why I say that maybe I speak 90 percent of K'iche', and . . . sometimes they put it in Spanish. Instead of saying, "oh . . . ," in K'iche' we call it [inaudible K'iche' utterance], it's a way of saying "sorry." And sometimes [when speaking] K'iche' [we say] *"Oh, disculpa,"* [in Spanish], we don't say the K'iche' phrase anymore. It's gotten combined, and that's why I say that it's 90 percent that I speak, not all of it, and there are also [K'iche'] words that I don't know.

Andrés compared his use of Spanish phrases in K'iche' utterances to immigrants' mixing of English and Spanish. Instead of seeing K'iche'-Spanish codeswitching in terms of linguistic *adaptación,* Andrés saw it as evidence of deficiency or as a lack of proficiency in any one language. This reflects a sociolinguistic context in which Mayan-speakers' language is continually stigmatized and derided as illegitimate, as "neither this nor that," as Andrés put it. Aarón, like Joel, remarked that Mayan speakers bore the scars of colonial language ideologies from Guatemala, which bred a sense of inferiority and *timidez* (shyness) in the US. They referred to Spanish colonizers who forced Mayan speakers to change their language, quoting the colonizers: "'Your language isn't worth anything,' if not simply 'You speak a dialect.'"

Participants' semilingual framings of Mayan-language proficiency also point to another function of percentage talk. It could be used to weigh the possibility of language shift, a community-wide trend away from Mayan languages, owing to immigrant speakers' contact with Spanish and English. Tomás, for example, said that he felt good about speaking K'iche' because it was his first language, but ruefully admitted that he struggled to speak fluently because Spanish speakers constantly surrounded him:

I feel good because it's my first language, but I don't know—well, where I'm living now, they just use nothing but Spanish. I realized that when some [Maya] friends came to visit, I don't know, it's a lot of work to speak K'iche' again . . . I stutter a lot.

Participants also connected language shift to family members' ongoing *preparación* and *adaptación* in Guatemala, through which, some hoped, further migration could be prevented. Aarón, who migrated to the United States in part because of his feelings of isolation as a K'iche' speaker in Guatemala, spoke of his attempts to socialize relatives in Guatemala into the languages he associated with social incorporation: "Now, they know Spanish maybe 60 percent, English maybe 40 percent, but we're getting there. We're getting there." It is hard to say how well Aarón's family members could actually get by in English, given his efforts to tutor them in anticipation of their possible migration. Still, he certainly thought that they were better prepared than he had been. He contrasted his family members' *preparación* (either to adapt to life in Guatemala or the US) with his own lack of *preparación* in Guatemala, which he thought accounted for his perceived inability to "adapt" to Spanish and non-Indigenous culture.

Despite Aarón's nuanced understanding of colonial language hegemony, he held K'iche' responsible, in part, for his being *atrasado* in Guatemala and at least initially upon his arrival in the US:

> Why was I suffering here for five years? Because no, I didn't adapt to the language. . . . That's why I suffered so much, [and] over there [in Guatemala] I suffered a lot because I didn't adapt to the language of the other culture, for example, Spanish, and arriving here it was the same thing: I didn't adapt, I felt discrimination, and so now, yes, since I'm learning Spanish as well. I no longer have a problem speaking Spanish with other cultures from Mexico, South America, [and] Central America.

Aarón blamed his suffering in Guatemala on a lack of linguistic *preparación* and a resulting inability to adapt. In contrast, he saw that he had gradually mitigated his suffering in the US through a different process of *preparación* that allowed him to adapt more effectively within his nested contexts of incorporation.[29] Through this experience, Aarón became a prominent advocate of language learning for his fellow Maya immigrants and his family members, as it was the form of *preparación* he most associated with adapting to address various forms of suffering. In addition to the labor-related suffering discussed previously, Aarón saw Spanish proficiency as important for overcoming feelings of social isolation and loneliness. If he had adapted more effectively and developed a similar sense of community in his hometown, Aarón mused, he might not have migrated to the United States. Hence, helping to improve the Spanish proficiency of his left-behind family might make their eventual migration unnecessary, sparing them the suffering Aarón experienced.

To summarize, *adaptación* was connected not just to developing and gauging one's proficiency in English and Spanish but also to moving away from Mayan languages, which were associated with the suffering participants had experienced in Guatemala and, to some extent, in the US. Even so, some youth, like Andrés and Tomás, expressed concern over what they saw as the attrition of their individual K'iche' competence. In community settings, participants grappled with what these individual-level changes might mean for K'iche'.

Furthermore, co-constructions of proficiency were not just used to measure individual Maya youth's competence against others' perceived competence; they also related to youths' desire to advocate for others' well-being through efforts at preparing *them* to adapt. This could apply to family members who were considering immigrating in the future as well as other Guatemalan immigrants to whom they were not directly related.

In the next section, we theorize an apparent paradox of Maya youth's percentage talk with respect to *sobrevivencia*. While participants' social co-construction of language proficiency was initially related to individual milestones (e.g., gaining access to easier and better-paying jobs, finding a girlfriend), it reflected collectivistic motivations over time. As youth perceived their English and Spanish proficiency to improve in the context of their overall *adaptación,* they began to rethink language proficiency, seeing it not exclusively as related to individual survival but as a resource for promoting other Maya immigrants' well-being.

Co-Constructing Language Proficiency for *Sobrevivencia*

Looking carefully at youth's talk about *sobrevivencia* illuminates their view of *preparación* and *adaptación,* along with the role of perceived language proficiency in these interrelated social processes. Percentage talk transformed perceived proficiency into measured proficiency, a strategy that youth linked to their ability to thrive in diaspora. On an individual level, youth's *sobrevivencia* was tied up with their role as workers and their imagined futures as active participants in social networks with diverse sociocultural ties. Constructions of proficiency emboldened youth to take social risks, such as those that enabled occupational mobility or expanded their social networks and social worlds.

As we saw above, Aarón was an outstanding example of pursuing individual *sobrevivencia* through linguistic adaptation for social integration. In his hometown in Guatemala, he felt isolated from peers because of his Maya identity and language and his self-professed inability to "adapt." Once in Los Angeles, however, Aarón assessed his Spanish and English proficiency to chart his *adaptación* within multicultural spaces and social groups in the US. Aarón believed language proficiency was necessary to adapt *"con todo el mundo"* (with the whole world). Outside of this, he said, language proficiency "has no purpose" if "one still feels lonely." Unlike in Guatemala, Aarón's linguistic abilities gave him the confidence to make friends and change his condition of loneliness to one in which he had *"un montón de amigos* ... a lot of friends from different cultures, and I feel good."

His comments affirmed that Maya youth espoused an ideology of language learning *as* an element of preparation and *for* adaptation, seeing Spanish and English as worthwhile because they allowed youth to expand their social networks beyond the Maya immigrant community. Moreover, Aarón's co-construction of proficiency underscored that language learning was not merely a matter of economics for the youth in this study. While language was key to securing better-paying and easier work, it was also crucial for combating loneliness and isolation and making friends across linguistic and cultural boundaries—a "convivial tool," per philosopher Ivan Illich, for youth in the Maya diaspora.[30]

In cases where language presented roadblocks, youth decided which linguistic resources were needed based on their perceptions of their proficiency and began seeking them out. Their experiences differed starkly from those of "accompanied" or parented immigrant youth, whose pursuit of English is frequently guided by adults and curricula in K-12 schooling. As in other ESL settings with refugee and immigrant adults, youth directed their own language learning efforts according to their keen awareness of exactly what communicative resources they needed to function competently in specific situations.[31] We have argued that this is a major way in which unaccompanied Indigenous youth's incorporation differs from their parented or accompanied counterparts: that youth must decide for themselves which types of *preparación* are most needed to facilitate the forms of *adaptación* most likely to promote *sobrevivencia*.

Widely shared dilemmas around everyday uses of English and Spanish were a hinge between individual and collective understandings of *sobrevivencia*. Individual youth needed particular phrases or forms of competence to deal with problematic speech situations in Los Angeles, but because the participants all faced similar linguistic issues, they made communal efforts to improve proficiency in everyday English and Spanish.

In the spring of 2015, a group of young people asked Stephanie to organize biweekly tutoring classes to review worksheets and exams from their English classes, either to reinforce lessons or to answer questions they felt too embarrassed to ask their instructors.[32] During the group's first meeting in March 2015, the conversation quickly turned to the translation of commonly used phrases such as, "*¿Cuál es la clave del baño?*" (What is the restroom door code?), "*¿Dónde están los probadores?*" (Where are the fitting rooms?), and "*¿Cuál es la próxima parada?*" (What is the next [bus] stop?). Similar lessons continued for the next several months. Throughout, youth continuously demonstrated their pressing concern for navigating specific everyday social interactions. Without the ability to manage such interactions, Maya youth would have to return home when they needed to use the restroom while at a restaurant or coffee shop, leave articles of clothing behind when unable to try them on, or walk back several miles after missing their bus stop to avoid awkward interactions with non-Mayan- or Spanish-language speakers, which might unmask them as Indigenous or L2 Spanish speaking. As a group, the youth had assessed their degree of proficiency and determined what phrases, exactly, group members needed to function more successfully in common social situations.

Individual gains in linguistic proficiency validated youth's ability to contribute to others' language socialization and to the *adaptación* of the community at large. Beyond developing interpersonal mentorship connections, the young people also practiced group-level mentorship. At a support group meeting in February 2013, a former piece-rate worker named Raúl and three Maya women talked about their work experiences in the garment industry, especially the stress associated with the instability of employment, their inability to find new job sites, and the insecurity of wages. The young women expressed their *timidez* in speaking with others—male and non-Maya coworkers specifically—which hindered their opportunities for social, financial, and cultural capital accumulation.

Raúl sympathized with the three women, explaining that before he left the garment industry, "I felt my energy draining, my mind was draining." However, Raúl explained that he was growing in confidence and courage in his new job in landscaping alongside his English-speaking employer and a bilingual Mexican coworker. He was learning some English words while he worked, and his timid demeanor among non-Mayan or Spanish-speaking coworkers also evolved: "When I was with three or four people, I felt afraid, but I am fine now."

As the group of four discussed their work and its effect on their wellbeing, Raúl equated his entry into landscaping with "recovery" from the violence and exploitation of the garment industry: "Gardening is healing for me. Now I know that things are possible, *tengo un año en recuperación*" (I have been in recovery for one year). Raúl modeled his adoption of Western ideologies of individualism and suggested to the group that their recovery—in his case, from mental health issues—was possible if they wanted it for themselves, just as he had wanted it for himself: "I can put effort into it, everything is possible. The road you take is your own, of course, but I have to value myself. I have to help myself." By establishing in a group setting that his linguistic *adaptación* had improved through interaction, such that his energy and mind were restored and his *timidez* had diminished, Raúl leveraged his individual story of *sobrevivencia* for the collective good. Juxtaposing his perceived proficiency in English with the women's was not a way of putting them down but of showing them that "everything was possible" despite the struggles they had shared in the garment industry.

Conclusion

This chapter has explored the social construction of language proficiency among Maya youth as one dimension of what the young people describe as *adaptación*. Maya youth participants often described perceived proficiency as a percentage of total proficiency. Percentage talk functioned to cast language ability as interaction- and context-specific. Using percentages, the young people quantified how much Mayan, Spanish, or English-language proficiency was necessary for them to participate actively and effectively in work, community, and family life in the US and Guatemala. Talk about perceived proficiency might come across as problematic to a listener without context, in the sense that it called attention to what the youth lacked rather than the assets they brought to interactions. Reflecting an internalization of colonial language ideologies, the youth typically viewed language ability through a deficit lens, characterizing their proficiency according to the *inability* to use a language for a particular purpose or in a specific way, such as the inability to speak English or the inability to speak a Mayan language without Spanish influence.

However, Maya youth's co-construction of language proficiency also testified to their agency, adaptability, and resilience in contexts without "adult supervision," as traditionally understood as parent-led households and K–12 schools. Having little formal schooling, Maya youth's proficiency percentages were based on perceptions developed within distinct interactional contexts. Mayan-speaking youth did not measure their linguistic abilities relative to an institutional standard in speaking, listening, reading, and writing but by their ability to interact with others in everyday scenarios and public spaces—grocery and clothing stores, coffee shops, and public transportation. They judged themselves to be well "adapted" if they were progressing toward trilingual proficiency and if their proficiency aligned with the futures they imagined and were actively making for themselves.

The young people assessed their linguistic *preparación* and *adaptación* relative to native English and Spanish speakers, other Indigenous Latin Americans, and their past selves. The point of doing so was not just to highlight their marginality but to understand where they were, where they wanted to be, and what they needed to get there. In comparing the language proficiency of native speakers to their perceived proficiency, the young people assessed their level of *preparación* relative to how much total *preparación* was necessary to attain various goals. Percentage talk informed youth's determinations of whether they had "enough" English or Spanish *preparación* to pursue imagined futures.[33] The precarity of Maya youth's social, economic, and political position as Indigenous migrants, low-wage workers, and unaccompanied, undocumented young people meant that these futures were both local and transnational, reinforcing the value of maintaining Mayan language and cultural practice in diaspora.[34] Furthermore, despite the individualized nature of percentage talk, Maya youth also drew on percentage talk to gauge their ability to support the linguistic *preparación* and social *adaptación* of other L1 Mayan speakers. Perceptions of language proficiency—in Spanish, English, and Mayan languages—were central to youth's understanding of their prospects for *sobrevivencia* as contributing immigrant community members.

In framing language learning as a dimension of *preparación*, the Maya youth, like the Latina/o youth in Katherine Mortimer and Gabriela Dolsa's study, treated bilingualism as "non-dichotomous . . . continuously emergent . . . and primarily about meaning making rather than an end in and of itself."[35] Maya youth's language practices blended "recursive" and "dynamic" forms of bilingualism—that is, those they had inherited from their families and communities, and novel or unprecedented forms that they discovered were necessary to survive in diaspora.[36]

In addition to meaning making, facilitating social connectedness and social integration were primary functions of bilingualism from Maya youth's point of view. An all-or-nothing view of language proficiency was not realistic for youth who had to struggle and advocate on their own behalf as soon as possible after migration. The young people recognized that even a relatively low percentage of an idealized full proficiency in Spanish or English might be sufficient to accomplish their interactional goals or to enact symbolic competence in certain situations.[37]

As unaccompanied Central American youth continue to migrate to the US without legal status and grow up without parents or adult caretakers, it is instructive to contrast the English-language learning experiences and emergent language ideologies of the youth in this study with those of Dreamers—undocumented or underdocumented youth who arrived in the United States at a young age and generally grew up attending US schools. Dreamers frequently feel assimilative pressure around English, in the sense that English is crucial to their struggle to assert themselves as legitimate "Americans" given the macro-ideology that associates "monoglot standard" English with American national identity.[38]

Unlike Dreamers, the youth in this study did not necessarily aim for advanced English proficiency. Rather, they wanted to attain the degree of proficiency they deemed necessary to function in US society in particular ways. Percentage talk about perceived proficiency allowed Maya youth to assert their agency, making it possible for them to articulate how they perceived their current level of proficiency and to determine for themselves what ways of speaking would be required for them to pursue their imagined futures.[39] Instead of feeling pressure to assimilate by achieving advanced proficiency in English, the youth generally aimed for the minimum "percentage" necessary to take certain kinds of advantageous risks. Youth's deployment of perceived linguistic proficiency for *sobrevivencia* demonstrated their alacrity in navigating the social, economic, and legal precarity they faced.

FOUR

Surviving as Future-Making

Earlier in the book, we introduced Lucy, a Maya K'iche' woman who arrived in Pico-Union as an unaccompanied teenager twelve years prior to when Stephanie met her. During Lucy's interview, she reflected on the early years following her arrival to Los Angeles as a time of disorientation. Speaking only K'iche' at the time of her arrival, Lucy struggled to interact with others, which she explained impeded her ability to obtain information that could ease her orientation. "You come [to the US], and you speak a dialect, you won't understand what people are saying, or you won't know how to ask for something," Lucy explained. "But if you know how to speak Spanish and your dialect, that's good." In saying this, she was not just speaking for herself but reflecting on what she "notice[d]" in public spaces in Los Angeles over the course of twelve years: that Mayan speakers faced challenges in communicating with Spanish and English speakers. By the time of the interview, she could cast a veteran eye on other characters in the story—more recent arrivals from Guatemala still navigating disorientation and *preparación,* US-born Latinas/os who acted *presumidos* (stuck up) toward their immigrant counterparts, and Guatemalans who attempted to flaunt their level of *adaptación* relative to others'.

One of Lucy's acquaintances, in particular, a man from a church youth group she attended, stood out in the final respect:

> I know a guy that is from Guatemala that I see at a group I go to with my friends. Sometimes he's there and he starts talking on the phone in English and I don't know if he's just making things up. Who really knows? But when he's speaking English, he speaks really loudly. He even stands up and goes outside. And he doesn't have an education, but people go along with him.

Lucy did not speak English and could not determine whether the man's flamboyant English performance would be intelligible to English speakers, but she knew he did not have much formal education. This led her to believe he was likely overselling his English-language proficiency to increase his status among their peers. Lucy saw his attitude as one of pretension or perceived superiority because of his English proficiency—no minor sin in a context where youth were constantly evaluating their own and one another's English, Spanish, and Mayan proficiency informally, with an eye to how it might benefit them materially and emotionally.

Lucy thought her acquaintance's attitude was reminiscent of the US-born youth and young adults she knew from church. "It's the same here," Lucy said, drawing a parallel between Guatemalan-born youth who exaggerated their English proficiency for personal gain and US-born Latinas, in this case, who appeared to be unconcerned with immigrant youth at the church:

> If you see the girls who are born here, they think that they are so cool. They get along with each other really well, but not with anyone else. To me, it's better to get along with others because it's not good to think you're better than others. But then there are good people who are friendly, and it's better like that. So, when people ask me, I say, "Yes, I speak dialect, I speak Spanish, and I use dialect when I need it."

Language maintenance and acquisition are critical components of Maya youth's long-term survival in the United States. While scholarship on immigrant incorporation in the US has traditionally emphasized English proficiency and use as a marker of social integration and adaptation, Lucy's comments, and those of others throughout this book, demonstrate that *sobrevivencia* required trilingual agility—at a minimum, some socialization into English and Spanish, along with the maintenance of one's Mayan language (or languages).

Lucy contrasted her verbal behavior with that of US-born and English-speaking churchgoers. When asked what *she* did—"Do you help those people?"—meaning Mayan speakers who were visibly struggling to make themselves understood, Lucy smiled, then said:

> I will be honest; I am not the kind of person that feels embarrassed to speak my dialect. Sometimes, I will ask the person who doesn't know how to speak Spanish, "Do you speak dialect?" "Yes." "Ok, I speak dialect. What is it that you want to buy?" Then they tell me what they want in dialect, so I just do them the favor.

Lucy's response clarified that she was *not* the type of person who felt embarrassed to speak K'iche', suggesting that many of her peers were, indeed, embarrassed to be heard speaking Mayan. She prefaced her response with "I will be honest," an "honesty phrase" meant to express her independent stance on an issue—in this case, speaking Mayan languages in public settings in the United States—on which some interlocutors might prefer a different assessment.[1] Lucy then elaborated on the other type of person, adding that some were so fearful of being identified as Maya that they pretended to speak Spanish or English: There "are people that speak dialect, they don't speak Spanish, but they act like they do. They act like they speak Spanish or English."

"Why do they do that?" Stephanie asked, "Because they're embarrassed?"

"I will be honest," Lucy repeated, "there are many people that pretend to be something they are not. I don't like people like that. I see that people from Guatemala do that."

Again Lucy framed her answer with an honesty phrase tuned to the sensitivity of the issue and continued with a dispreferred response[2] that was designed with a possibly disapproving audience in mind.[3] Lucy's criticism of "people like that" arose in part because youth tended to see *sobrevivencia* not merely as a matter of individual survival but as a social outcome that involved "get[ting] along with others," in Lucy's words. Youth did not mean "getting along" in the sense of facile niceness.[4] Rather, "getting along" was a community-minded orientation toward mobility and well-being in the US. In this case, it referred to some youth's willingness to continue speaking Mayan, which—along with English and Spanish—prepared individuals to advocate for other Maya in situations like the service encounter Lucy described above.

Lucy expressed this when saying, "They tell me what they want in dialect, so I just do them the favor." Her behavior contrasted with her Guatemalan peer's loud English-speaking at church: Her public bilingualism, unlike his, strengthened relationships within the Maya community and improved the well-being of more recent arrivals with relatively less linguistic capital.[5] That is, the other man's public display of bilingualism came off as self-serving, while Lucy's was community-oriented (at least in her account).

It took Lucy twelve years to gain the linguistic and social knowledge required to become a language broker for other Maya youth in Los Angeles.[6] She learned from experience how language can create social cohesion or tension. Some people, like the English-speaking Guatemalan man and US-born Latinas at church, were conferred power. In contrast, others, like Lucy and her Mayan-speaking community, were excluded from exercising symbolic power in work and community spaces. Thus, Maya young people, like Lucy, grappled with the role of language and cultural practice in their prospects for *sobrevivencia*.

Based on these accounts, we analyze Maya youth's experiences with and perspectives on how language and other symbolic and material resources can be used to set them up for socially and economically secure futures as immigrants and as teens transitioning to adulthood. We refer to this as *future-making*, an immigrant incorporation framework that takes into account young people's agency and strategic actions in ensuring their *sobrevivencia* in the time between arrival and becoming incorporated through processes of *preparación* and *adaptación*, leveraging individual skills, lessons, and resources acquired to make new collective futures.

To be sure, migration scholars have proposed "future-making activities," like having pride in one's neighborhood and giving back to one's community, alongside "creating a sense of security, familiarity, and autonomy," as a "practice whereby people try to make themselves at home in a certain social context."[7] But we theorize future-making more expansively here. Beyond everyday activities attached to any given place or the future of the place, future-making refers here to the ideological orientation that guides Maya youth's embodied and discursive presentation of self in day-to-day interactions and strategic efforts to increase their social, cultural, material, and emotional capital to attain an imagined future of mobility, well-being, and inclusion within and across societies.

Conceptualizing Maya Youth's Future-Making

Attention to Indigenous youth's future-making critically intervenes in two common assumptions about immigrant youth incorporation and coming of age. First, researchers and policymakers often take for granted that children have access to caregiving adults, especially within parent-led households and in K–12 schools, who are invested in identifying children's aspirations and invested in ensuring children achieve their goals.[8] This produces an empirical trap in which we remain focused on how children are socialized to future aspirations by adults and through adult-led institutions.[9] As we show, the unaccompanied Maya youth workers at the center of this research who grew up outside of parent-led households and K–12 schools are not precluded from imagining their futures, setting goals, and working toward them. Instead, they engage in future-making in ways that reflect their unique social position and distinct social contexts and relationships.

Second, immigrant incorporation research suggests that everyday encounters with racism can produce hopelessness and resignation and diminish aspirations for the future as individuals feel excluded from opportunities to achieve mobility and belonging, especially among adolescents.[10] This research posits that parents, extended family, and coethnic community spaces reinforce the value of ethnic and cultural identity, and act as buffers to the adverse effects of racialized and xenophobic exclusion. In the case of unaccompanied Indigenous youth workers, opportunities for mobility, well-being, and inclusion in everyday life are constrained by hybrid hegemonies (Chapters 1 and 2). Young people experience everyday discrimination and marginalization.[11] Yet, as we have shown, Indigenous youth's starting points are not necessarily where they remain in the longer term; young people, individually and in community, establish new metrics of *sobrevivencia* and pool resources, like language and other cultural practices, to counteract structural and symbolic exclusion for themselves and coethnics in the present and future.

Maya youth's future-making is an ongoing process during the transition to adulthood. It does not presuppose specific desired outcomes for newcomers but makes space for complex local dynamics of integration, such as those we have sketched in our theorization of Maya youth's movement through phases of (dis)orientation, *preparación,* and *adaptación* to promote their *sobrevivencia* in diaspora. It also pushes researchers to account for elements of incorporation that traverse scales of time and space—for example, how individual decision-making may respond to immediate circumstances of economic well-being or survival while also reaching across national boundaries to address the well-being of one's family members in the origin society.

In the rest of this chapter, we describe how some youth came to terms with the trauma of dislocation, displacement, and disorientation to pursue future-making in diaspora, or to secure social and economic futures in Los Angeles in a distinctive, bottom-up way.[12] Concealing Maya identity through embodied and discursive strategies allowed youth to cope with the social problems posed by being identifiably Maya in Los Angeles and to navigate the constraints on social, material, and emotional opportunities for mobility, well-being, and inclusion. Then, as time passed, youth found other strategies for dealing with the problem of marginalization within the immigrant community at best and invisibility and erasure from it at worst. Youth's awareness of how profoundly discrimination and abandonment had affected them before *preparación* and *adaptación* also "prepared" them, in a sense, to move toward a state of relative well-being and belonging. Crucially for our argument, coming to question the language ideologies that marginalized Mayan speakers in Guatemala and the United States was central to this process, as was challenging US individualism by imagining collective futures.

Notably, experiencing dislocation, displacement, and disorientation is no guarantee that an immigrant will be successfully incorporated into their social context; without *preparación* and isolated from meaningful social ties, it can deter or deny prospects of incorporation over the longer term.[13] Building on work on immigrant precarity and deportability,[14] research with female Mexican guest workers in the US seafood industry finds, for example, that women workers become "trapped in a form of 'permanent liminality,'" in part because "there is very little socialization or interaction" among the participants.[15] Their work schedules, living conditions, and the "permanently temporary" nature of their labor made it impossible to establish lasting social connections or to develop a sense of community.[16]

As we make the opposite point in this chapter—namely, that youth need not be permanently "homeless," notwithstanding their initial experiences of marginalization and disorientation in the US—two points are worth mentioning in light of prior research conclusions.[17] First, navigating migration and resettlement successfully did not merely depend on how long the youth had been in Los Angeles, though it was related to the time of residence in the United States for some youths. While most participants dealt with ups and downs during incorporation and did not necessarily experience it as a linear process, it was also the case that some long-settled youth felt "stuck" in disorientation and found themselves unable to make the transition to *adaptación* through *preparación*. Additionally, whether youth remained disoriented or moved toward *adaptación* hinged on their opportunities to interact with other Maya and non-Maya people in Los Angeles, particularly in settings where they could explore shared experiences of discrimination, unfair labor practices, and ethnic and linguistic pride.

Thus, this chapter emphasizes that engaging productively in future-making entailed first coping with racial and linguistic discrimination and then undergoing transformations to be able to articulate new ideologies around Mayan language and culture in diaspora—not just as Indigenous migrants, but as teenagers and young adults developing their sense of self and imagining futures. Disorientation implied surviving continued exposure to harmful beliefs and discriminatory practices; the type of *adaptación* that would lead to *sobrevivencia* in youth's future-making efforts involved speaking back to those practices.

In making this point, our analysis begins by revisiting existing understandings of how race is (un)made in discursive practice; we analyze participants' language behavior and embodied practice during the phase of disorientation and initial *preparación* when Maya youth saw themselves as relatively isolated and employed a range of strategies to mitigate discrimination and avoid being identified as Indigenous. Participants specifically mentioned the fears of getting beaten up, being made fun of, or not being served at commercial establishments as tangible examples of discrimination they wished to avoid. We then move to the point of *adaptación*, where some youth (again, like Lucy) arrived when they had gained enough knowledge, experience, and linguistic capital through *preparación* to adapt successfully to Los Angeles, turning it into their own place. In other words, *adaptación* meant that youth could move toward *sobrevivencia*, "a material and symbolic condition they [had] struggle[d] to reach" since their initial displacement.[18] As youth participants made sense of their prospects for *sobrevivencia* in relation to their Maya peers and other non-Indigenous immigrant groups in and around Pico-Union, they considered leveraging language and other symbolic and material resources to secure their own social and economic futures and, over time, supporting coethnics in doing the same.

(Un)making Race in Embodiment and Discursive Practice

Upon arrival in Los Angeles, Maya youth dealt with disorientation due to the enduring power of anti-Indigenous racism in the US and its intersections with their social positions as undocumented immigrants and unaccompanied teens. Youth responded actively through *preparación*, employing a range of strategies to protect themselves individually. Later, some found themselves capable of advocating for others in ways that strengthened the Maya community overall. For Maya youth, *race-bending*, both embodied and discursive, was necessary for surviving the intense disorientation of early arrival, when they felt particularly vulnerable to discrimination and mistreatment from perceiving subjects who might react negatively to their language or appearance.[19] The idea of race-bending refers to youth's "everyday strategic use of race labels" to variously contest and accept "commonsense" racial categories; we use the phrase more broadly to capture Maya youth's creative strategies for hiding and revealing race in diasporic interactions.[20] As time went on and youth began to evaluate different possibilities for identifying as Maya in diaspora, race-bending became less important as they found ways to respond to the racializing ideologies that had framed their bodies and ways of speaking as inferior.

Immigrants' bodies are central to the racialization of illegality, as bodies are used as markers of race and ethnicity and proxies for legal status.[21] Latinas/os are more likely to be racialized as illegal when they share "physical characteristics typically attributed to indigeneity, including darker skin tone, hair color, eye color, short stature, and social characteristics such as limited English language skills, heavy accent, lower socioeconomic position and education level, and low-wage occupations."[22] Hence, Latin American immigrants strategically position themselves in relation to Indigenous and non-Indigenous others through language use and by "employ[ing] the body as a resource"[23] to deal with racialized illegality. These strategies play out against a historical backdrop of shifting beliefs about who does and does not belong in the United States.[24]

Scholars have consistently found that Indigenous individuals and communities may respond to hybrid hegemonies in the United States—that is, the anti-Indigenous ideologies that travel with them from Latin America, along with anti-immigrant and nativist sentiment in the US—in two ways. In some cases, Indigenous communities may employ a "dampening" of their Indigenous identity through distancing from language, way of dress, and other cultural practices. Immigrants in some contexts go to great lengths not to "look Mexican" because of locally circulating discourses that associate Mexican (Indigenous) immigrants with illegality.[25] For Maya youth workers in Los Angeles, however, race-bending through attempting to look or sound Mexican—or, barring that, to look and sound like non-Indigenous Guatemalans—was a strategy for distancing themselves from features of Maya/Indigenous identity that could prompt discrimination and symbolic and material violence.

Given Mexicans' status as the most populous Latin American immigrant group in the US, "Mexicanization" has long been recognized as a survival strategy for Guatemalans who may "hide in plain view" within the larger Mexican immigrant population.[26] Discursively, these strategies may include "speaking in silence," or the avoidance of linguistic features or ways of speaking that might reveal one's country of origin.[27] In other cases, by contrast, Indigenous individuals and communities choose to "brighten" ethnoracial boundaries—rather than dampening their identities—through greater association with their Indigenous identity,[28] engagement in ethnic associations,[29] media, and reliance on cultural symbols.[30]

A robust body of work has examined discourse strategies for doing and undoing "race" among diverse youth in the US, calling attention to hegemonic discourses that racialize youth along with youth's ingenious ability to "bend" race through discursive practice.[31] Youth can "cloak" or conceal forms of linguistic competence to avoid indexing ethnoracial or other social identities associated with ways of speaking.[32] Other scholars have examined the relationship between racializing discourse and racialized bodies, arguing for the centrality of embodied practice to people's "everyday racial strategizing."[33] In this chapter, we examine how Maya youth who embodied *timidez y miedo* in discursive practice moved from cloaking Indigeneity as an adaptive strategy to imagining and experiencing communal *sobrevivencia*, and the role of multicultural language communities in prompting this passage.

As established earlier, Maya youth overwhelmingly spoke of their initial settlement experiences in terms of shyness and fear, or *timidez y miedo*. Having endured discrimination and mistreatment by non-Indigenous Guatemalans in the origin country, and with warnings of potential violence at the hands of non-Maya groups, including Latina/o immigrants and US-born people, Maya youth engaged in strategies that separated them from their Indigeneity. The utility of these strategies was reinforced when youth's fears of continued discrimination and mistreatment were confirmed through workplace and community interactions.[34] Thus, youth's relationship to and expressions of their Indigenous culture and identity were not static but changed over time, in many cases, as invocations of future-making wherein youth put their *preparación* to work in cultivating successful *adaptación* to secure *sobrevivencia*. In what follows, we first consider survival strategies predicated on youth's distancing themselves from Indigeneity and then turn to integrative strategies that youth employed later in resettlement.

Silencing Indigenous Identity as an Adaptive Strategy

Recently arrived youth in Los Angeles, who are typically disoriented, employed several strategies to mitigate their ever-present fear of discrimination and mistreatment. These strategies involved concealing Indigenous/Maya identity through forms of bodily concealment or discourse practices. Some participants spoke directly about the processes of subordination in Guatemala and the United States that pushed them to disassociate themselves from Indigenous/Maya heritage. When asked if he felt ashamed to be Maya or to speak K'iche', Felipe replied:

> I think so, that I am ashamed. I don't like it. Because I'm not like the people who speak Spanish and [laughs]. [Stephanie: And how do you identify yourself? As a Guatemalan, as a Latino, as Maya?] Guatemalan. Yes [laughs].

Felipe's choice to identify himself as Guatemalan, rather than Maya or K'iche', may have reflected his lack of access to a social setting where his Indigenous identity could be validated since he did not participate in the Voces group, unlike many other participants, or another group like it.

Still, his account recalls Lucy's condemnation of Maya people "pretend[ing] to be something they are not" and, therefore, separating themselves from those who might benefit from their linguistic expertise. This may account for his use of "coping laughter," often associated with a speaker's effort to mitigate a threat to their "face," or social standing, in others' eyes.[35] In this excerpt, coping laughter appears to have functioned as a way for Felipe to manage possible disagreement, or anticipate and deal with possible disapproval, with the interviewer, who—like Lucy—Felipe might have expected to look askance at his concealment of Maya/K'iche' identity. In saying "I don't like [being identifiable as Maya/K'iche']" because it distinguished him from "people who speak

Spanish"—as a first language, or in a "standard" way—Felipe articulated, however uncomfortably, the way that some youth felt their verbal behavior left them exposed to mistreatment from those whose mother tongues were English or Spanish.

Felipe's comments also exemplified one prominent discourse strategy among Maya youth: refusing to identify as Indigenous, and, relatedly, avoiding speaking K'iche' and other Mayan languages in public settings. Carlos, a garment worker in the study, reflected: "Yes, I was a little ashamed to speak K'iche' when I arrived, so I said, 'Well, no, then I have to learn Spanish.' I tried the method of understanding and learning in that way, and that's how I learned." With *"pues saber y por eso aprender"* (understanding and learning in that way), Carlos appeared to be referring to a period of relative silence, during which he developed receptive Spanish competence while avoiding exposure as a K'iche' speaker, before beginning to speak Spanish publicly.

In another conversation with Gonzalo, he also remarked on the dilemma of speaking K'iche' (and audibly self-identifying as Maya), on one hand, versus isolating oneself by avoiding one's native language, on the other:

> Well, I think that arriving in Los Angeles, it's like I said, we arrive with that *temor* [fear], we don't know whether to speak our language, which is K'iche'. . . . We think that we're less because we're afraid, we're ashamed of speaking K'iche'. . . . I'm telling you from experience.

In this way, youth's adaptive strategies in confronting *timidez y miedo* functioned to reproduce Indigenous erasure—in this case, from Latina/o immigrant community life in Los Angeles. While presumably voluntary in that youth made deliberate decisions to silence their language, cloak their Indigenous cultural practices, and/or conceal their bodies, the threat of physical, structural, and symbolic violence—rooted in colonial and imperial persecution and disappearance—compelled these decisions. Influenced by past experiences, as Gonzalo alluded to, Maya youth were sometimes brought to collude in their own erasure from Pico-Union and Los Angeles public life.

Gonzalo addressed the long-term social implications of this linguistic isolation for him and the wider Maya community on the survivance of Mayan languages: "I feel good [speaking K'iche'] because it is my first language," he said, but also shared that speaking K'iche' had become more difficult after living with fellow immigrants who spoke only Spanish, such that, when K'iche'-speaking friends visited, *"me cuesta hablar otra vez"* (it takes a lot of work to speak [K'iche'] again) and he stumbled over his words. Like Gonzalo, Felipe expressed the linguistic ambivalence that many Mayan speakers shared. Though he said that Spanish-English bilinguals admired his trilingual ability and told him, "You're the best!" he still hesitated even to acknowledge his K'iche' identity. He confessed, "Sometimes I regret the *dialecto* that I have [i.e., K'iche'] . . . [because] I'm worried that someone will hear me and feel like I don't speak Spanish well."

A related discourse strategy was attempting to "pass" as Mexican or as non-Indigenous Guatemalan. Joel said, "Yeah, it happens here in Los Angeles that a lot of people say . . . 'Where are you from?' 'I'm Mexican' [even though] you can barely speak Spanish." He made clear that he did not see this as a viable strategy for mitigating discrimination because of the obvious differences between Mayan-speakers' Spanish and that of (presumably) non-Indigenous Mexicans:

> You can't say that you're Mexican or Chilango (from Mexico City) or from whatever part of Mexico, and you can barely speak Spanish, and you say you're not Guatemalan. You can see it a thousand kilometers away. If you see us from far away, we resemble Mexicans, but when you talk to us, you realize how we speak.

Joel denied ever having tried to pass as Mexican but admitted to pursuing a related strategy: acknowledging his Guatemalan origins while denying his Indigeneity ("What I did do is that if they would ask me if I spoke K'iche', 'No, I don't speak K'iche'"). These discursive strategies worked, at times, in tandem with bodily techniques for cloaking Maya/Indigenous identity.

Omar's experiences dramatically demonstrated how unaccompanied Maya youth had to confront the implications of "looking Indigenous" in addition to sounding Indigenous.[36] Omar had an especially difficult experience of adapting to life in Los Angeles. Arriving at fourteen years old, Omar recalls the persistent feeling of being unsafe in his community. He described the neighborhood as *"peligroso"* (dangerous):

> There are a lot of gang members where I live. But I am living there because it's a bit more affordable. It's cheaper there than if you go to ... if you go to other places where it's not as dangerous. It's cheaper because there aren't many people that want to live there; they don't want to rent there because of that, because of the gangs.

These negotiations between what was desirable—survivable even—and what was affordable were common. But Omar was particularly aware of the dangers posed as his body and phenotype made him a frequent target of discrimination and violence: He was under five feet tall in stature, with long black hair that fell over his eyes, dark skin, and dark eyes. Even more problematic, a birthmark under his left eye drew people's attention, who thought it was a gang-affiliated tattoo. Public transportation was particularly dangerous for Omar. After twice being beaten up and robbed at bus stops near MacArthur Park by *pandilleros* (gang members) and people he called *morenitos* (dark-skinned people), who mistook him for a gang member, Omar feared for his safety each time he used public transportation.

If the body can be a resource for navigating illegality, as for the Indigenous and non-Indigenous immigrants in sociologist Andrea Gómez Cervantes's work in rural Kansas, it can also communicate information that people would prefer not to reveal (e.g., Maya/K'iche' identity vis-à-vis Indigenous phenotype) and meanings that people do not intend to convey (e.g., criminal identity vis-à-vis a birthmark along with Indigenous phenotype).[37]

In response to these factors, many of the participants referred to embodied practices for cloaking Maya/ Indigenous identity and mitigating the semiotics of the body that increased the risk of discrimination and mistreatment. This could mean hiding one's entire body, as with Delia, who tried not to leave her house because she was afraid that people were going to ridicule her, or with other participants who avoided specific settings like public transportation where they would be more visible. Others sought to conceal particular features of their bodies that, they believed, indexed Indigeneity. Raúl, for example, said that he would not leave his house until after sundown so that his dark skin would not be as noticeable. Aarón, among others, mentioned that some youth avoided even opening their mouths in public—not just because they would be identifiable as K'iche' speakers, but because they did not want to show their teeth, as having more rounded teeth was a supposed feature of Maya/Indigenous people.

As they grew older, some study participants invested their hard-earned wages into altering their appearance to minimize the risk of detection and, therefore, *peligro*. Andrés, for example, eventually saw an orthodontist about straightening his teeth. At twenty-eight years old, Andrés wore braces during Stephanie's last year in the field. For Marianna, a Maya domestic worker who looked after two small children on LA's west side, measures were riskier. During a late 2015 Voces meeting, Marianna brought an assortment of creams in white tubes to show Stephanie. Calling Stephanie over to a hushed conversation with another Maya woman, Marianna retrieved the three tubes from her purse, asking Stephanie to read the product description, ingredients, and instructions listed in English. Stephanie read the names of skin-lightening chemicals like glycolic acid, retinol, and hydroquinone on the bottles, each claiming to treat melasma and dark spots for a brighter complexion. When Stephanie asked Marianna what she wanted to use these products for, Marianna explained that she did not like the skin tone on her forehead, cheeks, and around her nose. She noticed her complexion getting darker from days of playing outside with the children she looked after. She worried she would get "*muy morena*" (too dark). Marianna seemed shy to admit this but continued to ask Stephanie if she thought the products would work to lighten her skin.

Stephanie clarified that she was unfamiliar with these products but that a quick Google search confirmed that these chemicals were meant to achieve a skin-lightening effect. Stephanie expressed her worry that using multiple skin-lightening treatments simultaneously without a clear understanding of how they were meant to work together could result in burning or a rash that would make the very issue Marianna was attempting to address worse. Marianna agreed, saying the few tubes she managed to purchase were expensive, perhaps making the treatment unsustainable; she understood the risk, too.

Importantly, Maya youth's relationships to their body and their physical appearance, and the perception of them by others they interacted with, mattered not only as a fact of being immigrants trying to adapt to life in Los Angeles but as teenagers trying to fit into peer groups in their neighborhoods, community organizations, and in interpersonal relationships. Teens and young adults in this research, like teens and young adults across all societies, care about belonging and being attractive to those to whom they are attracted. The Maya young people in this research were curious about romantic relationships, too. They knew their bodies and language proficiency mattered in attaining their imagined social and romantic futures.

In this way, Maya young people are hyperaware of their bodies and the implications of embodying certain characteristics in multiple senses, as immigrants and as adolescents. They are navigating the transformation of their bodies with little guidance. Alonso described his emotional, physical, and psychological changes as he was transitioning from teenager to young adult.

> The truth is that, yeah, I think that when I was seventeen, eighteen, nineteen, it was almost like the depression—well, I didn't know what to call it then—but it was like depression attacked me. I felt some kind of melancholy, like . . . well, you know what I did? I started to read books. I went to the library in Echo Park. From there, I started to go to church. I went to school for a little bit. I saw how life started to get a little bit better because some stuff sticks. Stuff sticks. But, you know, sometimes you want to have a trusted person who can talk to you because you feel alone. You feel empty. That's how I felt.

Alonso felt his moods drastically changing, what many young people referred to as "overwhelming emotions," and briefly describes his process of *preparación*—reading books from the Echo Park Library, going to church, and going to school—as a way to make sense of what he was experiencing. He figured talking to someone he could trust would likely offer support, too, though he did not say whether he eventually accessed such support.

Twenty-seven years old at the time of his conversation with Stephanie, Alonso went on to describe how he could look back and see these transformations as linked to his life stage:

> It was almost like when my adolescence was over, I would say, I was in one psychological state, and then, you know, it's natural because the chemicals are developing, right? I didn't know. I didn't know what was happening to me, you know? But, like, there is a biological explanation. There is a psychological explanation. But in that moment, you don't know what's happening to you. I didn't understand, like, why I was suddenly so sad.
>
> It turns out that I was developing, and all the chemicals, all those hormones, are going all out. That's why, well, that's what happens. I was struggling with that. And often, *jóvenes* will find refuge in alcohol or drugs to feel less alone. A lot of people get involved in those things because of the loneliness. But these are, these are stages of life. We have to live through them.

Alonso described the physical, emotional, psychological, and hormonal transformation processes that any adolescent transitioning to adulthood would undergo.[38] He alluded to the disorientation he felt, unable to name what he was enduring. This hyperawareness of the changing body in the transition from adolescence to young adulthood co-occurs with the hyperawareness of how one is situated within hybrid hegemonies and the violence they produce.

The outcome for many youth was a period of severe psychological distress. However, immigrant incorporation is a dynamic process of future-making, not a static material outcome, and the trauma that characterized the immediate post-migration phase for unaccompanied Maya youth did not last (in the same form, anyway) for the entirety of the young people's residence in the US. This phase coincided with various forms of *preparación* and *adaptación*, social practices through which youth prepared themselves for social, economic, and emotional adjustment to

US life. This meant stability, at least, and mobility, at best. Because of this, some youth were ultimately able to take on new roles and responsibilities within the immigrant community. Even Omar, who endured four desperate years, acknowledged that he arrived at a new outlook with the support of fellow Maya youth and other community members within the Voces setting: "I was really screwed for four years. I'm recovering. I feel happier, with inner peace. I'm discovering myself more." Maya youth awaken and discover themselves in distinct relational contexts.

Future-Making Through Ethnic and Linguistic *Sobrevivencia* in Diaspora

Youth's future-making emerged with reference to other immigrant groups they perceived as having achieved social and economic stability in Los Angeles. After the initial shock of migration (which could last for several years, as in Omar's case), many Maya youth found that *sobrevivencia* in Los Angeles afforded opportunities to question assumptions about Indigenous people and languages that were taken for granted in Guatemala, holding forth the possibility of a diasporic future that was more amenable to Maya linguistic and cultural survivance. Importantly, *sobrevivencia* in Los Angeles was not just a matter of reproducing a pre-existing Maya identity in a new setting; rather, "in [this] process of self-discovery and self-definition," "place becomes an identity" that characterizes youth's perceptions of whether, to what extent, and how Maya ethnic identity and language can survive in diaspora.[39] In engaging with frames of reference offered by different immigrant groups, as well as longer-settled Maya, youth also engaged critically with questions of how being Maya could look different in Los Angeles, freed—to some degree, anyway— from the persistent stigma of Indigeneity in Guatemala.

Two domains of youth's social activity were central to questioning and reframing ideologies of racial and linguistic inferiority. First, conversations with other Maya youth and supportive Latinas/os who were involved in Maya spaces allowed youth to explore topics around self-esteem, mental health, and Indigenous identity that were not frequently discussed at work or church. Second, youth developed emergent frames of reference through cross-cultural contact with individuals and groups they would have been unlikely to encounter in Guatemala, namely Korean immigrants and Korean Americans in the workplace. These interactions prompted Maya youth to question and reconfigure negative language ideologies about Mayan languages and Indigenous people. Participants benefited from having the chance to hear directly from others, Indigenous and non-Indigenous, who had dealt with similar issues and to make their voices heard as they articulated their imagined futures.

Sobrevivencia and Future-Making Alongside Other Maya Youth

The process of self-discovery or *descubrimiento* that Omar referred to above ("I'm discovering myself more") came, in part, from messages that youth received in the support group about self-appreciation, the value of multiculturalism, and the importance of valuing one's story.[40] During interviews, youth often talked about how no one had asked to hear their stories or asked them how they felt about living in the US and what their daily lives were like. As we suggested in Chapter 2, this was primarily because of cultural beliefs (in Guatemala) about the value of elders' wisdom and stories, as opposed to young people's. By contrast, in the Voces group setting, youth were encouraged to tell their stories, to value themselves, and to acknowledge even the small strides they had made toward *adaptación* in securing work, learning to spend or save money, making friends, managing their emotions, enrolling in English classes, and learning new languages.

How Voces functioned as a source of support for the Maya youth participants was perhaps most evident on the nights when the group welcomed visitors or newcomers. On these occasions, the core youth participants of Voces de Esperanza took turns during the introduction period of the meeting to describe the impact of the group on their lives. This was the case on July 25, 2015, when, one after another, participants described the interventions of Voces de Esperanza and the meaningful relationships youth developed with the group, its coordinators, and one another that altered the course of their lives in Los Angeles. For example, Geoffrey shared:

> Friends, hello; it's a blessing to be here with you again today. I am from Guatemala. My first language is K'iche', and my second language

is Spanish. I am learning a little bit of English. I have been a part of this group since it started. I have known Wilfredo for more than five years. I knew him before this group because I went to church with him. At that time, I didn't have any goals. I didn't know what I was doing. No. My self-esteem was to the ground. When I got here, I didn't want to speak. I closed myself off. I didn't know what to do with myself. But thanks to this group; thanks to the support of this group and of Wilfredo, Jorge, and Aarón, people who oriented me, I now have a goal. I have dreams [for a future], and I have this group that is a great source of support for me. That's all I can share. Thank you.

Though in the moment of open-ended sharing, Geoffrey did not specify what his newfound goal was, he was confident in his expression that he felt differently about himself and his future because of the supportive community he found among his peers.

Following Geoffrey's introduction, Eladio began to share:

Hi, everyone, good evening. I am Eladio. I am from Guatemala, too. I live close by. I have been coming to this group for a year. I knew about the group before that, but I was attending another group for people from my town before coming here. I had a lot of emotional problems then. I dealt with a lot of guilt. I was in a really emotional place. I met someone who told me about this group. I have been coming here for a year, little by little; I am learning to talk more. My heart is . . . my heart feels better. I have my *compañeros* [peers] to thank for that. Before coming here, I was in my own world, alone. I live alone in my apartment, in my world. But now, thanks to this group, I have somewhere to go on Friday nights, then we go out on Saturday and Sunday. We are always talking and sharing with one another. I see how you are; I see what you do. I learn from you. Thanks to this group, I feel like I am growing. That's all. Thank you.

Evident throughout the young people's expressions of individual and collective growth was the value of spending time with and talking with their coethnic peers, people they saw as similarly situated as unaccompanied and undocumented immigrant teen workers. With each introduction, young people drew parallels with one another, stating that they were "from Guatemala, too," often specifying what languages they spoke and their emotional struggles in isolation before finding one another and creating community.

Next in line to share was Brayant. He brought together several of the themes Geoffrey and Eladio had confided with the group. As others did, Brayant opened with a greeting, before proceeding with his reflection:

> Good evening, everyone. I hear each person saying that, well, it's important to be a part of a group because it helps us a lot. It helps to distract us from our problems or whatever we are going through in our lives. I hear you saying that you have problems with *timidez*. Well, that's my problem, too. I wanted to get out of that [head]space that was like internal fear. I was even scared of greeting people. I would tremble. I tried to find medicine for it, or some herbal thing that I could drink. I thought that would fix it, but what I found is that talking was the key. I think I'm starting to overcome the fear of talking in public. I think we can all overcome it. When Eladio gave his testimony, I was thinking . . . I think Voces gives us the opportunity to leave that negative energy here. We can lift each other up as a group, right? We have to keep going. Thank you.

Whether they had been part of the group from its inception or joined later, participants agreed that there was collective power in sharing their individual stories with one another. As Brayant made clear in his introduction, hearing that others struggled with similar issues, like the fear of speaking with others in public, opened a space for him to admit that he had adverse physical reactions to the fear of being negatively perceived by others and that he sought out remedies for his fear.

Being in community, with honesty and an open mind, being with other Maya youth helped young people to reconcile the messages they had heard about their individual and community value before and after migration. This was perhaps most explicitly expressed by Alejandro, who was among the last to share on that night in July. He stated clearly and confidently:

Good evening, everyone. My name is Alejandro. I've been in Los Angeles for four years. I met Wilfredo two years ago. Little by little, he encouraged me to come here to see what you were doing together, and I like it a lot. It's why I keep coming here. I feel like when we share, when we share about our weeks with the group, we are sharing about our lives. Well, one of the things I am dealing with this week is how to manage the lies. Since we are little, people tell us that we are nothing, *"eres un idiota o un estúpido"* [you are an idiot or you are stupid], and then you start to believe it. You become like a radio that functions well, but the messages you are playing are those negative messages. A lot of the time, I believe those negative messages. That's been my biggest problem.

That, and that I struggle with low self-esteem. I left the radio on for too long and believed all the messages it was playing. But you share these things and start to see that they aren't true. You hear other people sharing these same things because they have also gone through similar situations, but they've already overcome them, so you tell yourself, "I want to do that, too. *Yo también quiero superar*" [I also want to overcome]. That's when I realize that it's a lie.

So, when you come to Voces, you start to open yourself up and heal many of the things that you wouldn't be able to do alone. You can't do it [alone]. And sure, God can help you but even then, you are doing it alone. You are asking God for help on a small part of the problem. You leave a little bit of the problem there [at church]. [They say], "Ask God for help," but I'm on my own. Later, when the radio is playing in my mind when the radio is there saying things, I don't know whether it's God, it's a demon [meaning Satan], or if it's just me. I can start to lie to myself. But when I come here when I share with you, *es cuando voy descubriendo que es verdad* [it's when I start to discover what the truth is].

So, yeah, that's what others have already said today: that it's good to get it out, to share it, and that when we share, we grow. I have seen some people make a lot of progress and that helps me, that helps me to keep wanting to progress as a person too.

For many, like Alejandro, *desahogando* (unburdening) and truth-telling in the company of other Maya were necessary correctives to the inner "radio" that incessantly broadcasted messages of inferiority and negativity. It is important to remember that Voces de Esperanza was primarily comprised of young men and that it is often seen as taboo for men to detail their emotions, especially when associated with vulnerability, fear, and loneliness.[41] In this sense, the Maya youth participants of the Voces de Esperanza group were not just future-making as it related to their ethnoracial identities but their gender identities, too.

At a Voces meeting the following year, in 2016, participants candidly discussed their efforts in their everyday lives to ensure that they did not stay stuck in periods of disorientation or in feelings of *timidez y miedo* or that they would remain silent. Iván testified about his own experience of leaving silence behind and embracing education as a means to integrate himself more fully with the community. He emphasized that he was sharing this story for the benefit of others who, like him, only thought about "working and working" and neglected their education and personal development, and exhorted the attendees to seek the *preparación* they needed to escape their own silence:

> I finally realized that studying is more important [than work] in 2010. I couldn't [really] speak Spanish. [I spoke] very little. I was ashamed to speak. I still had to think about what I was going to say. Until I realized, I had a moment of desperation, why didn't I go to school? . . . And that's what I can tell you in terms of what you can do, to let you know that it's not just working, but studying too. So that you can communicate with whoever, for example, our fellow *paisanos* who can't communicate well in Spanish. Sometimes one wants to speak but doesn't know how to explain things. [It's] better to stay quiet. That's how it was with me before. I would want to speak with somebody, and they would say, "Why are you so quiet, so serious?" I wanted to talk, I wanted to express myself, but I couldn't do it well. But only until I said "not anymore."

As often at Voces meetings, the message was one of empowerment, specifically of how individual empowerment—telling yourself that you wouldn't stay silent anymore—could also contribute to breaking the community's relative silence by allowing trilingual youth to speak on behalf of their *paisanos* (fellow Maya).

More experienced, longer settled youth also sometimes spoke explicitly about the need to counter *timidez* with expressions of ethnic and linguistic pride. As opposed to seeing *sobrevivencia* in exclusively individualistic terms, youth like Lucy embraced new roles as advocates for other Maya. Aarón regularly spoke with Voces participants about the need to recognize the roots of *timidez* and to embrace their Maya/K'iche' identities:

> Aarón addressed this *timidez* when he talked about not being afraid to be identified as *Indio* or Maya, and that he no longer feels ashamed of being K'iche' in the US context because he sees the sense of pride that others feel. When Aarón spoke to the group in this way, which he did at nearly every meeting, the other youth nodded their heads, signaling perhaps their comprehension and/or agreement.
> —Fieldnotes, November 2012

Aarón believed strongly that "awakening" to the value of Maya culture could help to heal the trauma of displacement and disorientation and promote social mobility for other Maya youth. This is not to imply that Aarón or other youth were previously "asleep"; rather, the difficult work of individual adaptation had ultimately given Aarón the space to consider *sobrevivencia* in broad, community-oriented terms. His remarks about "see[ing] the sense of pride that others feel" in the excerpt above were especially telling, as they suggested that being Maya was no longer a reason to compare himself negatively to non-Indigenous others. They also showed Aarón's understanding of the pride that members of non-Maya communities took in their distinctive ethnic and linguistic identities, such as Salvadoran and Korean immigrants and their descendants, an approach to highlighting ethnoracial boundaries that Maya youth began to explore for themselves, which we return to at the end of this chapter.

These moments shared by Voces participants reveal that, as young people discussed their individual awakenings within collective spaces, they grew in admiration of one another and came to value the resilience and ingenuity of their peers. By extension, they came to value the histories, characteristics, and everyday experiences that they shared. The group became centrally organized around the youth's shared Maya identity. It included such rituals as beginning each meeting by decorating a display table with an intricately woven textile—purple with a yellow, green, red, orange, and blue embroidered pattern—as a table runner. A Maya calendar was also prominently displayed. Wilfredo encouraged the youth to bring objects that reminded them of home and their families. One young man brought a framed image of lush green hillsides, the Western highlands he'd left behind. As the group grew in trust and comfort among one another, the women in attendance began to wear their *huipiles* (white cotton fabric tunics with embroidered floral patterns) to the group meetings. On one occasion, Marianna wore a complete *traje*, including a blouse, skirt, and belt. She spoke about wanting to wear her *corte* (skirt) to church that Sunday.

The men in the group were not to be outshone or left out. A few weeks after Marianna's display of pride, they organized to wear their traditional Maya shirts and belts to the group meeting. That night, they gathered around the decorated table for photos, posting them to Facebook to share with local and transnational community members. After all, even as participants were unaccompanied and undocumented Indigenous youth workers, they were also teenagers and young adults wanting to feel good about themselves and to display positive and proud identities. As they engaged in processes of *preparación* and *adaptación* among their Maya peers, which allowed youth to move closer to *sobrevivencia* over time, they could imagine futures where they were no longer isolated or ashamed and were no longer timid or silent.

Valuing Indigenous Culture Within a Broader Latin American Immigrant Diaspora

In January 2014, Stephanie met with Wilfredo, Jorge, and Aarón at a McDonald's. Aarón was talking to Wilfredo about how, in Aarón's view, the process of *adaptación* must include working with other groups: "We have to work with other cultures." Wilfredo agreed: If youth do not encounter cultural diversity, he asked, how could they come to see themselves as part of the expansive social fabric of Los Angeles? Aarón agreed, saying,

"The truth is that we've been abandoned. But the fact that others are interested in us, that gives us energy." Aarón's comments implied that, while youth continued to employ multiple comparative frames of reference, recently arrived youth tended to relate to those frames of reference from a deficit perspective (i.e., as *abandonados*, seeing themselves as deficient compared to others) but longer-settled, better-adapted youth like Aarón could use other frames to explore new possibilities for ethnic and linguistic pride.

One of the difficulties of working with other cultures was that youth often only participated in work and church spaces, both of which were predominantly Latina/o but also notorious for marginalizing Indigenous groups. In response, and with the group's holistic view of human development in mind, Wilfredo commented, "[Maya youth] don't learn these things in church; they just sweep and move furniture. They are getting the spiritual [development], but they aren't moving forward. They aren't dealing with the problem of low self-esteem or their exploitation at work." Wilfredo's point was that merely being in contact with members of other cultural groups would not necessarily result in integration or empowerment for Maya youth. Rather, as Aarón put it, seeing evidence of others' "interest" in Maya culture in supportive interactions could give youth "energy" to persevere in maintaining Maya identity in diaspora.

A salient example from the local community and a frequent topic in Voces meetings was Día del Salvadoreño, a Salvadoran parade and festival that takes up several blocks in Westlake, the nearby Salvadoran corridor, during the late summer. The festival was brought up annually when the date was approaching but also when Maya cultural events were being organized, as an example of how Maya youth could use similar public gatherings as occasions for "brightening" their ethnic and linguistic identities. Wilfredo spoke forcefully with youth about this connection in the weeks leading up to the 2016 Día del Cristo Negro, a celebration honoring the Black Christ, a figure of veneration among Indigenous communities in Mexico and Central America, and one that is said to look phenotypically like the Indigenous youth who were in the room at the time.

At one meeting, Wilfredo pushed the youth to go even further in honoring their country and culture and to be just as loud and take up as much space as the Salvadorans did. Furthermore, Wilfredo framed the Día del Cristo Negro as an opportunity for Maya youth to critique the language ideologies that positioned K'iche' as inferior to Spanish (specifically, to Central American varieties of Spanish), observing that Indigenous youth often "feel lesser" (*se sienten menos*) but that Salvadoran language and culture were not superior to K'iche' or Indigenous culture:

> How are you going to believe that K'iche' isn't worth anything if the Salvadorans talk about "piece of shit this, piece of shit that"? . . . And besides that, Salvadorans already speak Spanish. It's the Maya that have the ability to speak their Mayan language, learn Spanish, and arrive here to begin to learn English.

In this passage, Wilfredo, who hailed from El Salvador himself, made a joke at his own and his fellow Salvadorans' expense, contrasting vulgar but public uses of Salvadoran Spanish with Maya youth's reluctance to speak K'iche'. Wilfredo exploited *cerote*, a mild profanity used widely in Central America, but which he associated with the speech of Salvadorans in Los Angeles, to humorously undercut discourses of K'iche'/Maya inferiority. He also reminded the youth that their multilingual dexterity could be seen as more impressive than other Latin Americans' L1 or "standard"-sounding Spanish, since Maya youth had to handle at least three languages, unlike Salvadorans. In doing so, Wilfredo invited the Voces participants to reconsider their reluctance to use K'iche' when Spanish-speaking immigrants seemed to have no qualms about using Spanish in public in an English-dominant society. Posing the question opened the door for further conversations among the youth about what role K'iche' (and other Mayan languages, to a lesser extent) might play in Maya diasporic communities in the future.

At other times, Maya youth interacted with non-Indigenous Latin Americans who urged them to confront discrimination and cultivate a strong sense of self-worth grounded in Indigenous culture. For example, Mireya, a social worker in Los Angeles County and a Mexican immigrant, visited Voces for several months in 2012 and 2013 to talk to the participants about mental health, social interaction, and emotional regulation. During a group discussion at one meeting in September 2012, she encouraged the attendees:

> If you are facing discrimination, learn self-appreciation. Learn how your body works, how your mind works so that you have physical self-appreciation. Remember, your multiculturalism isn't a bad thing. See it as a blessing that multiculturalism exists and that you have many cultural experiences to draw from.

Mireya's focus on different forms of self-appreciation in this excerpt reflects the support group's multifaceted understanding of *desarrollo* (self-development). Over time, as fellow Voces participants and allies affirmed that every story mattered, youth were invited to redefine Maya culture and what being Maya meant in a new, multicultural context. For Mireya to speak of Maya identity as a "blessing" and a welcome contribution to multiculturalism in Los Angeles encouraged youth to envision how they could make their presence more visible and audible, as opposed to concealing it—through participation in public events like festivals, or by speaking K'iche' and other Mayan languages without shame.

For some, these new possibilities also brought healing from the *timidez y miedo* that trailed them from Guatemala to the US, as better-adapted youth learned to reframe existing ideologies of Indigenous language and culture. Others felt compelled to do the same. This came into sharp relief by the summer and fall of 2015, one year after the sudden rise in unaccompanied child migration and apprehension rates at the US southern border in 2014. The persistently high rates of unaccompanied child migration were a frequent topic of conversation in Voces meetings.

One fall evening, a Voces group participant, Martin, detailed how he saw his experience reflected in those of children at the border and how the companionship and support shared in Voces meetings could serve as a model for supporting newly arrived children:

> Good evening, everyone. I am Martin. Well, you know, the name Voces de Esperanza says all you need to know about this group. Most of us are from Guatemala. We don't speak English. We all came as

jóvenes from Guatemala. We left our *aldeas* [towns] to be here in Los Angeles. Los Angeles is a totally different world. It's not something a fifteen- , sixteen- , or eighteen-year-old teenager is ready to face. We get here at fifteen years old, without our dads, without our moms. When you're over there and with your family, you never think about what it's like to be without them. I think this group has been a significant [source of] support for those who have been here. We are all teenagers who deal with challenges; we deal with loneliness. I mean, away from our moms and dads, outside of our country, it is totally dangerous. And I think what we are seeing now, what we see these days with the kids arriving at the border, is in the same process. Maybe the dynamic is different for them [because they are apprehended at the border], but they are leaving so much violence, so much poverty. We know what they are experiencing because we experienced those things ten years ago. It was a dream of mine to come to the United States, to come to build a house. Those kids are coming here to look for ways to feed themselves, to build a house. They will experience loneliness. They might fall into vices. This group, this way of sharing with one another, how we get together every week and try to be better people, we need more of that.

Maya youth's future-making included creating more welcoming spaces for recently arrived unaccompanied children in light of the loneliness and challenges they had experienced after their own migration. As Martin suggested, being uprooted from a Maya *aldea* to Los Angeles was not something a teenager was "ready to face"; though the youth present had indeed faced it, they sought to shield other youth from enduring the same form of disorientation following displacement.

Beyond spaces for companionship, young people in Voces also talked about other services recently arrived unaccompanied children would need, like legal representation, support in educational enrollment, and family support. Voces participants knew of these needs because these were the services they were locked out of as young people who needed to stay outside of the view of the state to work to survive. On several occasions, Voces participants asked Stephanie if she knew how they could help Indigenous Guatemalan children arriving as unaccompanied children in Los

Angeles. At Wilfredo's request, Stephanie asked an attorney at a prominent Central American immigrant community-based organization in Pico-Union about whether and how long-settled Maya youth could volunteer or work as translators for recently arrived children. This attorney reported that volunteers would need certification proving their formal training as translators. If long-settled Maya young people wanted to work as translators, they would need some form of work authorization. Both options were out of reach for the Maya youth of Voces de Esperanza, who, because of the conditions of their migration and arrival to Los Angeles, had neither formal education nor documentation to qualify for a role as translators.

This did not stop Maya young people from future-making, in particular, from imagining futures where they could leverage their multilingual skills and knowledge of life in Los Angeles to support their community. Around 2016 and into 2017, participants talked about finding employment with the Guatemalan consulate, where they could act as interpreters and liaisons for other Mayan-speaking compatriots. Here again, Maya young people's lack of documentation proving formal education and legal status would ultimately prohibit such occupational opportunities. However, even if hypothetical, these conversations proved that young people began considering where their language proficiencies might be an asset for future individual and collective social and economic mobility in Los Angeles. Embedded in their nested social context as Indigenous migrants within the Latina/o immigrant community, study participants' future-making included seeing themselves as distinctly skilled and capable members of the Latin American–origin immigrant diaspora.

Taking Inspiration from Korean Business Owners
Maya youth also observed members of other non–Latin American ethnolinguistic communities using their languages without apology, giving them another frame of reference for incorporation that did not entail cultural loss or assimilation. Joel recounted a conversation with a Maya friend who was policing Joel's language use, embarrassed to be heard in the company of K'iche' speakers:

> I had a friend that I was talking to in K'iche' and another friend was there and he said, "Hey, stop speaking K'iche'. Doesn't it embarrass

you?" He was listening and he did study a bit in Guatemala. And I told him, "I hear the Koreans speaking in their own language. Do you think they feel embarrassed to be speaking in their own language in front of us?" I told him that. [laughs] [Stephanie: So how did he respond?] "No, no, I don't think so," he said. [And I said] "So why do you feel embarrassed that we are speaking our language?"

Koreans, who owned many of the garment factories that employed youth, emerged as a foil for anti-*Indio* Latinas/os in the young people's discourses about the place of K'iche' and Maya culture in the diaspora. On one hand, Maya youth were unsparing in their evaluation of Korean bosses. As Justino put it, "The Koreans are the ones who exploit our people ... because they know we need to work." The participants blamed Korean factory managers for an array of workplace abuses, including being *gritones y abusadores* (yellers and abusers), paying below minimum wage to take advantage of youth's undocumented status, failing to compensate workers for time spent waiting for pay, and "making [youth] work to the limit" without regard for their well-being.

On the other hand, some youth, like Joel, recognized that Koreans were successful business owners who maintained their heritage language and took pride in their ethnic identity, offering a model of future-making that did not entail the erasure of culture and language. As youth came to consider how their linguistic and social *preparación* had equipped them to advocate for others in the community, they moved from an individualistic to a group-oriented understanding of *sobrevivencia* in the incorporation process. Korean bosses provided a useful model of an immigrant group that had attained a relatively secure economic and social position without sacrificing their language and cultural practices, even as their upward mobility relied on a deportable labor force that included Maya youth. In addition to providing a novel frame of reference, cross-cultural contact (whether with Salvadorans, Koreans, or others) invited Maya youth to view their own culture from a different perspective and to pose a version of the question Elizabeth Sumida Huaman's Indigenous (Wanka) participant posed: "I think people in other foreign places admire distant cultures like ours. Why can't we admire our own?"[42]

Aarón described interethnic contact as both a learning opportunity and a warning, demonstrating Maya youth's nuanced view of other immigrant groups, who could prompt them to think differently about acculturation even as the others sought to exploit Maya youth's vulnerable status:

> For example, the Asians. I have the idea how they work, how they help each other, how they support each other. . . . So I say, "Wow, that's another, different way of thinking," so when I listen to the other [groups], I learn a lot—their negative and positive [aspects]. The positive side, I learn what's going to help me and the negative side is a warning for me.

Thus, Maya youth's movements toward future-making took place in dialogue with myriad others—Maya and non-Maya, Latin American and non-Latina/o—whose encouragement (in the case of Wilfredo and Mireya) or example (in the case of Salvadorans and Koreans) invited them to explore what it could mean to be Maya in the diasporic context of Los Angeles.

Youth's curiosities about this possibility were most prominently displayed in their articulations of their future as workers. Recall that Maya youth left their origin country and communities to find work that would lift them and their families out of poverty and open doors for future mobility. Growing up as unaccompanied and undocumented adolescents oriented young people to their social role and responsibilities as workers in low-wage secondary labor market jobs. From this perspective, Maya youth saw Korean immigrants as illuminating the possibility that ethnoracial identity could be preserved—centered, even—while making inroads toward social and economic mobility. As such, Maya young people began envisioning being business owners, each within their own work context—like, for example, Joel and Fernando, who were among the longest-settled Maya youth participants in this research. Having come of age as garment factory workers, each envisioned a future of economic mobility within that occupation. They hoped to be factory owners who treated workers more equitably and who could speak with employees with dignity and respect.

In the five years since his arrival in Los Angeles at seventeen, twenty-two-year-old Gonzalo had experience working in garment factories, in restaurant kitchens, and as a florist in the Los Angeles Flower Market. Having enjoyed his time creating special events bouquets in the Flower Market, Gonzalo aspired to be a floral designer. During multiple conversations, including a one-on-one interview, Gonzalo expressed wanting to own his own flower shop. He explained that he only needed to save enough money to start his business and learn enough English to be able to interact with potential customers to turn that dream into a reality. He felt motivated by people like Wilfredo and Jorge who told him things like "*¡Échale ganas, échale ganas!*" (go for it, give it all you've got!), and he saw how other immigrants, including Koreans, had succeeded. "I've seen that it's possible. I've learned that you can do it," Gonzalo said.

Maya young people's material future-making did not stop at aspirations they had for themselves. Most of the youth portrayed in this book maintained material, social, and emotional attachments to the families they left behind in Guatemala well into young adulthood. Thus, while Gonzalo engaged in future-making for himself in Los Angeles, he was also deeply invested in the futures of his left-behind siblings and mother. (Gonzalo's father passed away when he was still a child living in Guatemala.) "That's what I talk about with my mom," Gonzalo explained, "I talk a lot with my family."

> I talk a lot with them about what they need. I think I can be like a dad to my brothers. I talk with them about finances and our [household] economy. We talk about what they need at home, everything. With my youngest brother, I talk to him about what he's studying. I try to motivate him to go to school and explain the importance of education to him. I ask him what his goals are. I tell him, "You need to discover what your goal is. If you don't have a goal in mind, you won't accomplish anything." And he did, he discovered his goal.

Gonzalo's use of the word "discover" (*descubrir*) alludes to the process of *orientación*, where young people are not told what to do but independently learn. When Gonzalo told his brother that if he did not "have a goal in mind," he would not "accomplish anything," he was also demonstrating his belief that if they did not become oriented to what it takes to *survive*, they would be unable to prepare themselves, and therefore unable to adapt. Gonzalo shared with Stephanie that his brother had, in fact, "discovered his goal." "He wants to be a teacher," Gonzalo said. When Gonzalo's brother shared this with him, Gonzalo replied, "Okay, excellent. You can do that now. *Te voy a echar la mano*" (I will lend you a hand). Gonzalo committed to sending remittances home for his brother's schooling expenses for several years after.

Nearly ten years after their first meeting, Stephanie saw Gonzalo again in July 2023. This time it was to celebrate the opening of Gonzalo's party supply and floral design shop, which he opened with the help of Voces coordinators. On the day of the shop opening, Gonzalo proudly showed Stephanie a certificate from the County of Los Angeles, signed by District Supervisor Hilda Solis, recognizing the store's grand opening. In black cursive letters under the store name, the certificate read, "With sincere congratulations and best wishes, the Board of Supervisors of the County of Los Angeles hereby joins your celebration." Gonzalo did not have legal status nor school completion certificates to boast of, but the future he imagined for himself nearly a decade prior had been realized. A signed certificate from the Los Angeles County Board of Supervisors was evidence of his successful future-making. What's more, his brother eventually migrated, but not as an unaccompanied teen. And, when he arrived in Los Angeles, Gonzalo's business employed him. Together, the brothers worked to support their left-behind family.

As Maya youth engaged in the processes of *preparacion* and *adaptación*, en route to *sobrevivencia*, they looked to other ethnic groups they encountered within distinct social contexts (in this case, Koreans in the workplace) as evidence of the possibilities of future-making in Los Angeles. This was uniquely possible in Los Angeles, as Maya communities are the marginalized and oppressed ethnoracial group in Guatemala. As Maya youth were exposed to other immigrant groups in Los Angeles, they learned that being assigned a subordinate ethnoracial position did not exclude them from opportunities for mobility.

The futures Maya young people imagined as they transitioned to adulthood included righting the wrongs they'd experienced at work by creating spaces where, as Lucy put it in the opening vignette, people can "get along with others." Because of his *preparación* and *adaptación* in Los Angeles, Gonzalo was able to delay his brother's migration. Gonzalo worked to support himself and his family and to keep his brother in school. Furthermore, his future-making a decade prior enabled him to create a more welcoming material and emotional space for his brother. Maya youth future-making thus included thinking about how they could be leaders in business, supporting compatriots and left-behind families to make new futures in Guatemala and the United States.

Conclusion

Growing up in Los Angeles was a dynamic experience that presented a range of opportunities for, and constraints on, future-making, including increased exposure to a multicultural society and continued encounters with anti-Indigenous attitudes, which led to diverse outcomes for Maya youth.[43] Some youth in the study who initially felt profoundly marginalized gradually moved toward immigrant community incorporation and brighter imagined futures for themselves and their coethnics through *preparación* for *adaptación*, while others continuously struggled with feelings of vulnerability and being out of place.[44]

Long-term residence in the new society presents myriad challenges, as we documented in the foregoing chapters; still, it can also provide Indigenous immigrants with a variety of opportunities to question and reframe existing ideologies that stigmatize Indigenous languages, cultures, and bodies.[45] Being able to imagine a brighter future was an opportunity afforded to those who first survived the loneliness and alienation of post-migration "abandonment." Our analysis of post-migration survival strategies leading to eventual future-making does not mean that all the participants' journeys unfolded in this way; nor do we intend to romanticize the experiences of unaccompanied youth who managed to overcome some of the social and linguistic difficulties associated with displacement and disorientation. Rather, we highlight youth's agency and the ingenious embodied and discursive tactics they relied on to pursue *sobrevivencia* over the long term without neglecting the myriad and distinctive challenges of Indigenous Latin American immigration.

Especially at first, Maya youth were acutely aware of the stigma attached to Indigeneity in Guatemala and the way this stigma "traveled" to Latina/o immigrant communities in the United States.[46] The youth sought to defend themselves from anti-*Indio* harm and discrimination through discourse practices oriented to the "listening subjects" of non-Indigenous Latin Americans and non-Latinas/os.[47] Youth also employed techniques of bodily concealment that, while they could isolate Indigenous youth, were also believed to make them less racially identifiable in physical terms.[48]

For some, however, this phase gave way to "a state of reflection" in which youth found opportunities to question stigmatizing ideologies of Mayan language and culture in dialogue with diverse others.[49] This allowed some of them to think creatively about what kind of home Los Angeles could be and how—given the example of Salvadorans, Koreans, and other groups—it might become a place with space for Maya identity and cultural practice. As Maya youth established themselves in the US, they felt less of a need to defend themselves from stigmas attached to Indigeneity and Guatemalan identity. They began to reflect on possibilities for ethnic and linguistic pride in communal settings. These reflections accompanied a shift in youth's understanding of *sobrevivencia* from an individual matter (i.e., one's need to *defenderse*, or defend oneself, to survive after migration) to a collective matter (i.e., one's responsibility to contribute to the thriving of the Maya/Guatemalan community over the long-term) as the process of incorporation unfolded.[50]

These findings point to the need for immigrant incorporation scholars to move beyond snapshots of immigrants' attainment of social and economic mobility and well-being and to engage with incorporation processes that occur over time. Attention to agency in migration and incorporation, including that of unaccompanied migrant children and youth, offers new insights into who agents of individual socialization and community change are. Moving beyond portraits of Indigenous migrants, including youth, as objects of anti-Indigenous racism—and seeing them as mobilizers of resources, skills, and capital, some rooted in Indigenous identity itself, and as makers of their futures—restores Indigenous community agency and Maya youth agency in their simultaneous passages as migrants and adolescents transitioning to adulthood.

Here, we have acknowledged the persistent anti-Indigenous stigma that manifested psychologically in youth's *timidez y miedo;* we have also argued that it is necessary to look beyond post-migration experiences of linguistic and cultural shame, fear, and discrimination to illuminate possibilities for language maintenance and cultural pride in the context of long-term *sobrevivencia* in diaspora. Existing work has largely focused on the potential for schools to function as linguistically and culturally sustaining spaces for Maya youth or on the experiences of youth enrolled in US schools who found ways to enact "resilient indigeneity" in and out of school.[51] In this chapter, by contrast, we have examined how youth outside of formal schooling could question and reframe language ideologies about Mayan languages and speakers, using multiple frames of reference to reevaluate possibilities for being Maya and speaking Mayan in the immigrant community.

Conclusion

In 2016, about fifty service providers from across Southern California gathered in the basement of an office building in Los Angeles. They were meeting for a training session on how to improve the treatment of unaccompanied Maya children who came to these organizations' doors, in addressing such issues as multilingual competence, Indigenous language diversity, and cultural sensitivity.[1] The training meeting was organized and facilitated by Perla, the executive director of an umbrella nonprofit immigrant-serving organization, and by other community advocates. Perla began with an exercise: She said a phrase in her natal language of Zapotec (an Indigenous language of southern Mexico), then asked the audience to tell her what she said. Attendees remained silent, unable to translate the phrase. Perla repeated the phrase in Zapotec again, more slowly the second time, and asked the crowd to tell her what she said. The attendees stayed silent, unable to translate. Perla spoke more loudly the third time while repeating the same phrase. Still, no one understood. She asked how this made the group feel. Workshop attendees reported feeling frustrated, confused, and incompetent, among other things.

Perla then explained, "Most people that speak Spanish or English tend to do that," referring to her exercise. "They speak to [Indigenous-language speakers] slowly and loudly so [they] will understand. In court, in hospitals, and in schools our Spanish-speaking friends think if they speak to us slowly and loudly, we will understand." Her point was that if someone does not speak the language that is being spoken to them, the pace or volume of the utterance does not matter. The addressee simply does not understand.

Perla made the point again at a similar workshop held virtually in 2023. She explained, "I said [the phrase] fast, I said it slow, I said it loud." So, why couldn't the group understand her?, she asked rhetorically. Perla explained to the hundreds of attendees that this is how Indigenous languages speakers are treated, as if the Spanish and/or English language were the standard of communication and that Indigenous language speakers were unintelligent (as well as unintelligible) and held accountable for their failure to understand. Indigenous language speakers, according to Perla, were treated as if they had a learning deficit in situations where the dominant society's ignorance of Indigenous languages became evidence of the intrinsic limitations of their speakers.[2] Framing Indigenous languages in this way—as lacking the capacity, along with their speakers, to express "modern ideas and complex thoughts"—can become another justification for excluding Indigenous people from full participation in modernity.[3] Instead, Perla suggested, it is the duty of the service providers to acknowledge the legitimacy of Indigenous languages as stand-alone modes of communication that the Spanish or English speakers did not understand, calling attention to the service providers' language needs as well as the clients'.

The volunteer-led nonprofit organizing the meeting developed out of a concern for what its leadership calls the ongoing violation of Indigenous immigrant detainees' linguistic human rights.[4] The group has argued that detainees are "de jure subjects of language rights in the United States" under a 2000 executive order that, based on Title VI of the Civil Rights Act, requires that they be given "meaningful access" to information about their interactions with federal agencies.[5] Building on Indigenous-led efforts to train Indigenous language interpreters since the 1990s, the nonprofit describes its mission as ending the "linguistic solitary confinement" of immigrants who are forced to accommodate one or both of "the unintelligible language[s] of the historical oppressor" (i.e., Spanish and English) in their dealings with the immigration detention and court systems.[6] In their workshops, the group offers interpreter training as well as practical decolonization activities intended to educate the broader immigrant-serving community about the distinctive situation of Indigenous language speakers in the United States.

Since the 2016 workshop, the concern for Indigenous language-speaking youth has risen to the level of the federal government. In 2023, the US Department of Health and Human Services (HHS) Office of Refugee Resettlement—the federal agency charged with the care and custody of unaccompanied minors until they are released to an adult sponsor—led a virtual two-part workshop series organized by the Diversity, Equity, Inclusion, and Accessibility Commission centered on increasing an "understanding of [Indigenous] populations and their cultures" and supported through the efforts of the Los Angeles-based nonprofit described above. According to the HHS organizers, over 530 people were present for the 2023 workshops.

Beyond demonstrating that Spanish is not the only spoken language of Latin America and that multitudes of Indigenous languages continue to exist, the workshops also focused on teaching attendees about the diversity of Indigenous languages and the experiences of Indigenous language speakers in diaspora. To this end, the organizers of the 2023 HHS Indigenous-language workshops dedicated one of their sessions to Guatemalan Indigenous language communities and the other to Mexican Indigenous language communities. In the first session focused on Guatemalan Indigenous communities, the facilitator articulated the rationale for the workshops in general, along with the group's specific attention to Indigenous languages of Guatemala. We quote his comments at length, as they exemplify how several threads from our argument in this book were woven together in the language workshops. After sharing that twenty-four different Indigenous languages are spoken in Guatemala, underscoring the country's linguistic diversity, the speaker stated:

> It is a mistake to think that we are a monolingual region that speaks Spanish. . . . [I]t is important to highlight that when we migrate to this country, we do not leave these ideas of the perceptions of In-

digenous people behind. Unfortunately, the Latino community brings these ideas, and they reproduce these ideas here and it triggers and it creates a lot of violence against Indigenous communities. When we are trying to make a better life for our communities, we get pushback from ideas of *mestizaje* and violence against Indigenous peoples.

As noted, the facilitator's comments touched on several themes from this book. First, rising rates of Indigenous unaccompanied youth migration from Central America to the United States were reflected in the elevation of an Indigenous language workshop from the local to the national level and the concomitant "scaling up" of Indigenous presence through new technologies to different audiences.[7] What was initially seen as a regional issue to be addressed at a small, in-person basement workshop had become an issue with national scope that called for a broadly accessible online workshop attended by hundreds around the country. Likewise, Perla's initial efforts to demonstrate that Indigenous Mexican and Latin American languages like Zapotec merely existed gave way, at the second workshop, to sessions dealing in detail with the extent of language diversity in specific contexts (Mexico and Guatemala).

Second, the workshops highlighted the reality that Indigenous migrants in diaspora experience the reproduction of ethnoracial and language hierarchies that oppress and disparage their communities and cultures, and that this manifests in structural disadvantage and interpersonal interactions. Third, the presenter's reference to different forms of erasure—on one hand, *mestizaje*, or a logic of cultural elimination through racial "mixing"; on the other, violence that directly threatens Indigenous migrants—made clear that Indigenous language communities continue to confront and wrestle with questions of the value and legitimacy of the various languages they speak. Finally, as in Maya youth's future-making practices, Indigenous language speakers—in this case Perla, her colleagues, and the organization they represented—were made responsible for showcasing complex Indigenous community presence and asserting their language rights, "speaking back" directly to stereotypical "perceptions" of language deficit.

In the foregoing chapters, we explored how unaccompanied Indigenous Maya youth workers navigated Spanish and English learning through *preparación* and applied it through *adaptación* to work toward the futures they desired in Los Angeles. In their future-making, the young people positioned themselves strategically to gain access to desired linguistic capital,[8] initially concealing Maya identity and proficiency to mitigate discrimination and ultimately arriving at the "other shore" of *sobrevivencia*, where they began to make space for Mayan language maintenance. We also demonstrated that unaccompanied young people associated their *preparación* with the *adaptación* and *sobrevivencia* of their broader community and Maya compatriots, including those who were still struggling with disorientation in Los Angeles and those still in Guatemala, weighing the risks and benefits of migration.

Understanding the place of *preparación* in longer-term efforts to secure *sobrevivencia* equipped the young people to support other Maya in need. We have argued that it also led many to adopt a more critical perspective on the language ideologies and social hierarchies they had taken for granted while growing up. Having "survived" displacement to Los Angeles and succeeded in his future-making efforts, and now proficient in Spanish, with a few years of English classes under his belt, Aarón commented:

> I know what my values are now, [I know] that we are all the same. If other people know more [than me], it's because they have prepared themselves. But the value of a human? We are all the same, whether they are White, Black or whatever they may be, Mayas or whatever, we are all the same. But now, what I am realizing is, wow, maybe this North American culture has prepared itself a lot, and they have everything [that they do] because they have prepared themselves. But why hasn't my community? Well, because we have lived through times of war where we are oppressed, where people said, "You don't know anything, you don't have anything."
>
> They change our language. They told us, "Your language doesn't have any value." But they didn't say it directly, like "your language doesn't have value," but simply said things like "you speak a dialect," "you are an *Indio*," instead of asking "are you Maya?"

Aarón and others included in this work grew up being denied the dignity of language, culture, and identity from the highlands of Guatemala to the city streets of Los Angeles. Across both societies, and in myriad quotidian forms, Maya youth were silenced and marginalized. Aarón, like Perla and her colleagues at the workshop, recognized that structural and interpersonal oppression born in the origin country and reproduced by the hybrid hegemony in the destination country created the structural conditions that shape resettlement for Indigenous migrants.[9]

In the passage above, Aarón recounted his experience of what other youth referred to as "awakening" or "self-discovery" in the immigrant context: Having "prepared himself" to adapt to Los Angeles, Aarón was well positioned to reflect on differences in "preparation" between (in this case) North American and Maya cultures and communities. Whereas he might previously have swallowed others' contention that "You don't know anything" because of the self-explanatory power of the dismissal "You are an *Indio*," Aarón had become conscious that differences in social status were not innate but could be traced to people's relative level of *preparación*—the resources they possessed for adapting to changing conditions. He understood that others might know more, but not because there was anything intrinsically different about them; rather, it would be the case "because they have prepared themselves" to a greater degree. He also recognized that certain groups, namely descendants of colonial powers, were better positioned ethnoracially and culturally and therefore better economically positioned to engage in formal systems of *preparación* for adulthood. Through his own *preparación*, then, Aarón could recognize that the status and power differentials between "North American culture" and Maya cultures were not a matter of quality of culture; rather, they were a matter of the quantity of material and emotional resources passed down from one generation to the next—the financial, social, and cultural capital accrued over one's lifetime—and recognition of the legitimacy of distinct ethnoracial and cultural groups within and across those groups.

Furthermore, Aarón's account displayed his awareness of the social processes of subordination through which Mayan language and people were made to *seem* inferior to their non-Indigenous counterparts. Historically speaking, the answer to "Why hasn't my community prepared itself?" is that they have endured war, genocide, and oppression, not that there is anything intrinsically wrong with them.

Aarón's analysis of linguicide[10] was especially acute: The oppressors sought to "change our language"—to force a shift into Spanish—and denied that Mayan languages had value (i.e., that they could be seen as resources). But they did so indirectly, denigrating Mayan speakers and languages in the same breath ("You speak a dialect" therefore "You are an *Indio*") with the presupposition that less than full languages belong to less than fully human beings.[11]

Anti-Indigenous racism in Central America and the US might no longer take the overt forms of war or genocide, but it continues to manifest in boundary-setting phrases like "you speak a dialect" or "you are an *Indio*," phrases that represent a minimization of Indigenous languages and othering of Indigenous people. As Aarón's remarks demonstrated, and as we discussed in Chapter 4, the culmination of many youth's *preparación* was the ability to recognize and question these ideologies to promote *sobrevivencia* among their fellow Maya, in affirming the common "value of a human" and the rights of humans to "brighten" their ethnoracial identities in diaspora.

Our hope for this work is, in part, to draw attention to the everyday efforts Maya youth and young adults have made (and continue to make) to support linguistic survivance and access outside of the purview of local and regional organizations and the state. Indeed, the youth at the center of this research came to terms with their need for distinct forms of *preparación* through their independent orientation to life in Pico-Union—as Indigenous migrants, as unaccompanied youth, and as low-wage child workers. Maya youth then take the additional step of engaging in the everyday work of *preparación*, guiding peers and compatriots in doing the same. Even as youth make inroads to *preparación* (and *adaptación*) in everyday life, the burden of linguistic survival should not rest solely on Maya children's shoulders.

We thus underscore the need for comprehensive language services and continued advocacy for immigrants' language rights. In addition, we call on organizations and advocates to include long-settled migrants as experts on the lived experience of language socialization and the navigation of oppressive systems and structures through language. A wealth of resources within Indigenous communities can support the future-making of newcomer children and youth as well as adults and families. As this work has shown, inviting long-settled Maya young people to draw on their *preparación* to support newcomers has the potential to increase the prospects for ethnic pride and community integration, which contributes to emotional *preparación*. Material and emotional *preparación* facilitate material and emotional *adaptación*. These are critically interconnected components of the *sobrevivencia* of unaccompanied Maya youth.

In this Conclusion, we show how the main empirical findings advance theories of immigrant incorporation and language socialization, especially in relation to Indigenous immigrants in diaspora. We then offer recommendations for supporting language learning and *preparación* in the service of future-making in diaspora. We end by sharing thoughts on what contemporary trends of Indigenous Maya youth migration foreshadow in a broader sense for Latin American migration in the years to come.

Maya Youth and Future-Making in Diaspora

Through an examination of the language socialization of Maya migrant youth workers in Los Angeles, we have advanced the theory of unaccompanied migrant youth incorporation as a process of disorientation and adaptation to include the distinct experiences associated with *preparación*, or socialization into ideologies, practices, and institutions that make up an initially unfamiliar *sistema*, or social system. We have argued that Maya youth in diaspora engage in *preparación*, a distinct phase of incorporation in which youth work to "prepare themselves" to secure *sobrevivencia* in multiple contexts: as undocumented immigrants in an anti-immigrant society, as Indigenous migrants in an anti-Indigenous Latina/o immigrant community, and as independent migrant youth workers.

Our data reveal that, even within the population of unaccompanied youth migrants, ethnoracial and language-based communities are differentially dislocated in and displaced from their origin country, as well as intersectionally disoriented once in the destination country. This last point deserves emphasis and attention in future research: Rather than treating race, ethnicity, and language background as proxies for community identification, researchers should consider how these social categories do and do not overlap in migration trends and immigrant destinations. To this end, our research reinforces the conclusions of sociologists Rogers Brubaker, Mara Loveman, and Peter Stamatov, who argued that "Race, ethnicity, and nationality exist only in and through our perceptions, interpretations, representations, classifications, categorizations, and identifications. They are not things *in* the world, but perspectives *on* the world—not ontological but epistemological realities."[12] The findings presented throughout this book might encourage scholars to ask questions such as how communities of speakers that span national borders may share common "push" factors driving migration, or how Indigenous migrants from different countries and backgrounds may experience the effects of racialization differently in diaspora, among others.

In our analysis, the hybrid and intersecting hegemonies that resulted in distinct forms of disorientation for Maya youth called forth equally distinct forms of linguistic and cultural maintenance and learning. *Sobrevivencia* in Los Angeles required that youth learn and adjust to life there—that is, they needed to move out of disorientation and acquire the social and linguistic capital necessary for adaptation. To do so, Maya youth engaged in what they termed a process of *preparación*. *Preparación* referred to the strategies they employed to increase their social, cultural, and linguistic capital to make *adaptación* possible, conceiving the latter primarily in terms of concrete advances in employability and social connectedness in the origin and destination societies. These adaptive advances, toward which youth worked incrementally once they felt themselves sufficiently "prepared," were predicated, in turn, on achieving specific language-related goals. Youth evaluated their progress toward broader life goals with reference to multiple others whose level of *adaptación* and language proficiency provided a helpful basis for comparison. Maya youth understood *preparación* and *adaptación* as prerequisites for *sobrevivencia,* particularly in their roles as independent youth workers, transnational family and community members, and as potential long-settled immigrants in the United States.

For unaccompanied Indigenous teens transitioning to adulthood outside of the often taken-for-granted socializing institutions of parent-led households and K–12 schools, youth's eventual *sobrevivencia* demanded forms of *preparación* that were not just material but emotional. In the collective space of Voces de Esperanza, where mentors emphasized positive self-development along different dimensions, young people unburdened themselves from their *preocupaciones*; they shared day-to-day experiences of defeat and triumph at work, in school, in local neighborhoods, and within transnational families. These interactions served as collective socialization, where young people gained a deeper understanding of the collective marginalization, shared worries of Maya migrants, and experimented with seeing themselves as "wise" experts whose words carried weight.

Engaging in such practices as a collective allowed the young people to cultivate an appreciation for the value of others and to see that others valued them and their shared identity and culture, further evidence that "organizations are vital conduits for identity formation processes."[13] The impact of Voces de Esperanza demonstrates the positive influence of grassroots organizations on immigrant well-being, and the power of supportive peer groups for unaccompanied children without parents and/or a central household family unit on which to rely in the United States, especially in the face of deep discrimination. Future research might consider whether and to what extent similar processes might play out for young people who are not embedded in neighborhood organizations or social communities, as well as for those who participate in various organizations that might not center emotional health and well-being (e.g., through the practice of *desahogo* or unburdening). Facing multiple marginalizations within nested ethnoracial and language communities, while also occupying social locations outside of the normative bounds of family and childhood *and* assuming the social role of independent youth worker (rather than dependent student), Maya youth developed distinct measures of their relative *adaptación* to life in Los Angeles.

Language, as constitutive of culture and identity, served as a key mechanism in youth's incorporation in that it enabled distinct future-making processes in diaspora, as youth co-constructed their language proficiency in relation to the sociolinguistic performance of US-born, immigrant-origin, and left-behind peers. They also reflected on their own past and future selves—where they had been and where they wanted to be—in light of their present abilities. Recalling the dislocation and displacement of Maya youth from their origin communities and country and their experiences of disorientation in response to persistent discrimination and social exclusion in Los Angeles, we observed how youth came to view *preparación*—especially in terms of language—as critical to their own *sobrevivencia* but also to that of their compatriots. Over time, Maya young people began to leverage their progress in *preparación* and *adaptación* to support that of their friends and peers, along with other Maya migrants who were experiencing disorientation in Los Angeles. A collective orientation to *preparación* and *adaptación* promoted future-making in that it bolstered local practices of community cohesion.

Another essential element of Maya youth's future-making was their exposure to examples of *adaptación* and ethnolinguistic survivance of other immigrant communities, including other Central American and Latin American-origin immigrants, non-Latina/o immigrants, like Korean Americans, and non-immigrants, like US-born White and non-White groups. Having grown up as *the* subordinate "other" in Guatemalan society, with a basically binary hierarchy (i.e., Indigenous versus Ladino), the emergence of multiple, overlapping frames of reference in Los Angeles (i.e., social groups with various ethnoracial identities and diverse cultural and language practices) made it possible to imagine different kinds of futures.

Whether and how immigrants achieve cultural adjustment in their destination society has been a central line of inquiry in immigration scholarship. Once analyzed as the sole dimension of immigrant "assimilation" (and the characteristic that immigrants should shed to achieve inclusion),[14] cultural values and practices are understood today as necessarily retained to achieve incorporation in a highly unequal US society.[15] In the study of immigrant children and children of immigrants, scholars have largely agreed that immigrant-origin youth are more likely to achieve economic mobility and social inclusion in an ethnoracially stratified society if they selectively acculturate, maintaining distinct components of their ethnic group's cultural values and norms and co-ethnic community ties to counteract the discrimination and exclusion they might face within the dominant mainstream society.[16] Existing theories posit that these processes are led by caregiving adults who provide the "moral and instrumental support" needed to strike the balance between the cultural norms and values practiced in immigrant parent-led households and coethnic communities and those upheld in "Americanizing" K-12 schools.[17] Our study shows that, outside of parent-led households and schools, youth undergo very different paths to incorporation and that incorporation can be youth-led. Maya youth participants approached language learning pragmatically, calibrating their efforts to attain the degree of proficiency needed to advance their goals within the distinct social spaces they inhabited. Their long-term language learning goals were informed by the futures they imagined for themselves, their families, and their compatriots within and across origin and destination societies.

Maya youth's linguistic *preparación* was complex. In the study of language and cultural retention among the children of Latin American–origin immigrants, it is often assumed that young people transition from one colonial language to the other—that is, from the assumed native Spanish language of their immigrant parents to the English language of their teachers, peers, and native-born counterparts in US classrooms.[18] Yet the Latin American immigrant community possesses more diverse language repertoires. As such, immigrants engage in variegated language socialization and learning processes. Maya youth's *preparación* not only included gaining some proficiency in each of the languages that comprised the nested language communities in which they were embedded (their Mayan language, Spanish, and English), but also learning how much proficiency in each language was required to navigate interactions within and across social spaces. Maya youth agentially learned to move from interactions with Mayan-speaking compatriots in a clothing store in one moment, to those with Spanish-speaking Latinas/os at church or other neighborhood spaces in another, to those with English-speaking employers. Being children in these non-normative institutions and social roles does not shield young people from anti-Indigenous racism; thus, their linguistic flexibility was a key element of adapting to survive in diaspora.

As we have drawn out throughout this work, our study participants' *sobrevivencia* required learning to navigate the intersecting social location of being undocumented in an anti-immigrant US society, being Indigenous in an anti-Indigenous Latina/o community, and being an unaccompanied minor in adult- and family-centric America. Youth's constant confrontations with such exclusionary and oppressive social boundaries had material and emotional consequences. Confronting these discriminatory social boundaries had detrimental effects on the young people's self-concept and self-esteem and shaped their hopes for the future. It was through participation in social spaces such as Voces in Esperanza that Maya youth could share about themselves and their lives with *honestidad* (honesty) and *mente abierta* (an open mind) alongside other Maya youth, and where the young people gradually honed a keen awareness of and appreciation for the cultural, social, and linguistic capital they possessed. Surviving within intersecting systems of oppression required an intersectional agency, the dimensions of which unaccompanied Maya youth workers gleaned from one another through stories about their successes, challenges, and failures. Developing these trusting and meaningful peer relationships was integral to their future-making in Los Angeles—not just as Indigenous migrants but as teenagers and young adults developing their sense of self and imagining futures in diaspora.

The question of immigrant cultural incorporation in the United States remains contentious due to its origins in the assimilation debate, which was founded on the premise that the dominant American culture (i.e., White Anglo-Saxon Protestant) was (and is) more legitimate and valuable than any immigrant culture. Today, public fears of immigration and immigrant population growth find a political footing in spurious cultural arguments. Indeed, sociologist Irene Bloemraad and her colleagues write that "much opposition to migration centers on worries that migrants are too culturally and socially different from the host population, that they will fail to integrate, or that they will change the demographics and culture of a destination society too dramatically."[19]

Our attention to colonial language learning among Indigenous migrants risks doing symbolic violence to Mayan languages and lifeways, in that it might be misunderstood to represent a community-wide shift to Spanish and English as "the price of incorporation." Because of this, we want to underscore that the young people did not view learning Spanish and English as prerequisites for "incorporation" into US society in an abstract or absolute sense. Instead, they oriented to the "colonial codes of power" in an almost purely instrumental sense,[20] to the extent that individuals like Jerónimo could lightheartedly admit that they disliked speaking English but allowed that it was necessary to achieve specific goals in their *adaptación* to immigrant life.

Our emphasis on future-making is not meant to suggest that imagining a future in Los Angeles implied moving on from Maya identity and cultural practice, but to highlight the young people's everyday efforts to gain minor advantages in the local language ecology, which, over time, might make the difference between surviving and failing—economically, socially, and emotionally. Future-making is not a rejection of Maya culture, but a strategic process of integrating past, present, and future selves and experiences, which takes place over the long term of youth's adolescence and young adulthood as immigrant workers. By and large, youth did not see their strategic acquisition of degrees of Spanish and English proficiency as incompatible with Mayan language maintenance, even as some struggled to overcome persistent stigmas associated with speaking and being Mayan in diaspora. Instead, as youth saw themselves as better prepared to adapt to life in Los Angeles, they also came to see new possibilities for "brightening" the lines of difference that marked them as Maya, including moving past shame at being identified as Maya and at using K'iche' and other Mayan languages in public.

Supporting Mayan-Language Survivance in Diaspora

Each of the foregoing chapters highlighted a particular dimension of unaccompanied Guatemalan Maya youth's language socialization. Chapter 2 documented how youth's pursuit of Spanish and English learning was intertwined with holistic efforts at *preparación,* or personal development, and aimed at specific future outcomes (for individual youth and coethnics/family members). In Chapter 3, we examined youth's social construction of language proficiency as a strategy for assessing their current level of *adaptación* relative to other individuals and groups and thereby estimating how close they were to achieving their goals. Chapter 4 discussed transformations in ethnic identification and discursive practice over time, as youth's post-migration tactics of concealment for individual survival gradually gave way to a self-discovery that coincided with increased advocacy for linguistic and cultural *sobrevivencia* in the Maya community. In all these cases, youth's efforts were mediated through interactions with others—from Voces attendees to coworkers and bosses to churchgoers—that provided youth with multiple, overlapping frames of reference for making sense of their own experiences.[21]

Taken together, Maya youth's developing critical awareness of possibilities for language advocacy in diaspora and the scenes from the language workshops described at the opening of this chapter give a picture of language policy emerging across heterogeneous scales of social practice.[22] In one sense, youth's negotiations around Maya sociolinguistic identity and performance—in dialogue with Wilfredo and other community members, and in reference to other ethnic groups—are evidence of what language revitalization scholar Teresa McCarty called "the grounded, improvisational, and grass-roots nature of [language policy] as it is realized in everyday social practice."[23] Daily linguistic interventions on behalf of Mayan languages and their speakers—from young people like Lucy, Aarón, and Joel—represented an incipient form of multilingual, community-based language policy in Los Angeles, in contrast to the bullying and silencing the youth had experienced in Guatemala.

A focus on "the individual and local community as active agents,"[24] in bottom-up efforts to carve out space for Mayan languages *and* identities in Los Angeles,[25] dovetails with our broader project of documenting Maya youth's future-making in the specific neighborhoods and social networks they inhabited.[26] From this perspective, moments of *adaptación* on the immediate scale of Los Angeles-centered future-making—Iván's speaking to Voces attendees about overcoming *timidez y miedo* through language learning, or Lucy's K'iche'/Spanish language brokering for more recently arrived immigrants—constituted a form of policy-in-practice. Enacting language policy for *sobrevivencia* was founded on a critical praxis of recognizing and questioning the raciolinguistic ideologies[27] that sought to relegate Mayan languages and speakers to the margins, both in Guatemala and the United States.

In another sense, the Indigenous language workshops are evidence that local communities' bottom-up efforts to promote linguistic survivance and end "linguistic solitary confinement" are being *rescaled*[28] on the level of top-down, superordinate language policy in small but important ways.[29] The workshop facilitator quoted above made several related points about the need for greater visibility of Latin American Indigenous languages—that Latin American immigrants are not linguistically homogeneous, that different languages are associated with different communities, and that stigmatizing language ideologies travel across borders with Indigenous speakers. The audience for these remarks suggested that things had changed substantially since the first workshop in 2016, at least in terms of awareness of unaccompanied Maya youth's needs. The fact that the same organization led both workshops also suggests that there are few organizations available to address the urgent language needs of Indigenous migrant families and communities, including unaccompanied minors. This underscores that there are relatively few experts for applying Indigenous-language learning, maintenance, and representation to these urgent needs for newly settled Indigenous families and migrants in detention.

Yet our research suggests that long-settled Indigenous youth can be a resource at local and national levels on these issues. Youth in the study—who had endured displacement and disorientation, passed through *preparación*, and adapted to life in LA to secure their own *sobrevivencia*—began to recognize these capacities in themselves. In later Voces meetings, following the much-publicized rise in rates of Central American migration, participants would sometimes talk about being able to interpret for recently arrived unaccompanied children. Thus, in addition to the more spontaneous forms of language brokering and language advocacy discussed earlier, youth displayed awareness that Mayan-Spanish-English multilingualism might have value in a more general sense, not just a situational one.

Recall when, seeking to build on this interest, Stephanie approached a Central American immigrant-serving community organization in Los Angeles about bringing in K'iche' speakers; but she was told the organizational leaders would not be able to hire the youth if they did not meet certain requirements for education, language certification, and legal status (see Chapter 4). This begs the question: What is holding back the US government, nonprofit agencies, local/regional service providers, schools, and others from seeing and treating Mayan languages as resources for the well-being of other immigrants—or, at least, from ensuring that people's language rights are not being violated under federal law?[30]

As the late language policy scholar Richard Ruiz[31] pointed out, such questions are underspecified in academic work that encourages a "language-as-resource" orientation, even as most efforts to support minority language speakers are premised on such an orientation:

> What kind of resource is [language]? What is the nature of the value that attaches to it? . . . Who is responsible for its development, cultivation, and management as a resource? To whom does it "belong"?[32]

In the present case, what does close attention to the role of language in Maya youth's *preparación* and *adaptación* for *sobrevivencia* reveal about youth's multilingualism as a *wasted* resource—not for the Maya community, certainly, but in light of the systemic incompetence (in the linguistic and everyday uses of the word) of the English- and Spanish-speaking social fields in which immigrant youth must function and in which their multilingual expertise is often invisible or viewed as a problem?

Current legal mechanisms for employment and social service provision exist within a system that has no space for youth—those who do not speak English or Spanish—nor for people lacking stable family networks. Another obvious difficulty, however, and one to which future research should address itself, is that researchers and practitioners know so little about the overall picture of Mayan-language diversity in the United States, despite the valiant efforts of groups like the one profiled above. No reliable estimate exists for the number of Mayan speakers in the US—one source places the probable range from 500,000 to 1.25 million—nor the number in immigrant detention.[33] The issues that make it difficult to estimate the Indigenous Latina/o immigrant population in the United States[34] mean that statistical information about Indigenous language communities is even harder to come by, especially considering well-documented problems with the US Census and American Community Survey's language questions for non-English speakers and speakers of less common languages.[35] Some have referred to this as evidence of statistical genocide of Maya peoples.[36] In an encouraging development, linguists have recently discussed the use of home language surveys in federal reporting from seven states to offer recommendations for better capturing the richness of Indigenous Mexican and Latin American languages in the school-age population.[37]

In terms of what we do know, attempts to sum up the scope of Mayan-language communities in the US sound mostly familiar themes: The Maya population is growing, though to what degree is an open question; different language communities have migrated at different times and to different areas of the United States; the situation varies depending on the sending and receiving contexts; Maya immigrants struggle to access interpretation and translation services and suffer as a result; Mayan languages continue to be stigmatized and marginalized in diaspora; and schools and service providers struggle to catch up with the diversifying population.[38] *Everyday Futures* advances our knowledge about Mayan-language communities in the US and the growing population of unaccompanied migrant youth among them; yet this research, conducted by a bilingual English-Spanish researcher, focuses on Maya youth who had some degree of Spanish-language proficiency and could speak to their Mayan, Spanish, and English-language socialization and maintenance processes. Research with monolingual Mayan-speaking youth or multilingual Mayan-speaking youth (those with proficiency in more than one Mayan language) can shed critical light on the meanings of *sobrevivencia* and forms of future-making for young people differently located within language ecologies than those portrayed in this book.

Researchers can help address this gap by writing interpretation services into proposals, directing resources from academic institutions and grant funding agencies to ameliorate existing communication barriers—for example, in schools, community-based organizations, and other public domains of Mayan language use. Making sure that Indigenous languages are accounted for in funding proposals would have both the practical effect of increasing access to services and the powerful symbolic effect of underscoring these languages' value as rights and resources.[39] Finding ways to support efforts underway to train interpreters or working with community-based organizations to start new efforts would address the lack of Mayan-language services in areas like medicine and education, which can require specialized interpretation. In the future, working with heritage speakers of K'iche' and other Mayan languages to build capacity for interpretation, along the lines of programs that "elevate" underappreciated linguistic resources in professional domains, may be an option.[40]

For now, it is imperative to consider creative solutions to institutional language incompetence in the United States and the systematic exclusion of language experts *from* those institutions. Might not trilingual proficiency and hard-earned interpretation experience in K'iche', Spanish, and English qualify someone for an H-1B visa for pursuing a "specialty occupation" or an O-1 visa on the basis of having "extraordinary ability in the sciences, arts, [or] education"[41]—and, what is more, committing to use that ability to improve outcomes in the US immigration system? The requirements for such nonimmigrant visa programs are notoriously prone to fluctuation with different presidential administrations,[42] which may pose challenges or present possibilities for creative redefinition of these categories.

Greater visibility of Mayan languages and recognition of their importance and utility might help shift the discourse around Indigenous Latin American immigrants' linguistic strengths and needs and even prompt institutions not only to accommodate newer immigrants but to reframe longer-settled immigrants' multilingualism as a resource, not a problem.[43] The basic difference in structure and intelligibility between linguistic codes like "K'iche'" and "Spanish," though, is only one dimension of the challenge facing Indigenous immigrants and the systems struggling to adapt to their presence. Nearly as important are the linguistic-ideological differences between K'iche' and Spanish (for example) as systems of *use*, which have already been documented to contribute to Indigenous Latina/o immigrants' relative disadvantage in the US court system, even when interpretation is available.[44] In such situations, bilingualism is no guarantee that cultural misunderstandings will not arise and non-Mayan interpreters and Maya clients may have "different expectations about the discourse appropriate for" particular fields of practice. María Luz García cites "body language, eye contact, and conversational and discursive norms" as some of the interactional differences that might shape such encounters.[45]

Labels like "Mayan languages" and "Indigenous languages," while necessary at times from the perspective of "strategic essentialism" in advocacy for Indigenous migrants,[46] also obscure real differences in diasporic affordances for language maintenance and revitalization, not to mention interpretation and translation. Problems of enumeration aside, "Mayan languages" describes a language family whose smallest members have a mere thirty speakers, while the largest, K'iche', has nearly 1 million.[47] In an environment where even K'iche' speakers have difficulty gaining recognition of their language as a resource, what does this imply for speakers of smaller Mayan languages? While Latin American Indigenous languages have made limited inroads in the US education system, the languages represented are generally those with robust populations of speakers, officially "threatened" though they may be.[48] It is not just a numbers game; the presence (or absence) of local communities of speakers plays a role, as do parents' bottom-up language policies and English "acquisition planning" for their children.[49] Still, in the greater scheme of things, it is likely that there are relatively more possibilities for larger languages like K'iche' in multilingual Los Angeles than for smaller language communities.[50]

Linguistic Expertise and Lived Experience as Valued Resources for Incorporation

We have made the point that unaccompanied Maya youth workers' experiences are distinctive—not just because of their racialized status and different linguistic backgrounds but because of their identities as *youth*—adolescents and young adults who struggle to be taken seriously by those who see them merely as children. Chapter 2 opened with the story of Enrique and Omar as an example of how the youth came to see that they possessed expertise that trusted adults in Guatemala did not, and that, because of this, it was possible to learn something from a fellow migrant, even if the other person was younger. Youth like Enrique and Omar found it was no longer true that youth "didn't have any weight to their words" (per Omar), as was assumed to be true in Guatemala. Rather, *preparación* coincided for many with an accelerated form of *madurándose,* growing up quickly through "dealing with life [in the US]," as Omar put it.

Youth's voices are frequently disempowered, if not ignored, within adult-centric societies. As anthropologist of education Norma González remarked, "Children are the ultimate 'others'" and are often represented as voiceless since adults tend to see their voices as "unformed and consequently uninformed"—as incomplete and lacking critical attention to the social issues that concern adults.[51] In opposition to this tendency, critical youth scholars are now arguing for the consideration of youth agency, opinion, decision-making, and desires across the life course, not simply upon reaching a certain definition of maturity. Of the many social roles that children have been assigned cross-culturally and in social analysis (e.g., as subjects in need of moral development, as a free source of labor, as immature adults, as apprentices, as intermediaries with the spirit world), our work aligns best with the recent tradition of analyzing youth and children as cultural brokers or social actors with the linguistic and cultural expertise to facilitate everyday boundary-crossing for themselves and others.[52]

In the context of other recent work on child language brokering,[53] our findings are additional evidence that youth's multilingual and intercultural expertise should be recognized and valued as a resource that adults depend on to make social life possible in diverse settings. The few existing studies of Maya and other Indigenous Latina/o youth in the US have largely focused on school-age children in school settings,[54] where possibilities for engaging directly with language ideologies and hegemonic practices—for example, in policies related to curriculum, instruction, and family/community engagement—look very different than the types of engagement we have glossed as "community-based language policy" in the lives of unaccompanied Maya youth coming of age out of school and without their parents.[55]

Another source of expertise, as Enrique and Omar indicated, is youth's lived experience of disorientation and *preparación,* which, as the preceding chapters make clear, encompasses immigrant language socialization but goes well beyond it. Indeed, many who conduct research with and advocate for unaccompanied minors argue that young people are "adultified" or are displaced and prematurely thrust into adult roles and responsibilities as they "hopscotch" over traditional rites of passage.[56] Those concerned with the well-being of unaccompanied minors and other youth of color discuss the hardships they face not only as a source of trauma but as a means both of learning valuable life skills and transferring these skills to less-experienced others.[57] Social work research even suggests that service providers, educators, and researchers may benefit from sympathetic attention to hard-earned lessons from youth, whose lived experience is described as an "underutilized" resource for strengthening the social safety net (however limited) around them.[58] Thinking of youth's expertise in this way reaches back to earlier work that challenged descriptions of migrant labor as "unskilled" and asserted the value and complexity of migrants' frequently invisible skilled work.[59]

Maya youth in this study found for themselves that they could transfer life skills gained through *preparación* (and from having endured disorientation, *timidez,* and *miedo*) to more recently arrived young people,[60] taking advantage of structured opportunities like Voces as well as informal teachable moments for doing so. However, Indigenous youth's ingenuity in figuring this out on their own is not an excuse for the systemic neglect of their distinctive cultural and linguistic needs in the US immigration regime and US immigrant communities. Making youth's expertise visible and leveraging it to support *preparación* and *adaptación* in a balanced way would formally and forcefully support their incorporation into the US legal system and regulated labor market. Arguing for a view of multilingual youth as skilled, expert interpreters and cultural brokers is also a way to bolster their case for legal inclusion in US society.

The Continued Diversification of Latin American Migration

The experiences and perspectives of unaccompanied Guatemalan Maya youth shared here demonstrate how incorporation processes unfold for Indigenous migrants coming of age as independent youth workers—without parent or guardian caregivers present and outside of K–12 schools—and the role of language socialization and learning in their *sobrevivencia* and future-making in diaspora. Understanding these processes will prove essential for meeting the needs of present and future immigrant populations. As Central American migration trends persist, scholars, advocates, and the public must become more aware of the ethnoracial, cultural, and language diversity they represent. Further still, we should set our sights on the future, heeding calls to attend to the rising rates of South American refugee migration to the United States in response to political and economic crises and natural disasters, especially from Colombia, Argentina, Peru, Chile, and Brazil.[61] With these migrations come many languages: for example, Colombians bring up to sixty-five Indigenous languages, Argentinians up to fourteen, and Peruvians up to ninety. As destination countries work to create welcoming and inclusive contexts of reception, they can be mindful of recognizing these languages, refusing to minimize them as "dialects" and advocating for their speakers' meaningful inclusion in all aspects of public life.

Finally, the growing diversity of Latin American-origin immigrants—and the language communities they represent—urges consideration of the mechanisms that prompt speech or language community displacement and whether and to what extent these might overlap with the mechanism of displacement of national origin groups more broadly. Our research suggests that Indigenous populations across the Americas might be subjected to quotidian dislocations in and displacement from their origin communities and countries. Furthermore, this displacement may continue to manifest as cultural disorientation in transit and upon arrival in their destination society, where migrants feel it acutely in institutional interactions, such as in the workplace or neighborhood organizations. Creating systems and structures that support Indigenous migrants' *preparación* and *adaptación* to secure *sobrevivencia* and promote future-making must be among our shared goals.

NOTES

Introduction

1. References to Indigenous communities as practicing witchcraft or described as "witches" are examples of the everyday racism, discrimination, and derogatory epithets Indigenous people encounter (Heidbrink et al. 2024).

2. Historical-present tense refers to instances in narratives where the present tense is used to depict events that happened in the past. Schiffrin (1981) argued that the historical-present has an evaluative function (i.e., it helps to convey the point of the narrative) as well as a structural function, in alternation with the past tense, of separating narrated events from each other.

3. Schiffrin 1981.
4. Hanks 2010: 4-5.
5. Hanks 2010: 4.
6. Canizales 2024b.
7. We are using the term "Latina/o" throughout our writing intentionally. Scholars have proposed using terms like "Latinx" or, more recently, "Latine" as more inclusive and gender non-binary terms. However, as this book will show, Indigenous communities experience Latina/o/x identity as categorically exclusive and gender binary on the ground, even as academics and advocates attempt to broaden the scope of the identity category. Indeed, our participants did not use the terms "Latinx" or "Latine," relying instead on "Latino" and "Latina," or "Hispano" and "Hispana" throughout our conversations. We opted to maintain

the use of "Latina/o" to more accurately reflect participants' lived experiences within the Latin American–origin immigrant community in Los Angeles, while standardizing for readability.

8. Portes and Rumbaut 2001.
9. Boccagni and Hondagneu-Sotelo 2021; Hondagneu-Sotelo and Pastor 2021.
10. Canizales 2024b.
11. For more on "revealing" and "concealing" legal status, see García 2019 and Patler 2018. For studies of Indigenous immigrants within predominantly non-Indigenous immigrant communities, see Asad and Hwang 2018; Gómez Cervantes 2021, 2023.
12. Barillas Chón 2022.
13. US Department of Health and Human Services 2023.
14. Canizales 2024b.
15. Congressional Research Service 2017.
16. US Customs and Border Protection 2023.
17. Congressional Research Service 2023.
18. Congressional Research Service 2021.
19. Chishti and Hipsman 2015.
20. US Customs and Border Protection 2023.
21. Heidbrink 2020:14.
22. Heidbrink et al. 2024.
23. Aleaziz and Flores 2019.
24. Greenberg et al. 2021; Pierce 2015.
25. Shepherd 2020; Wang 2014.
26. Medina 2019; Nolan 2019; Obinna 2021.
27. Abrego 2014; Andrews 2018; Duquette-Rury 2019; Hondagneu-Sotelo 2007; Levitt 2001.
28. Cranford 2005; Mahler 1995; Rosales 2019.
29. Canizales 2022; De Genova 2005; Gomberg-Muñoz 2019; Herrera 2016; Holmes 2013; Waldinger and Lichter 2003.
30. Canizales 2024b.
31. For more on bounded solidarity and enforceable trust, see Portes and Landolt 2000. For research on Indigenous community marginalization in the US, see Fox and Rivera-Salgado 2005 and Loucky 2000.
32. Gordon 1964; Park 1914; Thomas and Znaniecki 1918; Warner and Srole 1945.
33. Portes and Rumbaut 2001; Portes and Zhou 1993.
34. Ramírez 2020; see also Canizales and Vallejo 2021; Go 2024; and Oeur and Varga 2024.
35. Menjívar 2021.
36. Asad and Clair 2018; Canizales 2015; Chavez 2013; Molina 2010.
37. Fox 2006.

38. Zentella 1995.
39. Vallejo and Canizales 2023.
40. Ramírez 2020; Zamora 2022.
41. See Blackwell et al. 2017 for more on "hybrid hegemonies," and the work of Barillas Chón 2010; Canizales 2021; Casanova et al. 2016; Urrieta et al. 2019 for their impact on Indigenous immigrants' everyday lives.
42. Batz 2014: 195.
43. De Genova et al. 2015.
44. Ribas 2016.
45. Canizales 2024b; see also Asad 2023.
46. Canizales 2024b.
47. Diaz-Strong and Gonzales 2023.
48. Canizales 2024b.
49. Successful adaptation can be subjectively defined (Canizales 2024b).
50. Canizales 2024b.
51. Boccagni and Hondagneu-Sotelo 2021; Hondagneu-Sotelo and Pastor 2021.
52. Boccagni and Hondagneu-Sotelo 2021: 2.
53. Boccagni and Hondagneu-Sotelo 2021: 2.
54. Lévi-Strauss 1974: 17.
55. Millan et al. 2024; see also Flores 2009.
56. Estrada 2013: 167.
57. Estrada 2013: 174.
58. Boj Lopez 2017: 188.
59. Batz 2014.
60. Casanova et al. 2021.
61. Canizales 2024b.
62. Rymes 2014.
63. Bromham et al. 2022.
64. See Gorenflo et al. 2012; see also Nichols 1992 for more on "hotspots." See Mühlhäusler 2011 and Bromham et al. 2022 for more on how infrastructural and environmental forces put languages and people and risk.
65. Krauss 1992.
66. Fishman 1991.
67. Simons and Lewis 2013.
68. Bromham et al. 2022: 170.
69. Eberhard et al. 2023; Hammarström et al. 2023.
70. Bromham et al. 2022: 170.
71. Hill 2002.
72. Muehlmann 2012.
73. Leonard 2011.
74. Wolfe 2006.

75. Moore 2006.
76. Nelson et al. 2023: 188.
77. Meek 2011.
78. Leonard 2011: 137.
79. Leonard 2020: e6.
80. Vizenor 1999.
81. Skutnabb-Kangas 2000.
82. Wyman 2012.
83. Wyman 2012: 14.
84. Go 2024.
85. Kroupa 2013: 177–178.
86. Nicholas 2013: 83–84.
87. Weinberg and DeKorne 2016.
88. Avineri and Harasta 2021: 3.
89. Leonard 2021: 253.
90. Morales et al. 2019; Pérez Báez 2013, 2014; Velasco 2010, 2014.
91. Baquedano-López and Méndez 2023: 62.
92. Kramsch and Whiteside 2008; Whiteside 2013.
93. Casanova 2019.
94. Barillas Chón 2022.
95. Kroskrity and Meek 2023: 23.
96. Whyte 2013.
97. Doerr 2009; García 2011.
98. Hagan 1994; Menjívar 2001.
99. Canizales 2015: 1837; O'Connor and Canizales 2023.
100. Canizales 2019.
101. Deterding and Waters 2018.
102. Hammarström et al. 2023.
103. Menjívar 2011.
104. Casanova et al. 2016.
105. Boccagni and Hondagneu-Sotelo 2021: 155–156, emphasis in original.

Chapter 1

1. Lucy's experiences of spending most of her non-working time at home was shared by several women encountered during the fieldwork, which reinforces our hypothesis of why more Maya men participated in this research relative to Maya women.
2. Kramsch and Whiteside 2008: 646.
3. Barillas Chón 2019; Restall and Solari 2020.
4. Maxwell 2017: 120.
5. Go 2024: 13; emphasis in original.
6. Zamora 2022.

7. Heidbrink 2020: 34.
8. Bellino 2017.
9. Heidbrink et al. 2024.
10. Wellmeier 1998.
11. Hamilton and Chinchilla 2001: 1, 23.
12. Bellino 2017.
13. Táíwò 2021.
14. Baltimore County History Labs Program n.d.; US Department of State, Office of the Historian. n.d.
15. Striffler and Moberg 2003; Táíwò 2021.
16. Bellino 2017: 29, calling on the work of historian Cullather 2006.
17. Bellino 2017: 29.
18. Coutin 2001; Musalo 2018; Perla 2013.
19. Oster 2024.
20. Hamilton and Chinchilla 2001.
21. Burt and Estrada 2018; Heidbrink et al. 2024.
22. Hamilton and Chinchilla 2001; Jonas 2013; Manz 1988; Menchú 2010.
23. Heidbrink et al. 2024, quoting the Commission for Historical Clarification 1999.
24. Bellino 2017: 30.
25. US Institute of Peace 1997.
26. Heidbrink 2020.
27. Batz 2020.
28. Celigueta 2015.
29. Menjívar 2011.
30. Bellino 2017; USAID 2023b.
31. Arnett 2000; Youth.gov n.d.
32. Thirty-five percent of adolescents in Guatemala are out of school, compared to 9 percent in the region and 15 percent worldwide (USAID 2023a). Across the country, Guatemalan youth average ten years of total schooling, compared to twelve years across Central American and eleven years worldwide. About 83 percent of children complete primary education. Of these students, an estimated 37 percent complete secondary education. About 4 percent of Guatemalans twenty-five and older have a bachelor's degree or equivalent. Indigenous youth, girls, and queer youth experience the greatest challenges to educational attainment.
33. Bellino 2017; Rubin and Cervinkova 2019.
34. Bellino 2017.
35. Coutin 2011.
36. Bellino 2017.
37. Heidbrink 2020.
38. Bellino 2017: 10.
39. Canizales 2024b; Martinez 2019.

40. USAID 2018.
41. Heidbrink 2020.
42. Canizales 2024b.
43. Hagan 1994; Loucky 2000; Popkin 2005.
44. Canizales 2024a; Jonas 2013.
45. Nichols 2021: 2.
46. Heidbrink 2020.
47. Hagan 1994; Popkin 2005.
48. Canizales 2024b; see Feliciano 2020 for a review of how origin-country "immigrant selectivity" affects immigrants' outcomes in the destination country.
49. Hamilton and Chinchilla 2001.
50. Moslimani et al. 2023.
51. US Department of State 2023.
52. Canizales 2015; Obinna and Field 2019.
53. See Galli 2023.
54. Zamora 2022: 3.
55. Zamora 2022: 3.
56. Canizales 2024b; Menjívar 2001.
57. Oliveira 2018.
58. Menjívar 2008.
59. Allweiss 2021; Nichols 2021, 2024.
60. Bellino 2017: 33.
61. Nichols 2021: 4.
62. Barillas Chón 2022: 3.
63. Casanova 2023.
64. Bellino 2017: 9.
65. Golash-Boza and Valdez 2018.
66. Cranford 2005; Del Real 2019; Mahler 1995; Menjívar 2001.
67. Hagan 1994.
68. Migration Policy Institute 2019.
69. Canizales 2019, 2024b.
70. Hagan 1994; Waldinger and Lichter 2003.
71. Gómez Cervantes 2021; Perez 2009.
72. Canizales 2022, 2023a.
73. Canizales 2024b.
74. Canizales 2019.
75. Canizales 2022; see Suárez-Orozco 1987 for more on the dual frame of reference.
76. Barillas Chón 2022.
77. Acker 2006.
78. Acker 2006: 447.
79. Barillas Chón 2010; Blackwell et al. 2017; Casanova et al. 2016.

80. Maxwell 2017: 120.
81. Keane 2018: 75.
82. Cf. Brubaker 2005.

Chapter 2
1. Canizales 2024b; Diaz-Strong 2021.
2. Arnett 2000; Nurmi 1991.
3. See Stanton-Salazar 2011 for the importance of institutional agents in schools among poor and working-class students.
4. Darvin and Norton 2015; Kanno and Norton 2003.
5. Warriner 2007.
6. Canizales and Hondagneu-Sotelo 2022.
7. Estrada 2019; Estrada and Hondagneu-Sotelo 2011.
8. Suárez-Orozco et al. 2008.
9. Portes and Rumbaut 2001, 2006; Portes and Zhou 1993.
10. Canizales 2024b.
11. Canizales 2024b.
12. Research shows that gender shaped how boys and girls were received by the male and female long-settled relatives. Girls could experience sexualization by relatives or relatives' partners, creating hostile household environments that rendered them unaccompanied again, even after an initial welcome. See Canizales 2024b for more on how the relational dynamics make for receptive or hostile household environments.
13. Canizales 2024b; Small and Gose 2020.
14. Ruiz 1984.
15. Canizales 2019, 2022, 2024b.
16. Irvine 2004.
17. Mendoza-Denton and Boum 2015.
18. All Voces de Esperanza meetings were conducted in Spanish. We translated conversations into English for readability, leaving in Spanish the key emic terms we leverage for our analysis of incorporation and language socialization throughout the book.
19. Portes and Rumbaut 2001; Pugh 2009.
20. Baynham 2006.
21. Wyman 2012: 38.
22. As this book goes to press, Voces de Esperanza youth, now adults, continue to tend to plots of land at the Pico-Union community garden, formalizing their gardening program under Jorge's leadership and expanding to multiple garden locations.
23. Warriner 2016.
24. Warriner 2007: 11.
25. Pennycook 2001.

26. DeLuca et al. 2024.
27. Hornberger 2006.
28. Goffman 1963.
29. Canizales 2024a.
30. Canizales 2015.
31. Canizales and O'Connor 2022.
32. DuBord 2018.
33. Cf. Messing 2013.
34. Golash-Boza and Valdez 2018; Logan et al. 2002.
35. Casanova 2019.

Chapter 3

1. Collins 1995.
2. Boccagni and Hondagneu-Sotelo 2021: 155.
3. Kramsch and Whiteside 2008; Whiteside 2009, 2013.
4. Blommaert 2010; Rymes 2014.
5. Casanova 2019.
6. Kanno and Norton 2003; Warriner 2007.
7. Martin-Beltrán 2010; Watanabe and Swain 2008.
8. Olmedo 2003.
9. Martin-Beltrán 2010: 270.
10. Adawu and Martin-Beltrán 2012; Martin-Beltrán 2010.
11. Warriner 2007, 2016.
12. Irvine 1989: 255.
13. Duff 2019: 8; Riley 2011: 493.
14. Blommaert 2010; Rymes 2014.
15. Canagarajah 2014.
16. García 2011.
17. Mortimer and Dolsa 2020: 10.
18. Irvine and Gal 2000.
19. Canizales 2021.
20. Vásquez-Colina 2019; see also Baquedano-López 2021.
21. Milkman 2020.
22. Canizales 2021; Rosales 2020; Waldinger 2001.
23. Barillas Chón 2022.
24. Boccagni and Hondagneu-Sotelo 2021: 155.
25. Canizales 2023b.
26. DuBord 2018.
27. Blackwell et al. 2017; Whiteside 2009.
28. MacSwan 2000.
29. Golash-Boza and Valdez 2018.
30. Illich 1973.

31. Baynham 2006.
32. Canizales 2024b.
33. Canizales and O'Connor 2021.
34. Canizales 2021.
35. Mortimer and Dolsa 2020: 1.
36. García 2013; Wyman et al. 2013.
37. Kramsch 2006.
38. Gallo et al. 2014; Silverstein 1998.
39. Deters et al. 2015

Chapter 4
1. Edwards and Fasulo 2006.
2. Sacks 1987.
3. Bell 1984.
4. Laurier and Philo 2006.
5. Bourdieu 1991.
6. In US and non-US contexts, language brokering among immigrant youth and young adults is typically studied as family-based practice, in which children of immigrants broker on behalf of their immigrant parents (Kwon 2024; Melander and Gréen 2023; Orellana 2009).
7. Boccagni and Hondagneu-Sotelo 2021: 2.
8. Canizales and Diaz-Strong 2021.
9. Hardie 2022; Lareau 2000, 2011; Portes and MacLeod 1996; Vidal de Haymes et al. 2018.
10. Portes and Zhou 1993.
11. Portes and Rumbaut 2001; Zhou et al. 2008.
12. Boccagni and Hondagneu-Sotelo 2021: 165.
13. Sangaramoorthy 2019; Szakolczai 2009.
14. De Genova 2005.
15. Sangaramoorthy 2019: 559.
16. Sangaramoorthy 2019: 566–567.
17. Sangaramoorthy 2019.
18. Boccagni and Hondagneu-Sotelo 2021: 165
19. Pollock 2004.
20. Pollock 2004.
21. Menjívar 2021.
22. Gómez Cervantes 2021: 113.
23. Gómez Cervantes 2021: 100.
24. Ong 2006.
25. Gómez Cervantes 2021.
26. Castañeda et al. 2002.
27. Lavadenz 2005.

28. Canizales 2015; Casanova 2019.
29. Batz 2014; Boj Lopez 2017.
30. Estrada 2013.
31. Bucholtz 2011; Mendoza-Denton 2008; O'Connor 2016; Pollock 2004.
32. González and Arnot-Hopffer 2003; Mendoza-Denton 2008; Wyman 2012.
33. Roth-Gordon 2017: 6.
34. See Canizales 2021 and 2019, respectively.
35. Warner-Garcia 2014: 161.
36. Cf. Gómez Cervantes 2021; Rosa 2019.
37. Gómez Cervantes 2021.
38. Arnett 2000; Hogan and Astone 1986; Markey 2010.
39. Hondagneu-Sotelo and Pastor 2021: 253.
40. Canizales 2015.
41. Montes 2013.
42. Huaman 2015: 141.
43. Stepick and Stepick 2010.
44. Canizales and O'Connor 2021.
45. Barajas 2014; Batz 2014; Gómez Cervantes 2021.
46. Blackwell et al. 2017.
47. Flores and Rosa 2015.
48. Gómez Cervantes 2021; Roth-Gordon 2017.
49. Turner 1967: 105.
50. Canizales 2015, 2022.
51. Baquedano-López 2021; Casanova 2019.

Conclusion

1. The organization is fairly well-known, and its activities are public, but we choose not to name it here to provide at least a degree of confidentiality for its staff, since their work is potentially vulnerable to criticism from anti-immigrant forces.
2. Cf. Maxwell 2017.
3. Romero 2018.
4. Newdick and Romero 2019: 30.
5. Newdick and Romero 2019: 30.
6. Newdick and Romero 2019: 30.
7. Cf. Bauman 2016.
8. Bourdieu 1991.
9. Blackwell et al. 2017.
10. Skutnabb-Kangas 2000.
11. Maxwell 2017; Romero 2018.
12. Brubaker et al. 2004.
13. Bloemraad et al. 2022: 327.

14. Gordon 1964; Park 1914; Warner and Srole 1945.
15. Portes and Zhou 1993.
16. Kasinitz et al. 2008; Portes and Rumbaut 2001; Portes and Zhou 1993.
17. Neckerman et al. 1999: 948.
18. Alba 2004.
19. Bloemraad et al. 2023: 1.
20. Barillas Chón 2022; Ruiz 2010.
21. Cf. Golash-Boza and Valdez 2018.
22. Mortimer and Wortham 2015.
23. McCarty 2011: 5.
24. Hornberger 1996: 11.
25. Cf. Mortimer and Wortham 2015.
26. Cf. Hondagneu-Sotelo and Pastor 2021.
27. Flores and Rosa 2015.
28. Carr and Lempert 2016.
29. McCarty 2011.
30. Newdick and Romero 2019.
31. Ruiz 2010.
32. Ruiz 2010: 156.
33. García 2020; Newdick and Romero 2019.
34. Bazo Vienrich 2019.
35. Leeman 2018.
36. Heidbrink et al. 2024.
37. Zyskind et al. 2024.
38. García 2020.
39. Hult and Hornberger 2016.
40. Martínez and Schwartz 2012.
41. US Citizenship and Immigration Services (USCIS) n.d.
42. Goldfinger and Breçani 2019.
43. Ruiz 1984.
44. Brody 2017; Haviland 2003.
45. García 2020: 9.
46. Eide 2016.
47. García 2020: 2.
48. E.g., Baquedano-López 2021; Martínez and Mesinas 2019; Moran et al. 2024; Velasco 2014.
49. García 2020.
50. see, e.g., Anthony-Stevens and Griñó 2018 on efforts to promote the small language Ngigua in Mexican schools.
51. González 2005: 163.
52. Canizales and Hondagneu-Sotelo 2022; Lancy 2015.
53. E.g., Estrada 2019; Kwon 2022, 2024; Orellana 2009; Valdés 2003.

54. E.g., Baquedano-López and Méndez 2023; Kovats Sánchez et al. 2022; Morales et al. 2019; Moran et al. 2024.
55. Canizales 2024b.
56. Mendoza-Denton and Boum 2015.
57. Newman et al. 2021, 2022.
58. Mackay 2023.
59. Hagan et al. 2015.
60. Cf. Newman et al. 2021.
61. Batalova 2022; Selee et al. 2023.

REFERENCES

Abrego, Leisy J. 2014. *Sacrificing Families: Navigating Laws, Labor, and Love Across Borders.* Stanford: Stanford University Press.

Acker, Joan. 2006. "Inequality Regimes: Gender, Class, and Race in Organizations." *Gender & Society* 20: 441–464.

Adawu, Anthony, and Melinda Martin-Beltrán. 2012. "Points of Transition: Understanding the Constructed Identities of L2 Learners/Users Across Time and Space." *Critical Inquiry in Language Studies* 9(4): 376–400.

Alba, Richard. 2004. "Language Assimilation Today: Bilingualism Persists More Than in the Past, but English Still Dominates." *Lewis Mumford Center for Comparative Urban and Regional Research.* https://ccis.ucsd.edu/_files/wp111.pdf

Aleaziz, Hamed, and Alfredo Flores. 2019. "A 16-Year-Old Unaccompanied Boy Has Died in US Government Custody." *Buzzfeed News.* www.buzzfeednews.com/article/hamedaleaziz/unaccompanied-immigrant-boy-dies-us-custody

Allweiss, Alexandra. 2021. "'Too Dangerous to Help': White Supremacy, Coloniality, and Maya Youth." *Comparative Educational Review* 65(2): 207–226.

Andrews, Abigail L. 2018. *Undocumented Politics: Place Gender, and Pathways of Mexican Migrants.* Oakland: University of California Press.

Anthony-Stevens, Vanessa, and Paulina Griñó. 2018. "Transborder Indigenous Education: Survivance and Border Thinking in the Professional Development and Practice of *Maestros Indigenas*." *Association of Mexican American Educators Journal* 12(2): 92–120.

Arnett, Jeffrey Jensen. 2000. "Emerging Adulthood: A Theory of Development from the Late Teens Through the Twenties." *American Psychologist* 55(5): 469-480.

Asad, Asad L. 2023. *Engage and Evade: How Latino Immigrant Families Manage Surveillance in Everyday Life*. Princeton: Princeton University Press.

Asad, Asad L., and Matthew Clair. 2018. "Racialized Legal Status as a Social Determinant of Health." *Social Science & Medicine* 119: 19-28.

Asad, Asad L., and Jackelyn Hwang. 2018. "Indigenous Places and the Making of Undocumented Status in Mexico-US Migration." *International Migration Review* 53(4): 1032-1077.

Avineri, Netta, and Jesse Harasta. 2021. "Introduction: Exploring Agency, Ideology, and Semiotics of Language Across Communities." In *Metalinguistic Communities: Case Studies of Agency, Ideology, and Symbolic Uses of Language*, edited by Netta Avineri and Jesse Harasta, 1-23. Cham: Palgrave Macmillan.

Baltimore County History Labs Program. n.d. "RS #01: Background on the Guatemalan Coup of 1954." https://www2.umbc.edu/che/tahlessons/pdf/historylabs/Guatemalan_Coup_student:RS01.pdf

Barajas, Manuel. 2014. "Colonial Dislocations and Incorporation of Indigenous Migrants from Mexico to the United States." *American Behavioral Scientist* 58(1): 53-63.

Barillas Chón, David W. 2010. "Oaxaqueño/a Students' Un/welcoming High School Experiences." *Journal of Latinos and Education* 9(4): 303-320.

———. 2019. "Indigenous Immigrant Youth's Understandings of Power: Race, Labor, and Language." *AMAE Journal* 13(2): 15-41.

———. 2022. "K'iche', Mam, and Nahua Migrant Youth Navigating Colonial Codes of Power." *Urban Education* 59(4): 1224-1251.

Batalova, Jeanne. 2022. "Top Statistics on Global Migration and Migrants." Washington, DC: Migration Policy Institute. www.migrationpolicy.org/article/top-statistics-global-migration-migrants

Batz, Giovanni. 2014. "Maya Cultural Resistance in Los Angeles: The Recovery of Identity and Culture Among Maya Youth." *Latin American Perspectives* 41: 194.

———. 2020. "Ixil Maya Resistance Against Megaprojects in Cotzal, Guatemala." *Theory & Event* 23(4): 1016-1036.

Baquedano-López, Patricia. 2021. "Learning with Immigrant Indigenous Parents in School and Community." *Theory into Practice* 60(1): 51-61.

Baquedano-López, Patricia, and Cristina S. Méndez. 2023. "Stewards of the Language: Liminality and Transnational Sovereignty." *International Journal of the Sociology of Language* 279: 41-69.

Bauman, Richard. 2016. "Projecting Presence: Aura and Oratory in William Jennings Bryan's Presidential Races." In *Scale: Discourse and Dimensions of Social Life*, edited by E. Summerson Carr and Michael Lempert, 25-51. Oakland: University of California Press.

Baynham, Mike. 2006. "Agency and Contingency in the Language Learning of Refugees and Asylum Seekers." *Linguistics and Education* 17(1): 24-39.

Bazo Vienrich, Alessandra. 2019. "Indigenous Immigrants from Latin America (IILA): Racial/Ethnic Identity in the US." *Sociology Compass* 13(1): e12644.

Bell, Allan. 1984. "Language Style as Audience Design." *Language in Society* 13(2): 145-204.

Bellino, Michelle J. 2017. *Youth in Postwar Guatemala Education and Civic Identity in Transition*. New Brunswick: Rutgers University Press.

Blackwell, Maylei, Flori Boj Lopez, and Luis Urrieta Jr. 2017. "Introduction: Critical Latinx Indigeneities." *Latino Studies* 15(2): 126-137.

Bloemraad, Irene, Ali R. Chaudhary, and Shannon Gleeson. 2022. "Immigrant Organizations." *Annual Review of Sociology* 48: 319-341.

Bloemraad, Irene, Victoria M. Esses, Will Kymlicka, and Yang-Yang Zhou. 2023. "Unpacking Immigrant Integration: Concepts, Mechanisms, and Contexts." *World Development Report 2023: Migrants, Refugees, and Societies.* www.thedocs.worldbank.org/en/doc/454db131e2fb1cd039409bd6f78e1778-0050062023/original/Social-integration-FINAL-FORMATTED.pdf

Blommaert, Jan. 2010. *The Sociolinguistics of Globalization*. Cambridge, UK: Cambridge University Press.

Boccagni, Paolo, and Pierrette Hondagneu-Sotelo. 2021. "Integration and the Struggle to Turn Space into 'Our' Place: Homemaking as a Way Beyond the Stalemate of Assimilationism vs Transnationalism." *International Migration* 61(1): 154-167.

Boj Lopez, Floridalma. 2017. "Mobile Archives of Indigeneity: Building La Comunidad Ixim Through Organizing in the Maya Diaspora." *Latino Studies* 15(2): 201-218.

Bourdieu, Pierre. 1991. *Language and Symbolic Power*. Cambridge, MA: Harvard University Press.

Brody, Mary Jill. 2017. "Court Interpretation of an Indigenous Language: The Experiences of an Unexpected LSP Participant." In *Language for Specific Purposes: Trends in Curriculum Development*, edited by M. K. Long, 157-167. Washington, DC: Georgetown University Press.

Bromham, Lindell, Russell Dinnage, Hedvig Skirgård, Andrew Ritchie, Marcel Cardillo, Felicity Meakins, Simon Greenhill, and Xia Hua. 2022. "Global Predictors of Language Endangerment and the Future of Linguistic Diversity." *Nature Ecology & Evolution* 6(2): 163-173.

Brubaker, Rogers. 2005. "The 'Diaspora' Diaspora." *Ethnic and Racial Studies* 28(1): 1-19.

Brubaker, Rogers, Mara Loveman, and Peter Stamatov. 2004. "Ethnicity as Cognition." *Theory and Society* 33(1): 31-64.

Bucholtz, Mary. 2011. *White Kids: Language, Race, and Styles of Youth Identity*. Cambridge, UK: Cambridge University Press.

Burt, Jo-Marie, and Paulo Estrada. 2018. "Legacy of Guatemala Dictator Ríos Montt Shows Justice Is Possible." Washington Office on Latin America. www.wola.org/analysis/legacy-guatemala-dictator-rios-montt-shows-justice-possible/

Canagarajah, Suresh. 2014. "Theorizing a Competence for Translingual Practice at the Contact Zone." In *The Multilingual Turn: Implications for SLA, TESOL and Bilingual Education,* edited by Stephen May, 78–102. New York: Routledge.

Canizales, Stephanie L. 2015. "American Individualism and the Social Incorporation of Unaccompanied Guatemalan Maya Young Adults in Los Angeles." *Ethnic and Racial Studies* 38(10): 1831–1847.

———. 2019. "Support and Setback: How Religion and Religious Organisations Shape the Incorporation of Unaccompanied Indigenous Youth." *Journal of Ethnic and Migration Studies* 45(9): 1613–1630.

———. 2021. "Educational Meaning Making and Language Learning: Understanding the Educational Incorporation of Unaccompanied, Undocumented Latinx Youth Workers in the United States." *Sociology of Education* 94(3): 175–190.

———. 2022. "Ethnorace and the *Orientación* of Unaccompanied, Undocumented Indigenous Youth in Latinx Los Angeles." In *Latinx Belonging: Community-Building and Resilience in the 21st Century,* edited by N. Deeb-Sossa and J. Bickham Mendez, 31–55. Tempe: University of Arizona Press.

———. 2023a. "'*Si Mis Papas Estuvieran Aquí*': Unaccompanied Youth Workers' Emergent Frame of Reference and Health in the United States." *Journal of Health and Social Behavior* 64(1): 120–135.

———. 2023b. "Work Primacy and the Social Incorporation of Unaccompanied, Undocumented Latinx Youth in the United States." *Social Forces* 101(3): 1372–1395.

———. 2024a. "Between Obligations and Aspirations: Unaccompanied Immigrant Teen Workers' Transnational Lives and Imagined Futures." *Journal of Ethnic and Migration Studies* 50(10): 2510–2528.

———. 2024b. *Sin Padres, Ni Papeles: Unaccompanied Migrant Youth Coming of Age in the United States.* Oakland: University of California Press.

Canizales, Stephanie L., and Daysi X. Diaz-Strong. 2021. "Undocumented Childhood Arrivals in the U.S.: Widening the Frame for Research and Policy." *Immigration Initiative at Harvard* 1(11). https://immigrationinitiative.harvard.edu/wp-content/uploads/2021/05/brief_11_eng.pdf

Canizales, Stephanie L., and Pierrette Hondagneu-Sotelo. 2022. "Working-Class Latina/o Youth Navigating Stratification and Inequality: A Review of Literature." *Sociology Compass* 16(12): e13050.

Canizales, Stephanie L., and Brendan H. O'Connor. 2021. "From *Preparación* to *Adaptación*: Language and the Imagined Futures of Maya-Speaking Guatemalan Youths in Los Angeles." In *Refugee Education Across the Lifespan: Mapping*

Experiences of Language Learning and Use, edited by D. Warriner, 103–119. New York: Springer.

———. 2022. "'Maybe not 100%': Co-Constructing Language Proficiency in the Maya Diaspora." *International Multilingual Research Journal* 16(4): 328–344.

Canizales, Stephanie L., and Jody Agius Vallejo. 2021. "Latinos and Racism in the Trump Era." *Dædalus* 150(2): 150–164.

Carr, E. Summerson, and Michael Lempert, eds. 2016. *Scale: Discourse and Dimensions of Social Life.* Oakland: University of California Press.

Casanova, Saskias. 2019. "*Aprendiendo y Sobresaliendo*: Resilient Indigeneity and Yucatec-Maya Youth." *AMAE Journal* 13(2): 42–65.

———. 2023. "The "Other" Mexicans: Indigenous Yucatec-Maya Students' Experiences with Perceived Discrimination." *Journal of Latinos and Education* 22(5): 2178–2199.

Casanova, Saskias, Melissa Mesinas, and Sarait Martinez-Ortega. 2021. "Cultural Knowledge as Opportunities for Empowerment: Learning and Development for Mexican Indigenous Youth." *Diaspora, Indigenous, and Minority Education* 15(3): 193–207.

Casanova, Saskias, Brendan H. O'Connor, and Vanessa Anthony-Stevens. 2016. "Ecologies of Adaptation for Mexican Indigenous Im/migrant Children and Families in the United States: Implications for Latino Studies." *Latino Studies* 14(2): 192–213.

Castañeda, Xochitl, Beatriz Manz, and Allison Davenport. 2002. "Mexicanization: A Survival Strategy for Guatemalan Mayans in the San Francisco Bay Area." *Migraciones Internacionales* 1(3): 103–123.

Celigueta, Gemma. 2015. "¿Mayanización, indigeneidad o mestizaje? Clasificaciones étnicas y diversidad en Guatemala." *Revista de Dialectología y Tradiciones Populares* 70(1): 101–118.

Chavez, Leo R. 2013. *The Latino Threat: Constructing Immigrants, Citizens, and the Nation.* Stanford: Stanford University Press.

Chishti, Muzaffar, and Faye Hipsman. 2015. "The Child and Family Migration Surge of Summer 2014: A Short-Lived Crisis with a Lasting Impact." *Journal of International Affairs* 68(2): 95–XIV.

Collins, James. 1995. "Literacy and Literacies." *Annual Review of Anthropology* 24(1): 75–93.

Congressional Research Service. 2017. "Unaccompanied Alien Children: An Overview." Washington, DC. www.crsreports.congress.gov/product/pdf/R/R43599/25

———. 2021. "Unaccompanied Alien Children: An Overview." Washington, DC. www.crsreports.congress.gov/product/pdf/R/R43599cR

———. 2023. "Increasing Numbers of Unaccompanied Children at the Southwest Border." Washington, DC: www.crsreports.congress.gov/product/pdf/IN/IN11638

Coutin, Susan. 2001. "The Oppressed, the Suspect, and the Citizen: Subjectivity in Competing Accounts of Political Violence." *Law & Social Inquiry* 26(1): 63–94.

———. 2011. "Falling Outside: Excavating the History of Central American Asylum Seekers." *Law & Social Inquiry* 36(3): 569–596.

Commission for Historical Clarification. 1999. "Guatemala Memory of Silence: Report of the Commission for Historical Clarification, Conclusions, and Recommendations." https://hrdag.org/wpcontent/uploads/2013/01/CEHreport-english.pdf

Cranford, Cynthia J. 2005. "Networks of Exploitation: Immigrant Labor and the Restructuring of the Los Angeles Janitorial Industry." *Social Problems* 52: 379–397.

Cullather, Nick. 2006. *Secret History: The CIA's Classified Account of Its Operations in Guatemala, 1952–1954*, 2nd ed. Stanford: Stanford University Press.

Darvin, Ron, and Bonny Norton. 2015. "Identity and a Model of Investment in Applied Linguistics." *Annual Review of Applied Linguistics* 35: 36–56.

De Genova, Nicholas. 2005. *Working the Boundaries: Race, Space, and Illegality in Mexican Chicago*. Durham: Duke University Press.

De Genova, Nicholas, Sandro Mezzadra, and John Pickles. 2015. "New Keywords: Migration and Borders." *Cultural Studies* 29(1): 55–87.

Del Real, Deisy. 2019. "Toxic Ties: The Reproduction of Legal Violence Within Mixed-Status Familial and Friendship Ties." *International Migration Review* 53(2): 548–570.

DeLuca, Stefani, Nicholas W. Papageorge, and Joseph L. Boselovic. 2024. "Exploring the Trade-Off Between Surviving and Thriving: Heterogenous Responses to Adversity and Disruptive Events Among Disadvantaged Black Youth." *RSF: The Russell Sage Foundation Journal of the Social Sciences* 10(1): 103–131.

Deterding. Nicole M., and Mary Waters. 2018. "Flexible Coding of In-Depth Interviews: A Twenty-First-Century Approach." *Sociological Methods and Research* 50(2): 708–739.

Deters, Ping, Xuesong (Andy) Gao, Elizabeth R. Miller, and Gergana Vitanova, eds. 2015. *Theorizing and Analyzing Agency in Second Language Learning: Interdisciplinary Approaches*. Tonawanda: Multilingual Matters.

Diaz-Strong, Daysi X. 2021. "'*Estaba bien chiquito* (I was very young)': The Transition to Adulthood and 'Illegality' of the Mexican and Central American 1.25 Generation." *Journal of Adolescent Research* 37(3): 409–438.

Diaz-Strong, Daysi Ximena, and Roberto G. Gonzales. 2023. "The Divergent Adolescent and Adult Transitions of Latin American Undocumented Minors." *Child Development Perspectives* 17(3): 3–9.

Doerr, Neriko. Ed. 2009. *The Native Speaker Concept: Ethnographic Investigations of Native Speaker Effects*. Berlin: Mouton de Gruyter.

DuBord, Elise M. 2018. "Bilingual Tricksters: Conflicting Perceptions of Bilingualism in the Informal Labor Economy." *Language & Communication* 58: 107–117.

Duff, Patricia A. 2019. "Social Dimensions and Processes in Second Language Acquisition: Multilingual Socialization in Transnational Contexts." *The Modern Language Journal* 103: 6–22.

Duquette-Rury, Lauren. 2019. *Exit and Voice: The Paradox of Cross-Border Politics in Mexico.* Oakland: University of California Press.

Eberhard, David M., Gary F. Simons, and Charles D. Fennig, eds. 2023. *Ethnologue: Languages of the World,* 26th ed. Dallas: SIL International.

Edwards, Derek, and Alessandra Fasulo. 2006. "'To Be Honest': Sequential Uses of Honesty Phrases in Talk-in-Interaction." *Research on Language and Social Interaction* 39(4): 343–376.

Eide, Elisabeth. 2016. "Strategic Essentialism." In *The Wiley Blackwell Encyclopedia of Gender and Sexuality Studies.* https://doi.org/10.1002/9781118663219.wbegss554

Estrada, Alicia I. 2013. "Ka tzij: The Maya Diasporic Voices from Contacto Ancestral [Ancestral Contact]." *Latino Studies* 11: 208–227.

Estrada, Emir. 2019. *Kids at Work: Latinx Families Selling Food on the Streets of Los Angeles.* New York: NYU Press.

Estrada, Emir, and Pierrette Hondagneu-Sotelo. 2011. "Intersectional Dignities: Latino Immigrant Street Vendor Youth in Los Angeles." *Journal of Contemporary Ethnography* 40(1): 102–131.

Feliciano, Cynthia. 2020. "Immigrant Selectivity Effects on Health, Labor Markets, and Educational Outcomes." *Annual Review of Sociology* 46: 315–334.

Fishman, Joshua. 1991. *Reversing Language Shift: Theoretical and Empirical Foundations of Assistance to Threatened Languages.* Clevedon, UK: Multilingual Matters.

Flores, Nelson, and Jonathan Rosa. 2015. "Undoing Appropriateness: Raciolinguistic Ideologies and Language Diversity in Education." *Harvard Educational Review* 85(2): 149–171.

Flores, Samuel Luis Villela. 2009. "Cosmovisión indígena." Guerrero: Un estado multicultural. Programa Universitario México Nación Multicultural-UNAM y Secretaría de Asuntos Indígenas del Estado de Guerrero, México 465.

Fox, Jonathan. 2006. "Reframing Mexican Migration as a Multi-Ethnic Process." *Latino Studies* 4: 39–61.

Fox, Jonathan, and Gaspar Rivera-Salgado. 2005. "Building Migrant Civil Society: Indigenous Mexicans in the US." *Iberoamericana* 5(17): 101–115.

Galli, Chiara. 2023. *Precarious Protections: Unaccompanied Minors Seeking Asylum in the United States.* Oakland: University of California Press.

Gallo, Sarah, Holly Link, Elaine Allard, Stanton Wortham, and Katherine Mortimer. 2014. "Conflicting Ideologies of Mexican Immigrant English Across Levels of Schooling." *International Multilingual Research Journal* 8(2): 124–140.

García, Angela S. 2019. *Legal Passing: Navigating Undocumented Life and Local Immigration Law*. Oakland: University of California Press.

García, María Luz. 2020. "Mayan Languages in the United States." In *Handbook of the Changing World Language Map*, 791–804. Cham: Springer.

García, Ofelia. 2011. *Bilingual Education in the 21st Century: A Global Perspective*. Hoboken: John Wiley.

———. 2013. "Commentary: En/countering Indigenous Bi/Multilingualism." In *Indigenous Youth and Multilingualism*, edited by L. Wyman, T. McCarty, and S. Nicholas, 233–240. New York: Routledge.

Go, Julian. 2024. "Reverberations of Empire: How the Colonial Past Shapes the Present." *Social Science History* 48: 1–18.

Goffman, Erving. 1963. *Behavior in Public Places*. New York: Free Press.

Golash-Boza, Tanya, and Zulema Valdez. 2018. "Nested Contexts of Reception: Undocumented Students at the University of California, Central." *Sociological Perspectives* 61(4): 535–552.

Goldfinger, Desiree, and Drilona Breçani. 2019. "Redefining Specialty Occupation: How the Trump Administration Is Limiting the Use of the H-1B Visa Program." *The Federal Lawyer*: 30–32.

Gomberg-Muñoz, Ruth. 2019. *Labor and Legality: An Ethnography of a Mexican Immigrant Network*. Oxford: Oxford University Press.

Gómez Cervantes, Andrea. 2021. "'Looking Mexican': Indigenous and Non-Indigenous Latina/o Immigrants and the Racialization of Illegality in the Midwest." *Social Problems* 68(1): 100–117.

———. 2023. "Language, Race, and Illegality: Indigenous Migrants Navigating the Immigration Regime in a New Destination." *Journal of Ethnic and Migration Studies* 49(7): 1610–1629.

González, Norma. 2005. "Children in the Eye of the Storm: Language Socialization and Language Ideologies in a Dual-Language School." In *Building on Strength: Language and Literacy in Latino Families and Communities*, edited by A. C. Zentella, 162–174. New York: Teachers College Press.

González, Norma, and Elizabeth Arnot-Hopffer. 2003. "Voices of the Children: Language and Literacy Ideologies in a Dual Language Immersion Program." In *Linguistic Anthropology of Education*, edited by Stanton Wortham and Betsy Rymes, 213–243. Westport: Praeger.

Gordon, Milton M. 1964. *Assimilation in American Life: The Role of Race, Religion, and National Origins*. New York: Oxford University Press.

Gorenflo, Larry J., Suzanne Romaine, Russell A. Mittermeier, and Kristen Walker-Painemilla. 2012. "Co-Occurrence of Linguistic and Biological Diversity in Biodiversity Hotspots and High Biodiversity Wilderness Areas." *Proceedings of the National Academy of Sciences* 109(21): 8032–8037.

Greenberg, Mark, Kylie Grow, Stephanie Heredia, Kira Monin, Essey Workie. 2021. "Strengthening Services for Unaccompanied Children in U.S. Communities." Washington, DC: Migration Policy Institute. www.migrationpolicy.org/sites/default/files/publications/mpi-unaccompanied-children-services_final.pdf

Hagan, Jacqueline M. 1994. *Deciding to Be Legal: A Mayan Community in Houston.* Philadelphia: Temple University Press.

Hagan, Jacqueline, Ruben Hernandez-Leon, and J. L. Demonsant. 2015. *Skills of the Unskilled: Work and Mobility Among Mexican Migrants.* Berkeley: University of California Press.

Hamilton, Nora, and Norma Stoltz Chinchilla. 2001. *Seeking Community in a Global City: Guatemalans and Salvadorans in Los Angeles.* Philadelphia: Temple University Press.

Hammarström, Harald, Robert Forkel, Martin Haspelmath, and Sebastian Bank. 2023. *Glottolog 4.8.* Max Planck Institute for Evolutionary Anthropology. https://glottolog.org

Hanks, William F. 2010. *Converting Words: Maya in the Age of the Cross.* Berkeley: University of California Press.

Hardie, Jessica Halliday. 2022. *Best Laid Plans: Women Coming of Age in Uncertain Times.* Oakland: University of California Press.

Haviland, John B. 2003. "Ideologies of Language: Some Reflections on Language and US Law." *American Anthropologist* 105(4): 764–774.

Heidbrink, Lauren. 2020. *Migranthood: Youth in a New Era of Deportation.* Stanford: Stanford University Press.

Heidbrink, Lauren, Giovanni Batz, and David W. Barillas Chón. 2024. "Forced Family Separation: U.S. Crimes Against Indigenous People." *Maya America: Journal of Essays, Commentary, and Analysis* 6(1): 1–25.

Herrera, Juan. 2016. "Racialized Illegality: The Regulation of Informal Labor Space." *Latino Studies* 14(3): 320–343.

Hill, Jane. 2002. "'Expert Rhetorics' in Advocacy for Endangered Languages: Who Is Listening, and What Do They Hear?" *Journal of Linguistic Anthropology* 12(2): 119–133.

Hogan, Dennis P., and Nan Marie Astone. 1986. "The Transition to Adulthood." *Annual Review of Sociology* 12: 109–130.

Holmes, Seth. 2013. *Fresh Fruit, Broken Bodies: Migrant Farmworkers in the United States.* Oakland: University of California Press.

Hondagneu-Sotelo, Pierrette. 2007. *Domestica: Immigrant Workers Cleaning and Caring in the Shadows of Affluence.* Berkeley: University of California Press.

Hondagneu-Sotelo, Pierrette, and Manuel Pastor. 2021. *South Central Dreams: Finding Home and Building Community in South LA.* New York: NYU Press.

Hornberger, Nancy. 1996. "Indigenous Literacies in the Americas." In *Indigenous Literacies in the Americas: Language Planning from the Bottom Up*, edited by Nancy Hornberger, 3–16. New York: Mouton de Gruyter.

———. 2006. "Voice and Biliteracy in Indigenous Language Revitalization:

Contentious Educational Practices in Quechua, Guarani, and Māori Contexts." *Journal of Language, Identity, and Education* 5(4): 277-292.

Huaman, Elizabeth Sumida. 2015. "'Why Can't We Admire Our Own?': Indigenous Youth, Farming, and Education in the Peruvian Andes." In *Indigenous Innovation*, edited by E. S. Huaman and B. Sriraman, 129-148. Leiden: Brill.

Hult, Francis M., and Nancy H. Hornberger. 2016. "Revisiting Orientations in Language Planning: Problem, Right, and Resource as an Analytical Heuristic." *Bilingual Review/Revista Bilingüe* 33(3): 30-49.

Illich, Ivan. 1973. *Tools for Conviviality*. New York: Harper and Row.

Irvine, Judith. 1989. "When Talk Isn't Cheap: Language and Political Economy." *American Ethnologist* 16(2): 248-267.

———. 2004. "'Say When': Temporalities in Language Ideology." *Journal of Linguistic Anthropology* 14(1): 99-109.

Irvine, Judith T., and Susan Gal. 2000. "Language Ideology and Linguistic Differentiation." In *Regimes of Language: Ideologies, Polities, and Identities*, edited by Paul Kroskrity, 35-84. Santa Fe: School of American Research Press.

Jonas, Susanne. 2013. "Guatemalan Migration in Times of Civil War and Post-War Challenges." *Migration Policy Institute*. www.migrationpolicy.org/article/guatemalan-migration-times-civil-war-and-post-war-challenges

Kanno, Yasuko, and Bonny Norton. 2003. "Imagined Communities and Educational Possibilities: Introduction." *Journal of Language, Identity, and Education* 2(4): 241-249.

Kasinitz, Philip, John H. Mollenkopf, Mary Waters, and Jennifer Holdaway. 2008. *Inheriting the City: The Children of Immigrants Come of Age*. New York: Russell Sage Foundation.

Keane, Webb. 2018. "On Semiotic Ideology." *Signs and Society* 6(1): 64-87.

Kovats Sánchez, Gabriela, Melissa Mesinas, Saskias Casanova, David W. Barillas Chón, and

Kramsch, Claire. 2006. "From Communicative Competence to Symbolic Competence." *The Modern Language Journal* 90(2): 249-252.

Kramsch, Claire, and Anne Whiteside. 2008. "Language Ecology in Multilingual Settings. Towards a Theory of Symbolic Competence." *Applied Linguistics* 29(4): 645-671.

Krauss, Michael. 1992. "The World's Languages in Crisis." *Language* 68(1): 4-10.

Kroskrity, Paul, and Barbra Meek. 2023. "On the Social Lives of Indigenous North American Languages." In *A New Companion to Linguistic Anthropology*, edited by Alessandro Duranti, Rachel George, and Robin Conley Riner, 15-32. Hoboken: John Wiley.

Kroupa, Kuunux Teerit. 2013. "Efforts of the Ree-volution." In *Indigenous Youth and Multilingualism: Language Identity, Ideology, and Practice in Dynamic Cultural Worlds*, edited by Teresa McCarty, Leisy Wyman, and Sheilah Nicholas, 168-186. New York: Routledge.

Kwon, Hyeyoung. 2022. "Inclusion Work: Children of Immigrants Claiming Membership in Everyday Life." *American Journal of Sociology* 127(5): 1818-1859.

———. 2024. *Language Brokers: Children of Immigrants Translating Inequality and Belonging for Their Families*. Stanford: Stanford University Press.

Lancy, David. 2015. *The Anthropology of Childhood: Cherubs, Chattel, Changelings*. Cambridge, UK: Cambridge University Press.

Lareau, Annette. 2000. *Home Advantage: Social Class and Parental Intervention in Elementary Education*, 2nd ed. Lanham: Rowan & Littlefield.

———. 2011. *Unequal Childhoods: Race, Class, and Family Life: A Decade Later*, 2nd ed. Oakland: University of California Press.

Laurier, Eric, and Chris Philo. 2006. "Cold Shoulders and Napkins Handed: Gestures of Responsibility." *Transactions of the Institute of British Geographers* 31(2): 193-207.

Lavadenz, Magaly. 2005. "*Como Hablar en Silencio* (Like Speaking in Silence): Issues of Language, Culture, and Identity of Central Americans in Los Angeles." In *Building on Strength: Language and Literacy in Latino Families and Communities*, edited by Ana Celia Zentella, 93-109. New York: Teachers College Press.

Leeman, Jennifer. 2018. "Questioning the Language Questions: Federal Policy and the Evaluation of the US Census Bureau's Statistics on Language." *Survey Methodology* 11: m2015-02.

Leonard, Wesley Y. 2011. "Challenging 'Extinction' Through Modern Miami Language Practices." *American Indian Culture and Research Journal* 35(2): 135-160.

———. 2020. "Insights from Native American Studies for Theorizing Race and Racism in Linguistics (Response to Charity Hudley, Mallinson, and Bucholtz)." *Language* 96(4): e281-e291.

———. 2021. "Afterword: Reclamation and Metalinguistic Communities." In *Metalinguistic Communities: Case Studies of Agency, Ideology, and Symbolic Uses of Language*, edited by Netta Avineri and Jesse Harasta, 249-256. Cham: Palgrave Macmillan.

Lévi-Strauss, Claude. 1974. *The Savage Mind*. London: Weidenfeld and Nicholson.

Levitt, Peggy. 2001. *The Transnational Villagers*. Berkeley: University of California Press.

Loucky, James. 2000. "Maya in a Modern Metropolis: Establishing New Lives and Livelihoods in Los Angeles." In *The Maya Diaspora: Guatemalan Roots, New American Lives*, edited by James Loucky and M. M. Moors, 214-222. Philadelphia: Temple University Press.

Mackay, Tanya. 2023. "Lived Experience in Social Work: An Underutilised Expertise." *British Journal of Social Work* 53(3): 1833-1840.

MacSwan, Jeff. 2000. "The Threshold Hypothesis, Semilingualism, and Other Contributions to a Deficit View of Linguistic Minorities." *Hispanic Journal of Behavioral Sciences* 22(1): 3-45.

Mahler, Sarah. 1995. *American Dreaming: Immigrant Life on the Margins*. Princeton: Princeton University Press.

Manz, Beatriz. 1988. *Refugees of a Hidden War: The Aftermath of Counterinsurgency in Guatemala.* Albany: SUNY Press.

Markey, Charlotte N. 2010. "Invited Commentary: Why Body Image Is Important to Adolescent Development." *Journal of Youth and Adolescence* 39: 1387–1391.

Martin-Beltrán, Melinda. 2010. "Positioning Proficiency: How Students and Teachers (De)Construct Language Proficiency at School." *Linguistics and Education* 21(4): 257–281.

Martínez, Glenn, and Adam Schwartz. 2012. "Elevating 'Low' Language for High Stakes: A Case for Critical, Community-Based Learning in a Medical Spanish for Heritage Learners Program." *Heritage Language Journal* 9(2): 175–187.

Martinez, Isabel. 2019. *Becoming Transnational Youth Workers: Independent Mexican Teenage Migrants and Pathways of Survival and Social Mobility.* New Brunswick: Rutgers University Press.

Martínez, Ramón Antonio, and Melisa Mesinas. 2019. "Linguistic Motherwork in the Zapotec Diaspora: Zapoteca Mothers' Perspectives on Indigenous Language Maintenance." *Association of Mexican American Educators Journal* 13(2): 122–144.

Maxwell, Judith. 2017. "Kib'eyal taq ch'ab'äl: Mayan Language Regimes in Guatemala." *International Journal of the Sociology of Language* 246: 109–133.

McCarty, Teresa. 2011. "Introducing Ethnography and Language Policy." In *Ethnography and Language Policy*, edited by T. McCarty, 1–28. New York: Routledge.

Medina, Jennifer. 2019. "Anyone Speak K'iche' or Mam? Immigration Courts Overwhelmed by Indigenous Languages." *New York Times*, March 19. www.nytimes.com/2019/03/19/us/translators-border-wall-immigration.html

Meek, Barbra. 2011. "Failing American Indian Languages." *American Indian Culture and Research* 35(2): 43–60.

Melander, Charlotte, and Oksana Shmulyar Gréen. 2023. "Language Brokering as Acts of Care: Experiences of Young Migrants Born in Poland and Romania Living in Sweden." *Nordic Social Work Research* 13(4): 577–588.

Menchú, Rigoberta. 2010. *I, Rigoberta Menchú.* New York: Verso Books.

Mendoza-Denton, Norma. 2008. *Homegirls: Language and Cultural Practice Among Latina Youth Gangs.* Malden: Wiley-Blackwell.

Mendoza-Denton, Norma, and Aomar Boum. 2015. "Breached Initiations: Sociopolitical Resources and Conflicts in Emergent Adulthood." *Annual Review of Anthropology* 44: 295–310.

Menjívar, Cecilia. 2001. *Fragmented Ties: Salvadoran Immigrant Networks in America.* Berkeley: University of California Press.

———. 2008. "Violence and Women's Lives in Eastern Guatemala: A Conceptual Framework." *Latin American Research Review* 43(3): 109–136.

———. 2011. *Enduring Violence: Ladina Women's Lives in Guatemala.* Berkeley: University of California Press.

———. 2021. "The Racialization of 'Illegality.'" *Daedalus* 150(2): 91–105.

Messing, Jacqueline. 2013. "'I Didn't Know You Knew Mexicano!': Shifting Ideologies, Identities, and Ambivalence Among Former Youth in Tlaxcala, Mexico." In *Indigenous Youth and Multilingualism,* edited by L. T. Wyman, T. L. McCarty, and S. E. Nicholas, 111–129. New York: Routledge.

Migration Policy Institute. 2019. "Profiles of the Unauthorized Population: Los Angeles County, CA." https://www.migrationpolicy.org/data/unauthorized-immigrant-population/county/6037

Milkman, Ruth. 2020. *Immigrant Labor and the New Precariat.* Cambridge, UK: Polity Press.

Millan, Carlos Guerrero, Bettina Nissen, and Larissa Pschetz. 2024. "Cosmovision of Data: An Indigenous Approach to Technologies for Self-Determination." *CHI '24 Proceedings of the CHI Conference on Human Factors in Computing Systems* 617: 1–13.

Molina, Natalia. 2010. "The Power of Racial Scripts: What the History of Mexican Immigration to the United States Teaches Us About Relational Notions of Race." *Latino Studies* 8(2): 156–175.

Montes, Veronica. 2013. "The Role of Emotions in the Construction of Masculinity: Guatemalan Migrant Men, Transnational Migration, and Family Relations." *Gender & Society* 27(4): 469–490.

Moore, Robert E. 2006. "Disappearing, Inc.: Glimpsing the Sublime in the Politics of Access to Endangered Languages." *Language & Communication* 26(3–4): 296–315.

Morales, P. Zitlali, Lydia A. Saravia, and María Fernanda Pérez-Iribe. 2019. "Multilingual Mexican-Origin Students' Perspectives on Their Indigenous Heritage Language." *Association of Mexican American Educators Journal* 13(2): 91–121.

Moran, Dan, Theresa Catalano, and Héctor Palala Martínez. 2024. "Indigenous Latinx Students and Translanguaging: The Possibilities and Challenges of Using K'iche' in a Kindergarten Spanish-English Handwriting Classroom." *Bilingual Research Journal*: 1–17.

Mortimer, Katherine S., and Gabriela Dolsa. 2020. "Ongoing Emergence: Borderland High School DLBE Students' Self-Identifications as Lingual People." *International Journal of Bilingual Education and Bilingualism* 26(1): 7–19.

Mortimer, Katherine S., and Stanton Wortham. 2015. "Analyzing Language Policy and Social Identification Across Heterogeneous Scales." *Annual Review of Applied Linguistics* 35: 160–172.

Moslimani, Mohamad, Luis Noe-Bustamante, and Sono Shah. 2023. "Facts on Hispanics of Guatemalan Origin in the United States, 2021." Washington, DC: Pew Research Center. www.pewresearch.org/hispanic/fact-sheet/us-hispanics-facts-on-guatemalan-origin-latinos/

Muehlmann, Shaylih. 2012. "Rhizomes and Other Uncountables: The Malaise of Enumeration in Mexico's Colorado River Delta." *American Ethnologist* 39(2): 339–353.

Mühlhäusler, Peter. 2011. "Ecolinguistics, Linguistic Diversity, Ecological Diversity." In *The Postcolonial Science and Technology Studies Reader*, edited by Sandra Harding, 198–210. Durham: Duke University Press.

Musalo, Karen. 2018. "El Salvador—A Peace Worse Than War: Violence, Gender, and a Failed Legal Response." *Yale Journal of Law and Feminism* 30(3): 1–97.

Neckerman, Kathryn M., Prudence Carter, and Jennifer Lee. 1999. "Segmented Assimilation and Minority Cultures of Mobility." *Ethnic and Racial Studies* 22(6): 945–965.

Nelson, Diane, Nhenety Kariri-Xocó, Idiane Kariri-Xocó, and Thea Pitman. 2023. "'We Most Certainly Do Have a Language': Decolonizing Discourses of Language Extinction." *Environmental Humanities* 15(1): 187–207.

Newdick, Vivian, and Odilia Romero. 2019. "Interpretation Is an Act of Resistance: Indigenous Organizations Respond to 'Zero Tolerance' and 'Family Separation.'" *LASA Forum: The Languages and Literature of Abiayala* 1(50): 30–34.

Newman, Tarkington J., Dawn Anderson-Butcher, Kendra Bostick, and Sandra Black. 2021. "Psychological Processes Involved in Life Skill Transfer: Understanding the Lived Experiences of Youth Recognized as Being Socially Vulnerable." *Child and Adolescent Social Work Journal* 38: 423–436.

Newman, Tarkington J., Fernando Santos, Sandra Black, and Kendra Bostick. 2022. "Learning Life Skills Through Challenging and Negative Experiences." *Child and Adolescent Social Work Journal* 39(4): 455–469.

Nicholas, Sheilah E. 2013. ""Being" Hopi by "Living" Hopi." In *Indigenous Youth and Multilingualism: Language Identity, Ideology, and Practice in Dynamic Cultural Worlds*, edited by Teresa McCarty, Leisy Wyman, and Sheilah Nicholas, 70–89. New York: Routledge.

Nichols, Briana. 2021. "Nothing Is Easy: Educational Striving and Migration Deferral in Guatemala." *Journal of Ethnic and Migration Studies* 49(7): 1919–1935.

———. 2024. "Contesting Educational Imaginaries at the Intersection of Migration and Transnational Development in Guatemala." *Anthropology & Education Quarterly* 55: 1–23.

Nichols, Johanna. 1992. *Linguistic Diversity in Space and Time*. Chicago: University of Chicago Press.

Nolan, Rachel. 2019. "A Translation Crisis at the Border." *New Yorker*, December 30. www.newyorker.com/magazine/2020/01/06/a-translation-crisis-at-the-border

Nurmi, Jari-Erik. 1991. "How Do Adolescents See Their Future? A Review of the Development of Future Orientation and Planning." *Developmental Review* 11: 1–59.

Obinna, Denise N. 2021. "Alone in a Crowd: Indigenous Migrants and Language Barriers in American Immigration." *Race and Justice* 13(4): 488–505.

Obinna, Denise N., and Layton M. Field. 2019. "Geographic and Spatial Assimilation of Immigrants from Central America's North Triangle." *International Migration* 57(3): 81–97.

O'Connor, Brendan H. 2016. "Racializing Discourse in Public and Private: Social Differentiation and the Question of Mexicanness at an Arizona High School." *Anthropology & Education Quarterly* 47(2): 130–147.

O'Connor, Brendan H., and Stephanie L. Canizales. 2023. "Thresholds of Liminality: Discourse and Embodiment from Separation to Consummation Among Guatemalan Maya Youth Workers in Los Angeles." *International Journal of the Sociology of Language* 279: 155–179.

Oeur, Freeden Blume, and Donna Varga. 2024. "Colonialism, Racism, and Childhoods: Introduction." *American Behavioral Scientist*. Online first. https://doi.org/10.1177/00027642241268

Oliveira, Gabrielle. 2018. *Motherhood Across Borders*. New York: NYU Press.

Olmedo, Irma M. 2003. "Language Mediation Among Emergent Bilingual Children." *Linguistics and Education* 14(2): 143–162.

Ong, Aihwa. 2006. "Mutations in Citizenship." *Theory, Culture & Society* 23(2-3): 499–505.

Orellana, Marjorie Faulstich. 2009. *Translating Childhoods: Immigrant Youth, Language, and Culture*. New Brunswick: Rutgers University Press.

Oster, Ryan. 2024. "Guatemalan Civil War 1960-1996." US Department of Defense: Study of Internal Conflicts Case Studies, Study Sequence No. 36. https://media.defense.gov/2024/Mar/20/2003416572/-1/-1/0/20240306_GUATEMALANCIVILWAR_1960-96.PDF

Park, Robert E. 1914. "Racial Assimilation in Secondary Groups with Particular Reference to the Negro." *American Journal of Sociology* 19(5): 606–623.

Patler, Caitlin. 2018. "To Reveal or Conceal: How Diverse Undocumented Youth Navigate Legal Status Dislosure." *Sociological Perspectives* 61(6): 857–873.

Pennycook, Alastair. 2001. *Critical Applied Linguistics: A Critical Introduction*. Mahwah: LEA.

Pentón Herrera, Luis Javier. 2022. "Creating Positive Learning Communities for Diasporic Indigenous Students." *Journal of Multilingual and Multicultural Development*. https://doi.org/10.1080/01434632.2022.2159033

Perez, Carlos. 2009. "Indigenous Languages: Nahuatl, Quechua, and Maya: A Study of Multilingual Immigrant Students and Their Families." *Multicultural Education* 17(1): 22–26.

Pérez Báez, Gabriela. 2013. "Family Language Policy, Transnationalism, and the Diaspora Community of San Lucas Quiaviní of Oaxaca, Mexico." *Language Policy* 12(1): 27–45.

———. 2014. "Determinants of Language Reproduction and Shift in a Transnational Community." *International Journal of the Sociology of Language* 227: 65–81.

Perla, Héctor. 2013. "Central American Counterpublic Mobilization: Transnational Social Movement Opposition to Reagan's Foreign Policy Toward Central America." *Latino Studies* 11: 167–189.

Pierce, Sarah. 2015. "Unaccompanied Child Migrants in U.S. Communities, Immigration Court, and Schools." Washington, DC: Migration Policy Institute. www.migrationpolicy.org/research/unaccompanied-child-migrants-us-communities-immigration-court-and-schools

Pollock, Mica. 2004. "Race-Bending: 'Mixed' Youth Practicing Strategic Racialization in California." *Anthropology & Education Quarterly* 35(1): 30–52.

Popkin, Eric. 2005. "The Emergence of Pan-Mayan Ethnicity in the Guatemalan Transnational Community Linking Santa Eulalia and Los Angeles." *Current Sociology* 53: 675–706.

Portes, Alejandro, and Patricia Landolt. 2000. "Social Capital: Promise and Pitfalls of Its Role in Development." *Journal of Latin American Studies* 32(2): 529–547.

Portes, Alejandro, and Dag MacLeod. 1996. "Educational Progress of Children of Immigrants: The Roles of Class, Ethnicity, and School Context." *Sociology of Education* 69(4): 255–275.

Portes, Alejandro, and Rubén G. Rumbaut. 2001. *Legacies: The Story of the Immigrant Second Generation*. Berkeley: University of California Press.

———. 2006. *Immigrant America: A Portrait*, 3rd ed., rev., expanded, and updated. Berkeley: University of California Press.

Portes, Alejandro, and Min Zhou. 1993. "The New Second Generation: Segmented Assimilation and Its Variants." *The Annals of the American Academy of Political and Social Science* 530(1): 74–96.

Pugh, Allison. 2009. *Longing and Belonging: Parents, Children, and Consumer Culture*. Berkeley: University of California Press.

Ramírez, Catherine Sue. 2020. *Assimilation: An Alternative History*. Oakland: University of California Press.

Restall, Matthew, and Amara Solari. 2020. *The Maya: A Very Short Introduction*. Online edition. Oxford Academic. www.doi.org/10.1093/actrade/9780190645021.001.0001

Ribas, Vanesa. 2016. *On the Line: Slaughterhouse Lives and the Making of the New South*. Berkeley: University of California Press.

Riley, Kathleen C. 2011. "Language Socialization and Language Ideologies." In *The Handbook of Language Socialization*, edited by Alessandro Duranti, Elinor Ochs, and Bambi B. Schieffelin, 493–514. Malden: Wiley-Blackwell.

Romero, Sergio. 2018. "Ethnicity, History and Standard Ixhil (Ixil) Mayan." *Language & Communication* 61: 102–112.

Rosa, Jonathan. 2019. *Looking Like a Language, Sounding Like a Race: Raciolinguistic Ideologies and the Learning of Latinidad*. New York: Oxford University Press.

Rosales, Rocio. 2020. *Fruteros: Street Vending, Illegality, and Ethnic Community in Los Angeles*. Oakland: University of California Press.

Roth-Gordon, Jennifer. 2017. *Race and the Brazilian Body: Blackness, Whiteness, and Everyday Language in Rio de Janeiro*. Oakland: University of California Press.

Rubin, Beth C., and Hana Cervinkova. 2019. "Challenging Silences: Democratic

Citizenship Education and Historical Memory in Poland and Guatemala." *Anthropology & Education Quarterly* 51(2): 178–194.
Ruiz, Richard. 1984. "Orientations in Language Planning." *NABE Journal* 8(2): 15–34.
———. 2010. "Reorienting Language-as-Resource." In *International Perspectives on Bilingual Education: Policy, Practice, and Controversy*, edited by J. Petrovic, 155–172. Charlotte: Information Age.
Rymes, Betsy. 2014. "Marking Communicative Repertoire Through Metacommentary." In *Heteroglossia as Practice and Pedagogy*, edited by Adrian Blackledge and Angela Creese, 301–316. Dordrecht: Springer.
Sacks, Harvey. 1987. "On the Preferences for Agreement and Continuity in Sequences in Conversation." In *Talk and Social Organization*, edited by Graham Button and John R. E. Lee, 54–69. Clevedon, UK: Multilingual Matters.
Sangaramoorthy, Thurka. 2019. "Liminal Living: Everyday Injury, Disability, and Instability Among Migrant Mexican Women in Maryland's Seafood Industry." *Medical Anthropology Quarterly* 33(4): 557–578.
Schiffrin, Deborah. 1981. "Tense Variation in Narrative." *Language* 57(1): 45–62.
Selee, Andrew, Valerie Lacarte, Ariel G. Ruiz Soto, Diego Chaves-González, María Jesús Mora, and Andrea Tanco. 2023. "In a Dramatic Shift, the Americas Have Become a Leading Migration Destination." Washington, DC: Migration Policy Institute. www.migrationpolicy.org/article/latin-america-caribbean-immigration-shift
Shepherd, Katie. 2020. "Indigenous People Face Persistent Language Access Challenges in Immigration Detention." American Immigration Council: Immigration Impact. www.immigrationimpact.com/2020/10/12/indigenous-people-language-barriers-immigration/
Silverstein, Michael. 1998. "Monoglot 'Standard' in America: Standardization and Metaphors of Linguistic Hegemony." In *The Matrix of Language*, edited by D. Brenneis and R. H. S. Macaulay, 284–306. New York: Routledge.
Simons, Gary F., and Paul Lewis. 2013. "The World's Languages in Crisis: A 20-Year Update." In *Responses to Language Endangerment: In Honor of Mickey Noonan*, edited by Elena Mihas, Bernard Perley, Gabriel Rei-Doval, and Kathleen Wheatley, 3–20. Amsterdam and Philadelphia: John Benjamins.
Skutnabb-Kangas, Tove. 2000. *Linguistic Genocide in Education—Or Worldwide Diversity and Human Rights?* New York: Routledge.
Small, Mario L., and Leah E. Gose. 2020. "How do Low-Income People Form Survival Networks? Routine Organizations as Brokers." *The Annals of the American Academy* 689(1): 89–109.
Stanton-Salazar, Ricardo D. 2011. "A Social Capital Framework for the Study of Institutional Agents and Their Role in Empowerment of Low-Status Students and Youth." *Youth & Society* 43(3): 1066–1109.

Stepick, Alex, and Carol D. Stepick. 2010. "The Complexities and Confusions of Segmented Assimilation." *Ethnic and Racial Studies* 33(7): 1149–1167.

Striffler, Steven, and Mark Moberg, eds. 2003. *Banana Wars: Power, Production, and History in the Americas.* Durham: Duke University Press.

Suárez-Orozco, Carola, Marcelo Suárez-Orozco, and Irina Todorova. 2008. *Learning a New Land: Immigrant Students in American Society.* Cambridge, MA: Harvard University Press.

Suárez-Orozco, Marcelo M. 1987. "'Becoming Somebody': Central American Immigrants in US Inner-City Schools." *Anthropology & Education Quarterly* 18(4): 287–299.

Szakolczai, Arpad. 2009. "Liminality and Experience: Structuring Transitory Situations and Transformative Events." *International Political Anthropology* 2(1): 141–172.

Táíwò, Olúfémi O. 2021. "When the United Fruit Company Tried to Buy Guatemala." *The Nation.* https://www.thenation.com/article/economy/united-fruit-guatemala/

Thomas, William Isaac, and Florian Znaniecki. 1918. *The Polish Peasant in Europe and America: Primary-Group, Organization,* vol. 2. Chicago: University of Chicago Press.

Turner, Victor. 1967. *The Ritual Process: Structure and Anti-Structure.* Chicago: Aldine.

Urrieta, Luis, Jr., Melissa Mesinas, and Ramón A. Martínez. 2019. "Critical Latinx Indigeneities and Education: An Introduction." *Association of Mexican American Educators Journal* 13(2): 1–14.

USAID. 2018. "Education Links: Improving the Lives of Guatemalan Youth." www.edu-links.org/learning/improving-lives-guatemalan-youth

———. 2023a. "Guatemala: Education." Washington, DC. www.idea.usaid.gov/cd/guatemala/education

———. 2023b. "Youth in Guatemala." Washington, DC. www.usaid.gov/guatemala/our-approach/youth

US Citizenship and Immigration Services (USCIS). n.d. "O-1 Visa: Individuals with Extraordinary Ability or Achievement." Washington, DC. www.uscis.gov/working-in-the-united-states/temporary-workers/o-1-visa-individuals-with-extraordinary-ability-or-achievement

US Customs and Border Protection. 2023. "Southwest Land Border Encounters." Washington, DC. www.cbp.gov/newsroom/stats/southwest-land-border-encounters

US Department of Health and Human Services. 2023. "Fact Sheet: Unaccompanied Children (UC) Program." Washington, DC. www.hhs.gov/sites/default/files/uac-program-fact-sheet.pdf

US Department of State. 2023. "U.S. Relations with Guatemala: Bilateral Rela-

tions Fact Sheet." Washington, DC. www.state.gov/u-s-relations-with-guatemala/
US Department of State, Office of the Historian. n.d. "Guatemala 1952–1954." https://history.state.gov/historicaldocuments/frus1952-54Guat/comp1
US Institute of Peace. 1997. "Truth Commission: Guatemala." www.usip.org/publications/1997/02/truth-commission-guatemala
Valdés, Guadalupe. 2003. *Expanding Definitions of Giftedness: The Case of Young Interpreters from Immigrant Communities*. New York: Routledge.
Vallejo, Jody Agius, and Stephanie L. Canizales. 2023. "Ethnoracial Capitalism and the Limits of Ethnic Solidarity." *Social Problems* 70(4): 961–980.
Vásquez-Colina, M. D. 2019. "Teachers Know, but We Do Too: The Case of Mayan Parents' Assessment Knowledge." *Journal of Latinos and Education*: 1–13.
Velasco, Patricia. 2010. "Indigenous Students in Bilingual Spanish-English Classrooms in New York: A Teacher's Mediation Strategies." *International Journal of the Sociology of Language* (206): 255–271.
———. 2014. "The Language and Educational Ideologies of Mixteco-Mexican Mothers." *Journal of Latinos and Education* 13(2): 85–106.
Vidal de Haymes, Maria, Adam Avrushin, and Deidra Coleman. 2018. "Educating Unaccompanied Immigrant Children in Chicago, Illinois: A Case Study." *Children and Youth Services Review* 92: 77–88.
Vizenor, Gerald. 1999. *Manifest Manners: Narratives on Postindian Survivance*. Lincoln: University of Nebraska Press.
Waldinger, Roger. 2001. *Strangers at the Gates: New Immigrants in Urban America*. Berkeley: University of California Press.
Waldinger, Roger, and Michael Lichter. 2003. *How the Other Half Works: Immigration and the Social Organization of Labor*. Berkeley: University of California Press.
Wang, Hansi Lo. 2014. "Language Barriers Post Challenges for Mayan Migrant Children." *NPR: Code Switch*, July 1. www.npr.org/sections/codeswitch/2014/07/01/326426927/language-barriers-pose-challenges-for-mayan-migrant-children
Warner, W. Lloyd, and Leo Srole. 1945. *The Social Systems of American Ethnic Groups*. New Haven: Yale University Press.
Warner-Garcia, Shawn. 2014. "Laughing When Nothing's Funny: The Pragmatic Use of Coping Laughter in the Negotiation of Conversational Disagreement." *Pragmatics* 24(1): 157–180.
Warriner, Doris S. 2007. "Transnational Literacies: Immigration, Language Learning, and Identity." *Linguistics and Education* 18(3–4): 201–214.
———. 2016. "'Here, Without English, You Are Dead': Ideologies of Language and Discourses of Neoliberalism in Adult English Language Learning." *Journal of Multilingual and Multicultural Development* 37(5): 495–508.

Watanabe, Yuko, and Merrill Swain. 2008. "Perception of Learner Proficiency: Its Impact on the Interaction Between an ESL Learner and Her Higher and Lower Proficiency Partners." *Language Awareness* 17: 115–130.

Weinberg, Miranda, and Haley De Korne. 2016. "Who Can Speak Lenape in Pennsylvania? Authentication and Language Learning in an Endangered Language Community of Practice." *Language & Communication* 47: 124–134.

Wellmeier, Nancy. 1998. *Ritual, Identity, and the Mayan Diaspora.* New York: Routledge.

Whiteside, Anne. 2009. "'We Don't Speak Maya, Spanish or English': Yucatec Maya-Speaking Transnationals in California and the Social Construction of Competence." In *The Native Speaker Concept: Ethnographic Investigations of Native Speaker Effects,* edited by Neriko Musha Doerr, 209–232. Berlin and New York: Walter de Gruyter.

———. 2013. "Research on Transnational Yucatec Maya-Speakers Negotiating Multilingual California." *Journal of Applied Linguistics and Professional Practice* 3(1): 103–112.

Whyte, Michael. 2013. "Episodic Fieldwork, Updating, and Sociability." *Social Analysis* 57(1): 110–121.

Wolfe, Patrick. 2006. "Settler Colonialism and the Elimination of the Native." *Journal of Genocide Research* 8(4): 387–409.

Wyman, Leisy T. 2012. *Youth Culture, Language Endangerment and Linguistic Survivance.* Clevedon, UK: Multilingual Matters.

Wyman, Leisy T., Teresa L. McCarty, and Sheilah E. Nicholas, eds. 2013. *Indigenous Youth and Multilingualism: Language Identity, Ideology, and Practice in Dynamic Cultural Worlds.* New York: Routledge.

Youth.gov. n.d. "Adolescent Development." Washington, DC. www.youth.gov/youth-topics/adolescent-health/adolescent-development

Zamora, Sylvia. 2022. *Racial Baggage: Mexican Immigrants and Race Across the Border.* Stanford: Stanford University Press.

Zelizer, Vivianna. 1985. *Pricing the Priceless Child: Changing Social Values of Children.* Princeton: Princeton University Press.

Zentella, Ana Celia. 1995. "The 'Chiquitafication' of US Latinos and Their Languages, OR Why We Need an Anthropolitical Linguistics." In *SALSA III: Proceedings of the Symposium on Language and Society,* 1–18. Austin, Texas.

Zhou, Min, Jennifer Lee, Jody Agius Vallejo, Rosaura Tafoya-Estrada, and Yang Sao Xiong. 2008. "Success Attained, Deterred, and Denied: Divergent Pathways to Social Mobility in Los Angeles's New Second Generation." *The Annals of the American Academy of Political and Social Science* 620(1): 37–61.

Zyskind, Karen, Meagan Dorman, Yessenia Medina, and Gabriela Pérez Báez. 2024. "Visibility for Indigenous Students and Their Languages: Analysis of Home Language Data in Federal Reports Across Seven US States." *Social Sciences* 13(8): 427.

INDEX

Aarón, 4, 71-72, 132, 137, 143, 148, 159-61, 169; and adaptation, 101, 111-12, 142; and anti-Indigenous discrimination, 43-49, 52-55, 86, 109; and isolation, 40; and preparation, 87-88, 110-11; and shyness/fear, 53, 141
abandono (abandonment), 25, 33, 39-40, 53-54, 123, 143, 152
abuse, 35, 55, 57-58, 74, 148
acculturation, 149, 165. *See also* assimilation; incorporation, immigrant
activism, 16-18, 33
adaptación (adaptation), 3-9, 12-15, 19-25, 56, 159, 161-71, 176-77, 181n49; measuring, 95-98, 101-2, 108-17; and preparation, 65, 67, 69-70, 81, 84, 87-88, 91-94; and survival, 118-21, 123-25, 128, 134-36, 141-42, 151-52. *See also* adjustment
adjustment, 4-5, 12, 96, 134, 163, 165. *See also adaptación* (adaption)

adulthood, 4-5, 7, 98, 107, 160, 168, 175; and diaspora, 35-36, 46, 52, 61; and preparation, 63-66, 74, 90, 93-94; and survival, 121-23, 134, 150-53
advice. *See consejos* (advice)
agency, 5, 13, 17, 24, 65-66, 121, 152-53, 167, 175; and adaptation, 103, 115, 117
agricultural labor, 22, 27, 31-32, 39, 42, 84
Akateko language, 22
Alberto, 51-52, 55, 83
Alejandro, 138-40
Alonso, 133-34
American Community Survey, 171
Americanization, 165-66. *See also* assimilation; incorporation, immigrant
Andrés, 1-7, 9, 45, 58-60, 64, 78-79, 84-85, 92, 102-3, 105-6, 108-9, 111, 132
anthropology, 4, 11, 34-37, 174; linguistic, 16, 22, 59, 80

211

anti-immigrant sentiment, 4, 6, 10-11, 126, 162, 166, 188n1
anti-Indigenous racism, 4, 10, 13, 23, 106-7, 161-62, 166; and diaspora, 29-30, 34, 37, 43, 48-50, 53, 56-67; and preparation, 65, 86-87; and survival, 124-25, 148, 152-53. *See also* discrimination; racism
apprehensions, migrant youth, 7-9, 145-46. *See also* deportation; violence
Árbenz, Jacobo, 32
Arévalo, Juan José, 32
Argentina, 176
armed conflict, 30-34, 36, 38, 159-61
Arikara people, 18
arrival, US, 4-8, 10, 87-89, 118, 121, 125-27, 149, 177; and adaptation, 104, 110; and diaspora, 38, 50-54, 57
assimilation, 25, 80, 105, 117, 147, 165, 167
aunts, 68
auto industry work, 57, 106
autonomy, 63, 122. *See also* independence, youth
ayuda (help), 111, 114, 120, 138-41, 146, 149-51; and diaspora, 41-43, 52, 56-57; and preparation, 62-65, 78, 81, 88-92

balanced bilingualism, 99
banana production, 31-32
Barrio 18 gang, 36
Batz, Giovanni, 11
Bellino, Michelle J., 32
belonging, 18, 24, 34, 41, 97-99, 122-23, 133; and preparation, 66, 79, 83, 87-89
Bible, the, 78-79
bilingualism, 17-20, 89-91, 121, 130, 172-73; and adaptation, 97-99, 106, 114-16; balanced, 99. *See also* monolingualism; multilingualism; semilingualism; translanguaging; trilingualism
Black Christ, 143
Black people, 48, 159
Bloemraad, Irene, 167
borders, national, 10, 14, 30, 41, 60, 74, 80, 163, 170. *See also* US-Mexico border
bounded solidarity, 10
Brayant, 46, 138
Brazil, 176
breached initiations, 74
brightening, 126-27, 143, 161, 168
brothers, 39-40, 43, 56, 73-74, 87-88, 150-52
Brubaker, Rogers, 163
Bryson, 79

caregivers, 9, 12, 23, 63, 81, 122, 165, 176; and diaspora, 39, 42, 50
Carlos, 107, 129
Castillo Armas, Carlos, 32-33
Caterina, 41-43, 56-57
Catholic Church, 31, 33, 70-72, 79. *See also* church participation
Celigueta, Gemma, 34
Central American immigrants, 11, 48, 147, 165, 170, 176; as youth, 7-8, 20, 34, 116, 183n32
Central Intelligence Agency (CIA), 32
children, 7-9, 14, 26, 100, 161, 164-66, 170, 174-75; and diaspora, 33-36, 38, 40-42, 46, 48-57, 183n32; and preparation, 63-64, 67-68, 73-74, 84-85; and survival, 122, 132, 145-47, 150, 153, 187n6. *See also* adolescence; teenagers; young adults
Chile, 176
church participation, 54, 70-72, 79, 84, 94, 119-21, 133, 137, 139, 142-43,

166, 169. *See also* Catholic Church; Protestants
Civil Rights Act, Title IV, 156
climate change, 15-16, 34
clothing, 3, 14, 28, 48-49, 51, 115-16, 126, 142
coethnic communities, 13, 25, 50, 61, 102, 165, 168; and preparation, 67-68, 94; and survival, 122-25, 137, 152
Cold War, 32-33
colonial codes of power, 7, 19, 57, 167
collectivism, 13, 24, 37-38, 66, 89, 163-65; and adaptation, 98, 111-14; and survival, 121, 123, 127, 137-38, 141, 147-48, 153
Colombia, 176
colonialism, 3-7, 13, 15, 17-19, 129, 160, 166-67; and adaptation, 106, 109-10, 115; and diaspora, 28-31, 37-38, 46, 49, 54-55, 57; and preparation, 69, 80
coming of age, 23, 64-67, 90, 103, 122, 149, 175-76; and diaspora, 41, 58. *See also* teenagers
community-based language policy, 169, 174-75
community gardens, 3, 76-77, 81, 114, 185n22
community life, 6, 9, 12-14, 20, 155, 157-72, 174-77; and adaptation, 97-99, 101, 109-16; and diaspora, 36-37, 43, 48, 50, 58, 60; and language, 15, 18-19, 23, 25, 93-94, 96-101, 109-16; and preparation, 65-70, 73, 77, 81-83, 86-89; and survival, 121-27, 129-35, 137-44, 147-54
community organizations, 147, 155-56, 161, 164, 170-72; and preparation, 68, 70, 81, 93-94. *See also* Voces de Esperanza
concealment, 1, 3, 6, 24, 55, 88, 159, 168, 180n11; and survival, 123, 127-32, 145, 153

consejos (advice), 62, 64-65, 77-79, 81
convivial tools, 112
coping laughter, 128
Costa Rica, 31-32
country of origin, 6-12, 30, 87, 94, 127, 164, 177, 184n48
court systems, 9, 156-57, 173
cousins, 43, 68, 73
critical youth studies, 175

Democratic Spring (Eternal Spring), 32
deportation, 8, 34, 36, 124, 148. *See also* apprehensions, migrant youth
Delia, 131
delinquency, 36
desahogo (emotional unburdening), 24, 73-78, 140, 164
desperation, 40, 73-74, 135, 140
detention, 157, 170-71
Día del Cristo Negro, 143-44
Día del Salvadoreño, 143
dialects, 84, 107-9, 118-21, 130, 159-61, 177; and diaspora, 28-29, 45, 58-59
diaspora, 2, 5-7, 11-15, 18-20, 26, 157-58, 161-69, 172, 176; and adaptation, 97-99, 102, 112, 116; and preparation, 64-67, 81, 93; and survival, 123-26, 135, 142-43, 147-48, 154; youth becoming, 38, 50, 60
differential inclusion, 10-12
disappearance, 33, 129
discrimination, 3, 5-6, 9, 11, 23-24, 164-65, 179n1; and adaptation, 96, 105-7, 110; and diaspora, 29-30, 34, 44-49, 53-60; and preparation, 65, 68, 70, 84-88, 92; and survival, 123-31, 144-45, 153-54, 159. *See also* anti-Indigenous racism; harassment; marginalization; mistreatment; persecution; racism; stereotyping

INDEX

dislocation, 24–25, 74, 123–24, 162, 164; and diaspora, 29–30, 35–37, 39–43, 46–53, 56, 60; quotidian, 23, 29, 39–41, 49, 60, 177. *See also* displacement

disorientation, 4, 12, 21–24, 104–5, 159, 162–64, 170, 175–77; and diaspora, 29–30, 50–53, 60–61; and preparation, 64–66, 81, 93–94; and survival, 118, 123–25, 128, 134, 140–41, 146, 152. *See also orientación* (orientation)

displacement, 4, 24, 159, 162–64, 170, 175–77; and diaspora, 29–30, 35–40, 43, 53, 57–60; and preparation, 65, 74, 93; and survival, 123–25, 141, 146, 152. *See also* dislocation

Doll Test, 48

Dolsa, Gabriela, 116

domestic abuse, 35

domestic work, 57, 84, 132

Dreamers, 116–17

DuBord, Elise M., 90, 106

Echo Park Library, 133

economics, 4–11, 14, 21–23, 160, 165, 168; and adaptation, 101–3, 106, 112, 114, 116–17; and diaspora, 31–38, 41, 50–51; and preparation, 65–70, 73–76, 83, 87, 89–90; and survival, 121, 123, 125–26, 131, 134–35, 147–50, 153; and US interests, 32, 34–35

education, 6, 9–11, 19–21, 24–26, 95–96, 100, 170–75, 183n32; and diaspora, 32, 35, 37–39, 41–43, 46, 55–57; and preparation, 65, 71–72, 75, 80–91; and survival, 119, 126, 140, 146–47, 150, 157. *See also* language learning; schools

Eisenhower, Dwight D., 32

Eladio, 137–38

elders, 34, 62–65, 77, 80, 136

elimination, logic of, 17, 158

El Salvador, 32. *See also* Salvadoran immigrants

emotional resources, 5, 7, 12, 21, 24, 160–68; and adaptation, 95–96, 107–8; and diaspora, 37–38, 53, 56–57, 60; and preparation, 64–66, 69–70, 73, 77–78, 81, 93–94; and survival, 119, 122–23, 133–34, 137–38, 144, 150–52. *See also desahogo* (emotional unburdening)

employment, 5–6, 9–12, 20, 23–24, 163, 166, 171; and adaptation, 96–97, 101–6, 110–12, 114; and diaspora, 27–29, 36–37, 39–43, 51–53, 57–60; and preparation, 64–68, 71–73, 78, 82–87, 90–92; and survival, 124, 136, 140, 143, 147–51

empowerment, 5, 16, 57, 77, 88, 140, 143, 174

enforceable trust, 10

English as a Second Language (ESL), 71, 95, 100, 112

English language, 5, 7, 10, 15, 18–25, 155–59, 166–74; and adaptation, 95–117; and diaspora, 29, 50–57; monoglot standard, 117; and preparation, 66–69, 71–72, 80–85, 89–92, 185n18; and survival, 118–21, 126, 129–32, 136–37, 144–45, 150

Enrique, 62–66, 69, 76–77, 91–92, 95–96, 101, 103, 174–75

erasure, 11, 15, 17, 94, 123, 129, 148, 158; and diaspora, 33, 58

Estrada, Alicia, 14

ethnolinguistic communities, 98, 147, 165

ethnoracial identities, 4, 6, 8, 10–11, 158–65, 176; and diaspora, 29–31, 34, 38, 40, 50, 58, 60; and survival, 126–27, 140–41, 148–49, 151. *See also* coethnic communities

exclusion, 10, 84–85, 156, 165–66, 173, 179n7; and diaspora, 46, 58, 60; and survival, 121–23, 151
expertise, 16, 96, 128, 161, 164, 170–76
exploitation, 9, 11, 21, 114, 143–44, 148–49; and diaspora, 31, 50, 58; and preparation, 74, 85–86, 90
extractive industries, 34, 40

factory work, 20, 27, 83–85, 92, 105, 148–49
families, 6–7, 9–12, 18, 22–26, 161–66, 168–75, 187n6; and adaptation, 97, 100–101, 110–11, 115–16; and diaspora, 29, 32–43, 50–55, 61; and preparation, 63, 65–69, 72–76, 82–83, 86–90, 93–94; and survival, 122–23, 142, 146, 149–52. *See also* aunts; brothers; cousins; fathers; grandparents; mothers; parents; siblings; sisters; uncles
fathers, 2, 39–41, 146, 150
fear. *See miedo* (fear)
Felipe, 85, 90–91, 106–7, 128–30
femicide, 35
Fernando, 54–55, 59–60, 149
Fishman, Joshua, 16
Fourth Invasion, 34
friendships, 3, 27, 44, 156, 165; and adaptation, 106, 109, 112, 119; and preparation, 70, 75, 87; and survival, 119, 130, 136–37, 147
future-making, 5–7, 13–14, 17–19, 23–25, 96, 158–69, 172, 176, 177; and adaptation, 97–99, 101–3, 106, 111–12, 115–17; and diaspora, 30, 35, 37, 42, 50, 57; and preparation, 66–67, 69–70, 72, 74, 82–94; and survival, 121–27, 134–37, 140, 142, 144, 146–53

gangs, 34, 36, 79, 131
Garífuna people, 34

garment industry, 1, 20, 84–86, 95, 105, 114, 129, 148–50; and diaspora, 27, 51, 56–59
gender, 20, 77, 114, 140, 179n7, 182n1, 185n12; and diaspora, 35, 43, 58. *See also* men; women
genocide, 32–37, 60, 161, 171
Geoffrey, 136–38
Germany, 31
globalization, 90, 99, 103
Go, Julian, 29
God, 2, 70–71, 76–77, 83, 92, 107, 139. *See also* spirituality
Gómez Cervantes, Andrea, 131
González, Norma, 174
Gonzalo, 85–86, 101, 107, 129–30, 150–52
Graded Intergenerational Disruption Scale, 16
grandparents, 40–41, 43, 86
Guatemala City, Guatemala, 33, 40
Guatemalan Civil War, 32–36
Guatemalan Commission for Historical Clarification Report, 33
Guatemalan history, 28–38, 90, 160

Hagan, Jacqueline, 57
Hanks, William, 4
harassment, 46, 78–79, 85. *See also* discrimination; oppression
health care, 5, 9, 11, 37, 91–92, 101. *See also* mental health; well-being
Heidbrink, Lauren, 36
help. *See ayuda* (help)
hierarchies, 4, 9–12, 29–30, 36, 40, 58–60, 158–59, 165. *See also* inequality; inferiority; subordination
Hill, Jane, 16
hispano/as, 44, 179n7
homemaking, 6, 13, 25
homogenization, 8, 11
Honduras, 31–32

hopelessness, 40, 78, 122
Hopi people, 18
housing, 7-11, 28, 51, 72, 131
Huehuetenango, Guatemala, 8, 47
humanity, 29, 59-60, 159, 161
human rights, 32-35, 52, 156, 158, 161, 170-72
hybrid hegemonies, 11-13, 80, 86, 93, 160, 163, 175, 181n41; and diaspora, 35, 53; and survival, 110, 123, 126-27, 134

identities, 11, 17-18, 23-26, 117, 148-49, 162-65, 174, 179n7; and diaspora, 31, 43, 48-50, 60; and preparation, 66-67, 93. *See also* Indigeneity; Mayan identities
ideologies, 5-7, 10, 17-20, 25, 55, 159-62, 169-70, 173-75; and adaptation, 97-102, 104-9, 112-16; and preparation, 65-69, 84, 86, 92-93; and survival, 122-26, 135-36, 144-45, 152-54
"illegal" (term), 10-11, 126
Illich, Ivan, 112
inclusion, 4, 60, 85, 165, 176-77; differential, 10-12; and survival, 122-23, 142, 157, 161-62
incorporation, immigrant, 4, 6, 9-15, 20, 23-26, 162-67, 174-76, 185n18; and adaptation, 95-96, 110, 113; and diaspora, 38, 41, 46, 50, 53; and preparation, 64-67, 80, 84, 93-94; and survival, 120-24, 134, 147-48, 152-53
independence, youth, 7, 51, 107, 120, 150, 161-64, 176; and preparation, 65-69, 81, 94. *See also* autonomy
indígena (term), 34, 46
Indigeneity, 14, 25, 94, 97, 107, 125-32, 135, 152-54; and diaspora, 34, 53-54, 57

indigenización, 34
Indigenous land, 31-33, 37
Indigenous languages, 3, 9, 15-18, 21, 26, 155-58, 161, 169-76; and adaptation, 106, 108; and diaspora, 29, 49; and preparation, 67, 80, 84, 92, 94; and survival, 135, 145, 152. *See also* Mayan languages
Indios (term), 2, 52, 108, 141; discrimination against, 31, 34, 45, 48, 55, 58, 84, 106, 148, 153, 159-61
individualism, 25, 98, 114, 123, 141, 148
inequality, 25, 36, 57, 97. *See also* hierarchies; inferiority; subordination
inequality regimes, 57-58
inferiority, 5-7, 24, 93, 96, 107-9, 160; and diaspora, 28, 45, 48-49, 54-56; and survival, 126, 135, 140, 144. *See also* hierarchies
institutions, 5, 9, 12-13, 122, 162-63, 166, 172-73, 177; and adaptation, 98, 115; and diaspora, 29, 34-36; and preparation, 65-67, 93-94
interpretation services, 9, 26, 147, 156-57, 163, 170-73, 176
intersectionality, 12, 41, 50, 66-67, 93, 162-63, 166-67
isolation, 1, 3, 25, 40, 53; and adaptation, 98, 110-12; and preparation, 64, 68, 80, 86-87; and survival, 124-25, 129-30, 138, 142, 153
Iván, 140, 169

Jerónimo, 103-6, 167
Joel, 109, 130, 147-49, 169
Jonny, 39-41, 43
Jorge, 21, 62, 64, 70-71, 74-81, 137, 142, 150, 185n22
Juan, 90-91, 105-7
Justino, 148

Kaska people, 17
K'iche' language, 2-3, 7-8, 11, 15-16, 19, 22, 24, 168-74; and adaptation, 98, 106-11; and diaspora, 28-29, 39, 43, 46, 49, 59; and preparation, 62, 88-89, 92-93; and survival, 118-20, 128-32, 136, 141, 144-48
knowledge, 11-12, 17, 45-47, 121, 125, 147, 172; and adaptation, 96, 99-101; and preparation, 65-66, 90-93. *See also* skills
Korean immigrants, 85-86, 104, 136, 141, 147-51, 153, 165

L1 speakers, 19-22, 96-98, 101-2, 106, 108, 116, 144. *See also* language proficiency
L2 speakers, 22, 85, 108, 113. *See also* language proficiency
labor, 7, 9, 20, 30-32, 175-76; and diaspora, 35, 38, 43, 51, 54, 57-59; and preparation, 74, 84, 90-91; and survival, 103-6, 110, 124, 148-49. *See also* low-wage laborers
Ladinos, 31, 34, 44, 47, 49, 55, 60, 165
landscaping work, 57, 114
language brokering, 121, 169-70, 175-76, 187n6
language diversity, 15-16, 26, 155, 157-58, 171, 176
language ecologies, 15, 28-29, 50, 67, 80, 97, 168, 172
language learning, 23-25, 56, 97-107, 110-12, 116, 119, 162, 166-70; and preparation, 66, 72, 81-83, 87-92
language loss/extinction, 16-17, 161
language maintenance, 14, 16-18, 22, 25, 158-59, 168-69, 173; and adaptation, 101, 104, 111; and preparation, 67, 82, 93; and survival, 119, 130, 154. *See also* linguistic survivance

language proficiency, 5, 18-20, 23-25, 28-29, 54, 159, 163-68, 172-73; and adaptation, 96-106, 108-17; and preparation, 67-69, 82-85, 88-94; and survival, 119-20, 133, 147. *See also* L1 speakers; L2 speakers
language reclamation, 18
language rights, 156, 158, 161, 170
language socialization, 3, 14-15, 22-26, 161-62, 166-68, 172, 175-76, 185n18; and adaptation, 99, 101, 113; and preparation, 94; and survival, 120
languaging continuum, 99
Latin America, 29, 32, 55, 69
Latina/o (term), 179n7
Latina/o communities, 4-13, 17-20, 23-26, 158, 165-66, 169-77, 179n7, 180n7; and adaptation, 96, 100-101, 104-6, 115-16; and diaspora, 28, 50, 58-60; and preparation, 66-68, 83-84, 86, 89; and survival, 119, 126-29, 143-44, 147-49, 152-53, 162
left-behind families, 7, 9, 65, 69, 73, 83, 87-88, 100, 111, 150-52, 164
legal status, 6-12, 20, 93-94, 116-17, 170-71, 180n11; and diaspora, 38, 41, 51; and survival, 126, 131, 146-47, 151
Lenape people, 18
Leonard, Wesley, 17
Leopoldo, 48-49
linguicide, 16-17, 161
linguistic capital, 105, 121, 125, 159, 163, 167
linguistic survivance, 17-18, 26, 130, 135, 161, 165, 168-74
literacy, 82, 95. *See also* language learning; language proficiency
loneliness, 111-12, 134, 140, 146, 152; and preparation, 68, 75, 78, 86-88
long-term (re)settlement, 2, 5-7, 12, 24, 161-63, 170, 173, 185n12; and adaptation, 97, 119; and diaspora, 40-41,

long-term (re)settlement (*cont.*) 45, 51–53, 61; and preparation, 63, 65, 68, 75, 83, 90–93; and survival, 124, 141, 143, 147, 149, 152–54

Los Angeles County Board of Supervisors, 151

Los Angeles Flower Market, 107, 150

Loveman, Mara, 163

low-wage laborers, 9, 23, 65–67, 103, 116, 126, 148–49, 161; and diaspora, 32, 38–40, 51. *See also* wage theft

Lucy, 27–30, 45, 58, 118–21, 125, 128, 141, 151, 169, 182n1

Luz García, María, 173

MacArthur Park, Los Angeles, 20, 22, 38, 50, 72–73, 131

Mam language, 8, 15, 22

marginalization, 4–6, 9–14, 21, 96, 115, 160, 164, 172; and diaspora, 29, 35–37, 55–56; and preparation, 66, 71, 74; and survival, 123–24, 143, 151–52

Marianna, 79, 84, 132–33, 142

Martin, 145–46

Martin-Beltrán, Melinda, 98

material resources, 5, 7, 12–13, 21, 108, 160–63, 166; and adaptation, 96, 99; and diaspora, 37–38, 56–57, 60; and preparation, 64–65, 68–70, 76–77, 93; and survival, 119–26, 134, 150–52

Mayan cultural practices, 2, 6, 14–19, 25, 68, 159, 163–68, 175; and adaptation, 97, 116; and diaspora, 33–34, 48; and survival, 121–23, 126, 129, 142–45, 148, 153

Mayan identities, 6, 14, 23–26, 92, 112, 159–61, 168–69; and diaspora, 34, 45, 53–54; and survival, 122–23, 126–31, 135, 140–45, 153

mayanización, 34

Mayan languages, 4–11, 14, 19–20, 23, 28, 157, 172; and survival, 120–21, 124, 136. *See also* Akateko language; K'iche' language; Mam language; Q'anjob'al language

Mayan religion, 14, 54–55. *See also* God; spirituality

McCarty, Teresa, 169

Meek, Barbra, 17

men, 20, 35, 37, 47, 75, 79, 119, 140, 142, 182n1, 185n12

mental health, 1, 5, 52–53, 114, 133–39, 144–45, 153, 164. *See also desahogo* (emotional unburdening)

mentors, 64–68, 71, 73, 89, 113–14, 163

mestizaje, 158

methodology of book, 19–27

Mexican immigrants, 8, 11, 20–21, 84, 88, 157–58, 171; and adaptation, 110, 114; and diaspora, 38, 48, 50; and survival, 124–27, 130, 143–44

Mexicanization, 127

Mexico, 8, 31, 49, 85, 87, 106, 110, 130, 143, 155, 158

Mexico City, Mexico, 130

miedo (fear), 1–3, 6, 24, 167, 169, 176; and adaptation, 106–7, 114; and diaspora, 30, 44–45, 49, 53–57, 60; and preparation, 67, 70, 73, 78, 80–81, 86–87; and survival, 120, 125, 127–29, 131, 138, 140, 145, 153–54. *See also timidez* (shyness)

migranthood, 36, 52

Mireya, 144–45, 149

mistreatment, 45, 79, 125, 127–29, 131. *See also* discrimination

mobility, 4, 6–7, 10–13, 26, 165; and adaptation, 96, 99, 103–5, 112; and diaspora, 37, 40–45, 60; and preparation, 70, 82–84, 93; and survival, 121–23, 135, 141, 147–49, 151–53

monolingualism, 23, 157, 172. *See also* bilingualism; multilingualism; semilingualism; translanguaging; trilingualism
morality, 21, 36, 165, 175
Mortimer, Katherine, 116
mothers, 39–42, 48, 63–64, 85–86, 146, 150
MS-13 gang (Mara Salvatrucha), 36
multiculturalism, 25, 112, 127, 136, 145, 152
multilingualism, 19, 23, 28, 144, 147, 155, 169–76. *See also* bilingualism; monolingualism; semilingualism; translanguaging; trilingualism

nationalism, 10, 29, 43, 49, 117
neoliberalism, 90, 103
Nichols, Briana, 37, 46

Oliveira, Gabrielle, 42
Omar, 62–66, 69, 77–79, 89, 130–31, 135–36, 174–75
opportunities, 4, 10, 12–13, 25, 176; and adaptation, 96, 103–5, 114; and diaspora, 27–28, 35–37, 40–42, 54, 56, 60–61; and preparation, 69, 77, 81, 84–85; and survival, 122–24, 135, 144, 147–48, 151–53
oppression, 30, 33, 37, 54, 78, 151, 157–61, 166–67. *See also* harassment; persecution
orientación (orientation), 4–6, 12, 82, 161, 164, 171; and survival, 118, 121–22, 150. *See also* disorientation

parents, 5–7, 14, 18–24, 122, 163–66, 174–76, 187n6; and adaptation, 100, 103, 111–12, 115–16; and diaspora, 27, 34, 36, 40, 43, 48–54, 61; and preparation, 62–68, 83, 86, 93–94. *See also* fathers; mothers

passing, 130
Peace Accords (1996), 34, 60
percentage talk, 24–25, 93, 95–111, 115–17
Perla, 155–56, 158, 160
persecution, 33, 40, 129. *See also* disappearance; discrimination; displacement; genocide; oppression
Peru, 176–77
phenotypes, 6, 9, 48–49, 59, 131, 143
physical appearance, 3, 44, 49, 55, 59, 78, 126–33, 152–53
Pico-Union, Los Angeles, 3, 20–22, 62, 72–73, 161, 185n22; and diaspora, 27, 38–39, 48–50; and survival, 118, 125, 129, 147
plantation labor, 30–31, 38
policing, 79–80
policy recommendations, 26, 155–7
politics, 9–11, 23, 90, 116, 167, 176; and diaspora, 28, 31, 36–38, 41, 51; and US intervention, 32–35
poverty, 9, 24, 83–84, 146, 149, 185n3; and diaspora, 32–37, 41–43, 49–50, 57–58
preocupaciones (worries), 73–74, 76–77, 164
preparación (preparation), 4–6, 9, 12–15, 19, 24–25, 159–66, 168–71, 174–77; and adaptation, 96–102, 110–13, 115–18; and the future, 64–74, 77–85, 87–94; and survival, 121–27, 133–34, 140, 142, 148, 151–52
pride, 2, 106, 122, 124, 141–43, 148, 151–54, 162; and preparation, 68, 73, 83, 92, 94
Protestants, 55, 167
public life, 11, 20, 115, 167–68, 170–72, 176–77, 182n1, 188n1; and diaspora, 28, 34–35, 47–48, 60; and preparation, 78, 87, 89–91; and survival, 118, 120–21, 129, 132, 138, 143–45

public transportation, 5, 40, 79, 104, 115, 131

Q'anjob'al language, 8, 15, 22, 48, 55–56
Quetzaltenango, Guatemala, 8, 47
quotidian dislocations, 23, 29, 39–41, 49, 60, 177
Quiché, Guatemala, 8

race-bending, 125–27
racial baggage, 41
racialization, 4–8, 11, 24, 158–65, 169, 174, 176; and diaspora, 29–34, 37, 40–43, 45–50, 55, 58, 60; and preparation, 68–69, 79, 84, 87; and survival, 122, 124–27, 135, 140–41, 151–53
racism, 2–3, 5, 13, 23, 161, 166, 179n1; and adaptation, 106–7; and diaspora, 30, 43, 48–50, 55–56; and preparation, 68, 74; and survival, 122, 125, 153; White supremacist, 10. *See also* anti-Indigenous racism; discrimination; harassment; mistreatment; violence
rape, 33–34
Raúl, 114, 132
reducción (reduction), 4
refugees, 9, 33, 37–38, 112, 157, 176
religion, 14, 21, 54–55, 66. *See also* Catholic Church; church participation; Protestants
resettlement, 7, 9, 24, 67, 90, 124–25, 128, 157, 160
resilience, 19, 94, 97, 115, 141, 154
resilient Indigeneity, 94, 97, 154
responsibility, 7–12, 107, 135, 149, 153, 158, 171, 175; and diaspora, 30, 35–36, 40, 52, 60; and preparation, 65–66, 74
rhematization, 59

roles, 12, 65, 135, 141, 163, 166, 175; and diaspora, 29–30, 35–36, 52, 60; and preparation, 70, 81, 89, 93–94
romantic relationships, 27, 89, 111, 133
Ruiz, Richard, 170–71

safety, 1, 9, 37, 80, 84, 131, 176
Salvadoran immigrants, 21–22, 141, 143–44, 148, 153
San Antonio Sija, Guatemala, 43–44
San Carlos Sija, Guatemala, 39–40, 44, 47–48, 55
San Marcos, Guatemala, 8
San Pedro Soloma, Guatemala, 47
schools, 4, 9, 12, 15, 18, 22, 26, 156, 163–66, 170–76, 183n32; and adaptation, 95, 100, 103–6, 112, 115, 117; and diaspora, 27, 29, 35, 39–47, 51–56, 61; and preparation, 66, 68, 74, 79–84, 91–94; and survival, 122, 133, 140, 150–54. *See also* education
secondary labor market, 103, 149
self-discovery, 135–36, 160, 168
self-esteem, 1–2, 24, 107, 135–39, 143–45, 167; and diaspora, 45–47, 52–56, 60; and preparation, 77–78, 80, 88–89. *See also* sense of self
semilingualism, 108–9. *See also* bilingualism; monolingualism; multilingualism; translanguaging; trilingualism
sense of self, 65–66, 77, 87, 124, 136, 144–45, 167; and diaspora, 30, 35, 46–47, 55. *See also* identities; self-esteem
Serenity Prayer, 77
shame, 3, 21, 80, 107, 168; and survival, 128–29, 140–42, 145, 154
shyness. *See timidez* (shyness)
siblings, 43, 56–57, 68, 94, 139, 150. *See also* brothers; sisters

silencing, 56, 80, 127-35, 140-41, 155, 160, 169, 174
sisters, 39, 43, 56, 75
skills, 9, 12, 38, 58, 175-76; "low-skilled" labor, 38, 58, 84, 176; and preparation, 66, 84-85, 91; and survival, 121, 126, 147, 153. *See also* knowledge
sobrevivencia (survival), 2, 5-7, 9, 13-15, 19, 24, 159, 166-68; and adaptation, 111, 116; and diaspora, 38, 40, 50; and future-making, 119, 121, 123-25, 127-31, 135, 146, 151-53; and preparation, 75, 82-83, 89, 91-92. *See also* thriving
social class, 10, 50, 58, 185n3
social dimensions, 4-12, 159-72, 174-75; and diaspora, 35-36, 40-41, 51-53, 57, 60-61; and language, 19, 28, 96-102, 105, 110-17; and networks, 37-38, 176; and preparation, 65-68, 83, 87; and survival, 120-29, 133-35, 141-44, 147-53; and Voces de Esperanza, 21, 70-73, 77-81
socialization, 18, 20, 35, 120, 124, 153; and adaptation, 97-99, 110; and preparation, 60-61, 65-66, 69-71, 77. *See also* language socialization
sociolinguistics, 90, 109, 164, 169
sociology, 29, 41, 131, 167
Solis, Hilda, 151
Spain, 3, 30-31, 44, 48, 54-55
Spanish language, 3-7, 15, 18-25, 155-61, 167-73; and adaptation, 96-117; and diaspora, 27-29, 39, 43-52, 54-55, 58; and preparation, 66-67, 69, 77-78, 81-90, 92, 185n18; and survival, 118-21, 128-30, 137, 140, 144
speaking in silence, 127
spirituality, 2, 5, 18, 21, 33, 54, 143, 175; and preparation, 65, 72-73, 79. *See also* God; Mayan religion

Stamatov, Peter, 163
stereotypes, 3, 11, 34, 58-59, 83-86, 108, 158
stigma, 6-7, 11, 23-25, 109, 152-53, 170-72; and diaspora, 46, 54-55, 60; and preparation, 69, 84, 92
storytelling, 2-7, 104, 114, 118, 136, 140, 145, 174; and diaspora, 41, 43, 47, 59; and preparation, 63, 75, 77, 83, 85
strategic essentialism, 173
students, 18-19, 95, 164, 183n32, 185n3; and diaspora, 29, 32, 39-41, 45-46. *See also* education; schools
subordination, 9-11, 128, 151, 160, 165. *See also* hierarchies
substance use, 73-75, 78
suffering, 1-3, 104, 110-11, 172; and diaspora, 30, 54-57; and preparation, 70-72, 87-88, 92
Sumida Huaman, Elizabeth, 148
survivance, 17-18, 26, 130, 135, 161, 165, 168-74
survival. *See sobrevivencia* (survival)

teachers, 3, 18, 46, 66, 100, 112-13, 151, 166; and diaspora, 32, 39, 46
teenagers, 1, 5-8, 20-21, 103, 118, 163, 167, 176; and adaptation, 121, 124-25, 131-33, 137, 142, 146, 149, 151; and diaspora, 27, 30-31, 34-35, 39-47, 50-53, 59-60; and preparation, 68, 73-75, 82-84, 94. *See also* children; young adults
thriving, 2, 7, 14, 25, 66, 112, 153. *See also sobrevivencia* (survival)
timidez (shyness), 6, 24, 109, 114, 169, 176; and diaspora, 30, 53-55, 60; and preparation, 67, 70, 73, 78; and survival, 127, 129, 138, 140-41, 145, 153. *See also miedo* (fear)
Tomás, 109, 111

Totonicapán, Guatemala, 8, 27, 39, 43
transition to adulthood, 5, 7, 35, 163; and adaptation, 98, 107; and dislocation, 36, 46; and future-making, 121, 123, 133-34, 151, 153; and preparation, 65, 90, 93-94
translanguaging, 17, 92. *See also* bilingualism; semilingualism; trilingualism
transnational care constellations, 42
transnationalism, 9, 11, 14, 18, 25; and adaptation, 97, 116; and diaspora, 37-38, 42, 47; and preparation, 66-69, 82, 87, 92-94; and survival, 142, 163-64
trauma, 3, 123, 134, 141, 175
trilingualism, 107, 115, 120, 130, 141, 173. *See also* bilingualism; monolingualism; multilingualism; translanguaging
Truth Commission, 34

unaccompanied youth migrants, 1, 3, 6, 58, 61, 118, 157-58, 164, 167, 170, 174-76; and adaptation, 96-100, 113, 116, 158, 162; definition, 7; and diaspora, 27, 29, 38; and disorientation, 12, 50-53; and displacement, 47; and future-making, 122, 125, 130, 134, 137, 142, 145-46, 149, 151-53; history of, 7-10; and methodology of book, 14-15, 19-23; and preparation, 63-74, 81-83, 86-94, 96, 158, 161-63; and sexual violence, 185n12; and shyness/fear, 53, 55
uncles, 68
undocumented migrants, 4-6, 9, 12, 21, 50-51, 116, 162, 166; Dreamers, 116-17; and preparation, 67-70, 74, 81-82, 90, 93-94; and survival, 125, 137, 142, 148-49
United Fruit Company (Chiquita), 32

United Nations, 33
US-born people, 118-21, 127, 164-65
US Census, 171
US Department of Health and Human Services (HHS): Diversity, Equity, Inclusion, and Accessibility Commission, 157; Office of Refugee Resettlement, 9, 157
US Immigration and Customs Enforcement (ICE), 40
US Institute of Peace, 34
US intervention, 31-34
US-Mexico border, 7-8, 106, 126, 145-46

violence, 9-10, 23-24, 114, 158, 167; and diaspora, 33-37, 40, 43, 46, 49-50; and preparation, 78-80, 85; and survival, 125-31, 134, 146
Vizenor, Gerald, 17
Voces de Esperanza, 3, 15, 20-22, 163-64, 167-70, 176, 185n18, 185n22; and diaspora, 47, 54-55; and preparation, 62, 64, 66, 70-75, 77-79, 81; and survival, 128, 132, 135-36, 138-41, 143-47, 151
vulnerability, 148, 152

wage theft, 85-86, 92, 101. *See also* low-wage laborers
Wanka people, 148
warehouse work, 57
Warriner, Doris, 82
well-being, 5, 9, 26, 43, 60, 164, 170, 175; and adaptation, 101, 111, 114; and preparation, 69-70, 75, 91-92; and survival, 121-23, 148, 153
Westlake, Los Angeles, 20, 22, 38, 50, 143
White Anglo-Saxon Protestant culture, 167
White people, 39-40, 44, 55, 159, 165, 167

White supremacy, 10
Wilfredo, 21, 39–40, 47, 56, 169; and preparation, 62, 64, 70–72, 75–81; and survival, 137, 139, 142–44, 147, 149–50
witchcraft, 2, 4, 55, 179n1
women, 8, 20, 114, 118, 124, 142, 182n1, 185n12; and diaspora, 33–37, 47–48; and preparation, 79, 89
workplaces, 29, 101, 177; and diaspora, 57–60; and preparation, 65, 67, 78, 82, 84–86, 91–92; and survival, 127, 136, 148, 151
World War II, 31
worries. *See preocupaciones* (worries)
Wyman, Leisy, 17, 80

Ximena, 47–49, 55–56
Xinka people, 34

Ydigoras Fuentes, Miguel, 33
young adults, 7, 13, 20, 46–47, 161, 167–68, 174, 187n6; and diaspora, 74, 82, 90; and survival, 119, 124, 133–34, 142, 150. *See also* children; teenagers
youth workers, 3–4, 19–20, 29, 158, 162–63, 167, 174–76; and adaptation, 98–99, 103, 105; and diaspora, 58, 60; and preparation, 64–70, 82, 90, 92–93; and survival, 122, 126, 142

Zamora, Sylvia, 41
Zapotec language, 155, 158

The authorized representative in the EU for product safety and compliance is:
Mare Nostrum Group
B.V Doelen 72
4831 GR Breda
The Netherlands

www.ingramcontent.com/pod-product-compliance
Lightning Source LLC
Chambersburg PA
CBHW020836160426
43192CB00007B/675